Moral Demands and
Personal Obligations

Moral Demands and Personal Obligations

Josef Fuchs, S.J.

Translated by BRIAN MCNEIL

GEORGETOWN UNIVERSITY PRESS / WASHINGTON, D.C.

Georgetown University Press, Washington, D.C.   20057–1079
© 1993 by Georgetown University Press. All rights reserved.
Printed in the United States of America
10 9 8 7 6 5 4 3 2 1   1993
THIS VOLUME IS PRINTED ON ACID-FREE OFFSET BOOK PAPER.

Library of Congress Cataloging-in-Publication Data

Fuchs, Josef, 1912-
        Moral demands and personal obligations / Josef Fuchs.
        p.   cm.
        1. Christian ethics--Catholic authors. 2. Absolute, The.
        I. Title.
BJ1249.F755   1993   241'.042--dc20   93-3804
ISBN 0-87840-537-2   ISBN 0-87840-543-7 (pbk.)

Contents

7
Innovative Morality 109

8
Ethical Problems in the Christian Prayer of the Psalms 122

9
The Magisterium and Moral Theology 138

PART 3
CONSCIENCE AND MORAL OBJECTIVITY

10
Conscience and Conscientious Fidelity 153

Foreword

In the realm of normative morality, no doubt an absolute exists that knows of no exceptions. In the same area, much exists that would like to present itself as an absolute: on looking more closely, however, one finds that it is not an absolute.

It follows that the fundamental statement about normative morality is that many of its requirements are not univocal, but necessarily permit a certain plurality.

In addition, the normative statements of morality do not simply stand by themselves; they must also be understood in relation to the person who acts. Thus, problems arise for concrete behavior that cannot be solved on the basis of normative morality alone.

The essays collected in this volume, which were written in the last few years, deal with the questions indicated in the title of this book and this foreword. As papers previously published in various languages and journals, they have been freshly edited for this collection.

Rome   JOSEF FUCHS, S.J.

Acknowledgments

Acknowledgment is gratefully made to the publishers and others for permission to use again, in edited form, the following:

Introduction The difficult Golden Rule: "Die Schwierige Goldene Regel," *Stimmen der Zeit* 209(1991): 773–81.

Chapter 1 The Absolute in Moral Theology: "Das Absolut in der Moral," *Stimmen der Zeit* 207: 825–38.

Chapter 2 Natural Law or Naturalistic Fallacy? "Naturrecht oder naturalisticher Fehlschluss?" *Stimmen der Zeit* 206 (1988): 407–23.

Chapter 3 What Responsibility? "Verantwortung," *Stimmen der Zeit* 209 (1991): 485–93.

Chapter 4 Structures of Sin, "Strukturen der Sünde," *Stimmen der Zeit* 206(1988): 613–22.

Chapter 5 "Soul" and "Ensoulment," *Soul* and *Ensoulment*, in the Individual Coming into Being of the Human Person. Presentation. Workshop on Human Life—Personhood: FIAMC Biomedical Centre, Bombay, 7–9 December 1988. First published: "Seele und Beseelung im individuellen Werden des Menschen," *Stimmen der Zeit* 207 (1989) 522–30.

Chapter 6 Historicity and Moral Norm, "Storicità e norma morale." Presentation. Morle e coscienza storica: Naples, 7–8 May 1987. Published in S. Ferraro, ed., Morale e coscienza storicà in dialogo con Josef Fuchs. (Saggi 26) Rome, Ave, 1988. German translation: "Geschichtlichkeit und sittliche Norm," *Stimmen der Zeit* 207(1989): 15–31.

Chapter 7 Innovative Morality, "Innovative Morality: The Bellarmine Lecture, St. Louis University. Published in *Theology Digest* 37 (1990): 301–12. German original: "Innovative Moral," *Stimmen der Zeit* 209 (1991): 181–91.

Chapter 9 The Magisterium and Moral Theology, "Magisterium und Moral theologie. Address to the Department of Theology, University of Fribourg, December 1988. Published in *Freiburger Zeitschrift für Philosophie und Theologie* 36 (1989) 395–407.

Chapter 10 Conscience and Conscientious Fidelity, "Gewissen und Gefolgschaft," *Stimmen der Zeit* 207 (1989) 308–20.

Chapter 11 "The One who Hears You Hears Me": Episcopal Moral Directives, "Wer euch hört, der hört mich": Bischöfliche Moralweisungen, in *Stimmen der Zeit* 210 (1992): 723–31.

Chapter 12 Ethical Self–Direction: "Sittliche Selbststeuerung," *Stimmen der Zeit* 210 (1992): 553–59.

Chapter 13 The Faithful Must Not Be Unsettled, "Die Gläubigen nicht verunsichern, Kirke zwischen angst und Zuversicht," *Stimmen der Zeit* 208 (1990): 453–62.

Chapter 14 Spiritual Foundations of the Structural Change in Western Society. Presentation. Bonn, 1988. First published: "Geistige Gründlagen des Struktkurwandels in der Gesellschaft," *Stimmen der Zeit* 207 (1989): 171–80.

Chapter 15 Law and Grace: A Theme of Moral Theology, "Getsetz und Gnade: ein Thema der Moraltheologie," *Stimmen der Zeit* 209 (1991): 317–22.

*Moral Demands and
Personal Obligations*

Introduction:
The Difficult Golden Rule

We find this logion of the Lord in the Sermon on the Mount in Matthew's Gospel: "Do unto others whatever you would have them do unto you" (Matt 7:12); and the text continues, "this [word] is the law and the prophets." We read in the parallel text of Luke's Gospel: "What you expect from others, do the same to them" (Luke 6:31). These logia from the synoptic gospels, though written decades after Easter, are quite possibly the genuine words of Jesus.

Here we have the Golden Rule in its positive formulation as it was known and applied in contemporary Judaism. But it was probably better known in its negative form: "What you do not want others to do to you, you must not do to them." In this form it occurs as a universally valid ethical norm in various highly developed cultures.[1]

R. Bultmann believed that the Golden Rule was nothing other than a naive, egotistical self-protection; other theologians hold the view that it is a rule concerned with the avoidance of conflicts and the preservation of peace so that persons may live together. For still others, the Golden Rule may even be a *talio*, a *do ut des*: "as you do to me, so I will do to you." Such an ethical norm does not occupy a particularly elevated position. The closeness of this rule in the synoptics to the commandment of love and to the "law and the prophets" leads us to expect something different.

The commandment to "love your neighbor as yourself" (Matt 22:39) and the position given to it—it is on equal footing with the commandment to love God—makes it a demand for greater ethical purity (G. Ebeling) in relationship to others, with respect for their personal dignity; that is, it is the reverse of the Golden Rule understood as an expression of naive egotism. This view accounts perhaps for the presence of the Golden Rule as a moral demand in so many of the world's epochs and highly developed cultures.

Presumably it is easy to grasp the Golden Rule in its negative formulation. If I must and do say to someone that it is absolutely wrong to commit adultery, then it follows that I must say precisely the same to everyone, even to my best friend in a similar situation, and possibly even to myself. Should my friend who is suffering from AIDS expect me to accept in a particular situation that he may act in a "carefree" manner which, however, could put others at risk, I may not concede this notion to him, any more than I can concede it to any sick person who lives in a similar situation. One must pay heed to two factors: first, the Golden Rule insists on the equality of the personal dignity of all individuals, and therefore cannot take sides in any *acceptio personarum*; second, in each case, the evil that is to be avoided must be similar in kind.

The problem becomes a little more difficult when the Golden Rule is formulated positively as it is in the Sermon on the Mount. Without any doubt, it would be ideal to be always ready to grant to another what I believe that I have good and just reasons to expect from him in a particular situation. And would not the lack of such a willingness be, in principle, a genuine ethical deficiency? Would this not imply an *acceptio personarum*, the use of different criteria in dealing with persons who have the same personal dignity?

INDIVIDUAL ETHICS

The Golden Rule holds good with regard to ethical right behavior between persons in our world. It demands personal ethical *goodness* of us, that is, acts of seeking, discovering, and putting into practice a behavior between persons that is ethically *right*. The Golden Rule is the basis of every attempt at right behavior. In this universality, it enters absolutely into all conduct between persons: it demands that we take no sides in interpersonal behavior. Thus, it is a basic ethical requirement, which is also extremely simple in this formal and personal sense.

The question, however, of "what" this impartial conduct means is, in many cases all the more difficult. For "I" and "the other" are personal individuals and not simply identical, with the exception of personal dignity in which we are equal. But the human concreteness in which personal dignity is incarnate is not the same in different human beings, even if the dignity itself is the same for all: this concrete difference is the source of the "difficulty" of the Golden Rule. To what extent are the individualities that are compared with one another on the basis of the Golden Rule substantially the same so that one can *straightforwardly* apply the Golden Rule to them in a justified manner?

In many cases, when particular problems are to be resolved, the material and intellectual sameness of individualities that are to be compared impartially with one another are so large and unambiguous that ethical problems do not arise at all in an explicit way. But this equality is certainly not the case always and in all situations. In order to arrive at good results on the basis of the Golden Rule, it would, in fact, be necessary to "get under the skin" of each of the persons involved: but this experience is in many cases scarcely possible, or only to a certain extent.[2]

In any case, the Golden Rule says nothing about this. The impartiality that it demands requires simply that one take individual differences into account. Herein lies the difficulty.

Precisely for this reason, ethical life in accordance with the Golden Rule is much more difficult than ethical life in accordance with the data of ethical natural law.[3] In this formulation, however, the natural law is static, a sum total of norms that are in principle always available for one to make use of at any moment. Many moral theology books written in the past can be read in this fashion, but it would seem that this tradition, broadly speaking, has come to an end.

A contemporary moral theology formulated in categories of the natural law requires, as does a moral theology based on the Golden Rule, that one reflect on the interior and the exterior dimensions of oneself and the other, totally and in detail, and understand and judge them under their ethical aspect. There is no antithesis between a moral theology conceived in terms of natural law and a concrete moral theology based on the Golden Rule; ultimately and at their base, these theologies are identical—and equally "difficult." The moral theology of the Golden Rule, like the theology of natural law, depends on ethical reflection in each case in order to be made concrete.

Both modes of moral theology also belong to what we are ready to acknowledge as Christian moral theology. On the other hand, neither starting point is distinctively Christian; this assertion does not exclude the possibility that a Christian anthropology and the light of Christian revelation can suggest decisive interpretations and even de facto individual concrete attempts at solutions to ethical problems that non-Christian starting points would scarcely be able to discover. But it does suggest that non-Christian moral theologies can understand and grasp these Christian interpretations and that they also have their own abilities and sufficient plausibility.

In recent years, a noticeable trend within the Catholic Church and its moral theology has been to insist emphatically on the observance of objective ethical norms and to set this demand in antithesis to another tendency, also acknowledged, that determines the rightness of ethical conduct not by the simple application of existing "objective" ethical norms, but by responsible ethical judgment on the part of those who act, although this tendency involves taking into account all the demonstrable elements and circumstances in the act and in the subject who carries it out.[4] The former trend is a trend against the justification and the task of conscience—and of the conscience alone—to attempt to form for itself the most *objective* (though not, as we have been occasionally but mistakenly warned, *infallible*) ethical judgment about the *correctness* of a concrete action in the totality of its reality. Attempting this judgment involves drawing on all available means; for example, the use of previously formulated norms and traditions in their hermeneutical interpretation, the counsel of wise persons, and the dicta of theologians.

Is it perhaps the case that this trend is threatened by the wisdom of the inherited Golden Rule? For the rule demands impartiality, while leaving it up to the responsible judgment (i.e., to the conscience) of the one who acts to decide about the objective justification of one's own wish ("what you *wish*/what you do not *wish*") and about the justification or nonjustification of the action of the other. Thus, the Golden Rule operates in a manner similar to that of a moral theology conceived in the categories of the natural law; it starts from the universally valid (but fundamentally formal) principle that good is to be done, and not evil.

Here one must note the possibility that one's own action and the action of the other can have an essentially different context, so that it can perhaps be justified in the one case but not in the other. When the Golden Rule is applied, one must pay heed, not only to impartiality, but also to the fundamentally similar or dissimilar situation in which the one person and the other find themselves. One who lives in extreme indigence will justifiably wish that no one should steal his extremely scanty possessions; he himself must heed this in the same way vis-à-vis another extremely poor person, but possibly not in abso-

ETHICS OF LIFE

In traditional formulations, the Golden Rule is conceived above all for problems of individual ethics. But it is also significant, in analogous terms at least, in the field of societal ethics. Is it perhaps also a source of orientation to the *bonum* of human life? That is, does it apply by analogy at least to the most acute problems of the *bonum*, the end and the beginning of human life that are so much debated today?

It is possible to prolong life, that is, to postpone the threat of death, in various ways. This reprieve can certainly be something subjectively and reasonably desired. But the tradition of moral theology and the traditional teaching of the Catholic Church, while not forbidding this possibility, have never made the prolongation of life an absolute obligation. Instead they suggest a comparison between the desirable value of prolonging a life and the conscious sacrificial commitment that is necessary to attain this goal.

Various opinions will be held about whether it is meaningful and defensible in situations of extreme risk to link the patient to costly and complicated apparatus, or for doctors to treat the patient through artificial nourishment with food and drink. How are doctors to behave, if they themselves would reject such a treatment in the extreme case: "What you do not wish others to do to you. . . ."? The case is resolved without problems for the doctor, if the patient—or if personal decisions cannot be made by the patient, a qualified representative—agrees, unless legislation specifies otherwise. If the decision of the patient or the patient's qualified representative is different, the doctor will presumably try to convince them of the meaninglessness of such measures.

If the doctors must make the decision, they will no doubt recall, "What you do not want others to do to you . . ." and "the treatment that you would wish for yourself. . . ."

If, however, the patient is already de facto dead, according to sober competent judgment and despite artificial apparatus that keeps the heart beating, then the doctor will presumably see to it that an apparent continuation of the "treatment" does not deprive other patients of a meaningful and necessary treatment and will doubtless not oppose the possibility of organ transplants.

How do doctors behave if they not only do not reject but explicitly wish euthanasia for themselves at the close of an extremely painful life, when they are confronted concretely with patients who hold the same view? Their view presupposes that they are substantially justified not to disallow the patient's wishes despite possible contrary statements from the religious society to which they belong. It cannot be excluded as a possibility that such doctors will agree with other philosophers who reject the full plausibility of the arguments based on the natural law for the absolute inadmissibility of euthanasia and will perceive (with a large number of theologians) that the arguments adduced in their own religious community are not conclusive.[6] May or must they refuse the patient's wish for help or intervention—presuming that no law opposes this—because of the rule: "What you wish others to do to you. . . ."? Will they perhaps see this not as something that "usurps the place of nature," but as something that "assists nature"? Here we have the difficulty of the Golden Rule!

Does the Golden Rule also have something to do, at least by analogy, with human life at its beginning? Here the fundamental question is, "Who is the other person, in comparison with whom I lay my own desire on the scales?" If the only outcome that can be expected of a particular pregnancy is a stillborn child, what conduct would I wish and expect vis-à-vis such a *nasciturus*, in keeping with the Golden Rule and following my own orientation?

What treatment would I expect for myself, if it is clear that my chances of survival as a *nasciturus* are nonexistent: ought the pregnancy to be continued to birth as a mode of treatment for the life that has begun, or not? One answer would be: "What you do not wish. . . ." Or what ought the answer to be in the case of the anencephalic—the child who has no prospect of interpersonal communication? Doubtless, a different answer from that in the case of the child who has Down's syndrome, who is not without hope of a certain quality of life. The Golden Rule requires only that we apply to others what we would reasonably wish or not wish in our own case. But if the life of the mother is in danger in one of these situations, should I and every doctor consider her only as the mediator of new life, that is, do we or do we not have the obligation of unconditional intervention?

The dignity of human life demands our respect. This fundamental demand is acknowledged; nevertheless, it is here that problems arise. Is the respect that I myself expect, the same respect that I claim vis-à-vis my father? Do I claim for the newborn baby the same respect and protection that I expect for myself? Does the principle, "What others do to you, you also ought to do for others," hold good here? Do I owe the same respect to the four-month-old fetus in its primitive self-development that I owe to my wife? Ought the zygote, which does indeed definitively bear in itself the qualities of its life, though it is not yet definitively individualized in the first fourteen days and therefore is surely not yet personalized (as I hold, unlike others of my colleagues), to claim the same respect and the same rights as an adult who is fully developed in personal terms?

The answers to these questions generate far-reaching consequences for problems in bioethics. Is the same protection owed to the relationship between the gametes that results from sexual intercourse or from fertilization *in vitro*, as to the new life implanted in the womb which is definitively individualized, even if perhaps not yet personalized? What about the protection that we owe to the masculine sperm and the female ovum? In all these questions, particular modes of human life are involved. Do we simply accept the principle that what you wish others to do to you, do also to them, and apply it to every mode of human life? Or must we not pay heed here to the various stages of human life in their *differentiation* with a correspondingly differentiated protection of life? One can note the difference, but the essential principle here is impartiality.

NOTES

1. H. Reiner, "Die goldene Regel" in his *Die goldene Regel: Die Grundlagen der Sittlichkeit*, Meisenheim 1974, 348-379. H. van Oyen, "Die goldene Regel und die Situationsethik," in *Ethik ohne Normen?* ed. J. Gründel and H. van Oyen, Freiburg 1970, 91-136. Ph. Schmitz, "Die goldene Regel—Schlüssel zum ethischen Kontext" in *Christlich Glauben und Handeln*, ed. K. Demmer and B. Schüller Düsseldorf 1977, 208-222. B. Schüller, "Die goldene Regel," in *Die Begründung sittlicher Urteile. Typen ethischer Argumentation in der Moraltheologie*, Düsseldorf 1973, 2d ed., 89-106.
2. Cf. J. Fuchs, "Innovative Moral," *Stimmen der Zeit* 209 (1991): 181-191.
3. Cf. H. van Oyen, "Die goldene Regel und die Situationsethik."
4. One can also discern this trend in Cardinal Ratzinger's speech at the extraordinary Consistory of the Cardinals, 4-7 April 1991. See *L'Osservatore Romano*, 5 April 1991, pp. 1 and 4.
5. *L'Osservatore Romano*, 24 March 1991, p. 4.
6. See my essay, "Christian Faith and the Disposing of Human Life," in *Christian Morality: The Word Becomes Flesh*, Dublin/Washington 1987, 62-82.

PART I

The Absolute in Moral Theology

1

The Absolute in Moral Theology

In 1914, Victor Cathrein, published a three-volume work on the unity of the ethical conscience.[1] He wished to show that there somehow exists in humanity a unified ethical consciousness, an absolute. What do ethicists and Catholic moral theologians think about this subject today? Dietmar Mieth, professor of moral theology at Tübingen, holds that the only metaethical principle known to theological ethics is "the moral capacity of the human person," the primary natural law insight that "good is to be done and evil left undone." Everything further requires empirical mediation.[2]

Thanks to our knowledge of the enormous variety in the ethics developed in Asia, Europe, America, Africa, and other places and the obvious ethical pluralism in people influenced by Christianity and even within Christian ethical proposals, we tend to suppose that the empirical mediation of metaethical insight de facto leads to a variety of ethical systems. This is not merely de facto the case, but the result of an inner necessity in the opinion of Gerard J. Hughes, professor of philosophical ethics at Heythrop College in the University of London.[3]

Is it true to say that the biblical or Christian revelation contributes not only to an unquestioned deepening but also to the recognition of a more extensive absolute, for those who accept Christian revelation and other groups influenced by them? Many Christian theologians in the past held this notion of a revealed absolute to be true, as did the church's magisterium—and the view is held among many even to the present day—with regard to general ethical principles, and in many concrete questions of life. A more conscious hermeneutic calls into question the validity of such a supposition; otherwise, the statements of Catholic ethicists such as Mieth and Hughes would be very difficult to understand.

Problems about the ethical absolute also exist within the realm of ethical norms that are broadly or, in some measure, universally accepted. Within the fellowship of the Catholic Church, do accepted ethical norms—the concrete behavioral norms—possess a validity that absolutely excludes exceptions? Even today, many Catholic ethicists and, in part, the magisterium maintain that this absolutism applies to norms, for example, those concerning life as a good for the human being, those concerning sexuality, and those that connect speech with one's commitment to the truth. Others, however, tend to see the supposition of an absolute in concrete ethical questions as a fallacy and an unjustified hindrance to the discovery of objective ethical truth.[4]

What is the meaning of the "absolute" in the title, "The Absolute in Moral Theology," the problem that is posed here? We are concerned with the thesis that there is but one single ethical order and one single ethical consciousness *for* and *in* humanity—corresponding to the fact that humanity is one—and that this ethical order is concrete; that is, it goes far beyond the very general principle of "doing good and avoiding evil." It follows that "absolute" in the contrary thesis should not mean "universally valid," or "broadly and generally acknowledged," but "objectively" and "unconditionally" valid within each relevant ethical system and taking into consideration all the ethically relevant circumstances.

THE ETHICAL ABSOLUTUM

Without an ethical absolutum, there is no moral theology. To say, with D. Mieth, that the person is a being with a moral capacity is to say that the person essentially has a spiritual experience of an absolutum, an experience of nonarbitrariness in a situation or reality that absolutely concerns one and determines one's sense experience. This concerns one's self-realization as a person known by oneself and one's concrete action and behavior which expresses that self-realization.

Personal beings experience, however, not only that they are capable of free self-realization, but also that they are capable of free self-alienation, and this distinction cannot and must not be a matter of indifference. They experience in consequence that their action and behavior are not abandoned to total arbitrariness. Both ethical objectives and intuitionists will admit this, but even decisionists experience and must admit that the decision about what counts as "ethically" correct or false, evil or good, cannot and must not be abandoned to total arbitrariness. Human self-experience is always also the experience of a fundamental ethical *absolutum*.

This experience is embraced in the fundamental experience of a "primal confidence," an experience that Bernhard Welte calls a "transcendental faith." Primal confidence is an "openness," an essential aspect of human life; it is an openness that accepts life and gives one courage to exist, to affirm that life has a meaning. It gives one a readiness to accept freedom. The self-experience that is the kernel of ethical experience, like the fundamental experience of primal confidence, need not be the object of conscious reflection. It is, however, capable of being the object of reflection, although this capability implies that it can be misunderstood or even denied in explicit reflection. The outcome of this self-experience can depend on a long education, a slow ethical growth, or a freely developed image of the human person.

This capability implies that while the ethical experience *in its kernel* is the same experience of absoluteness in all human persons; as a fundamental experience, it will also display an *individual nuance* in different groups and in the individual person. The fundamental experience of the absolute is the same in all cases; however, it is always found in an analogous particularity. This particularity and nuance begins in one's experience of self and world, and grows slowly into a particular understanding of morality on the part of the growing person, eventually reflecting also the individuality of other persons in one's milieu who influence this process of growing up and into morality. In short, the experience of an absolute as the ethical kernel is fundamentally present and identical in all human persons, although it is individualized in accordance with each one's experience of the world.

Naturally, the universally present experience of an absolute ethical kernel in human experience is a phenomenon that theoretically requires a plausible explanation. This explanation, however, is not identical everywhere; it is different in the believing Christian (and indeed in the teaching of the churches); Christians explain this absolute on the basis of the Creator God directly, or at least on the basis of the reality of the person as the work of the Creator. Agnostic humanists, on the other hand, acknowledge the existence of an ethical absolute that is somehow "mysterious," but they cannot accept a Creator God as the reason for this absolute. The explanation is different again among atheists of empirical color, who believe that they must deny the existence of everything that is not part of the human world.

In other words, the attempt to explain the kernel of ethical experience (which is already acknowledged to exist) is fundamentally determined by the "prior judgment" of the image of the person that each one (for whatever reasons) bears within the self. One should not deny the plurality of theoretical explanations of the fundamental experience of the ethical "absolute." Plurality is apparent among more or less convinced Christians, among deeply convinced Christians, and among Catholic theologians as surely as it is apparent in the larger world. Immanuel Kant saw the matter rather differently: "And thus, while we do not grasp the practical unconditional necessity of the moral imperative, we do grasp its incomprehensibility, and this is all that can reasonably be required of a philosophy that carries its endeavors to the boundary of the reason in principles."[5]

Such various explanations of the "absolute" ethical experience are coherent and satisfactory on the basis of the fundamental understanding of the person held by those who propose them. For the same reason, it is not easy to correct them or to call them into question *ab extra*. In certain circumstances, we might call into question the underlying image of the human person; but that, too, is difficult because the image is not the product of solitary reflection, but a product of the most various influences of an intellectual and emotional life lived within humanity as a whole and by modes of "seeing" and "appearing" that are themselves partly determined by the image.

As has already been indicated, the attempt to explain the fundamental kernel of morality has often involved the appeal within Christianity to the one who—unlike every created reality—is alone the absolute: God, as the basis and the only theoretical justification of the ethical *absolutum*. This appeal, however, would mean that every nontheistic explanation of the ethical experience of the absolute is null and void.

Bruno Schüller has pointed out that this argument, though proposed by many Catholic theologians, among others, is the victim of an ambiguity in the concept of the "absolute." But if so, the frequently-heard formulation that without the knowledge of God everything is permitted, would be seen to be unsound; therefore, agnostic humanists and others oppose such a formulation. It is true, says Schüller, that God—and God alone—is absolute in the sense of aseity, that is, that God "proceeds solely from godself"; but absoluteness in the sense of being unconditioned, that is, of having "unconditional validity," exists also in the realm of the creaturely; it is a valid *absolutum* created by the *absolutum* of the God who "proceeds from godself."

If one employs the formulation "good" or "evil," "correct" or "false," in the ethical sense, one is speaking of "unconditional" in the sense of absolute validity—or else one is not speaking at all about the realm of the ethical. In Schüller's formulation, if one speaks about what is "good" and "correct" without using these words as "gerundives," that is, in the sense of unconditional requirement and validity, then one is using these words in the same nongerundive sense as one who says that it is good to learn Greek or to go for a walk, namely, in a nonmoral sense. The agnostic humanist can and does speak in a gerundive way of good and evil. The reason, as has just been mentioned, is founded in the human being created *as a human person* (in autonomy) by the God who "proceeds solely from godself" (and who in this sense is "absolute"). Thus, the agnostic humanist is not speaking from a knowledge of the absolute as of a God who creates us and therefore lays obligation upon us.[6]

This explanation does not mean that persons without an explicit knowledge of God can have no intimate personal and intellectual (even if athematic, and therefore not explicit) experience of the *divine* foundation of all human existence. Not only the Christian, but also the agnostic and the atheist can experience the divine foundation, and every true knowledge of morality is fundamentally and de facto—even if athematically—oriented to God.

The primal experience of the person as an ethical being is formulated in the principle, "Do good and avoid evil," understood ultimately as the commission, based in creation and addressed to the created being, to show forth the self in and through the life one lives and to bring this self to development. When we say "oneself" we mean oneself as a person; ethical *goodness* is required of one as a person. But one's personal existence is incarnate—embodied and shared through interpersonal experiences and socialization in the world. These realities are entrusted to the personal human being, as is God's free relationship to them, in an unconditional, or absolute, manner so that one may realize them correctly.

"Do good and avoid evil" is therefore more than a personal moral imperative; it is also a commission to achieve the good (though not yet the ethically good) in this reality that is entrusted to one; that is, to achieve good for the person or persons in the world, and to avoid or prevent as far as possible evil in the world. When one realizes the imperative to "do good and avoid evil" understood in this way, one is also good in the personal ethical sense and lives the imperative, "do good and avoid evil." personally.

From this beginning proceed ethical absolutes in the plural, even though they are strongly formal. They include the following: do good by permitting the individual and the community to keep what is its own, or by giving them their own (i.e., be just); do good by honoring the truth in your communications with others (i.e., be honest); do good by taking care of those who need you (i.e., be merciful); do good by being concerned for marital love and fidelity (i.e., be chaste), and so forth. These plural absolutes translate the *one absolutum* "Do good and avoid evil" into the language of various areas of life. They say only that the good person will always seek to do what is right in these areas; they do not indicate what act is to be done as the right conduct by the good person in these areas. Right conduct is concerned with the non-absolute realm of the contingent human world that alters in the course of history.

The contingent human world must be accepted as it is. But it also requires our interpretation and evaluation, which, because of the givenness and the meaning of its realities, are not abandoned to total arbitrariness. Every attempt at an interpretation and evaluation must correspond to the givenness of various realities. Nevertheless, one must certainly admit that different interpretations of individual realities exist, each of which is coherent and humanly satisfactory. One may, for example, think of realities in the area of human sexuality. In this realm, the presence of different interpretations may be particularly true with regard to the occasional coexistence of such realities with particular and morally relevant circumstances. In such cases, it is clearly necessary to take the entire reality into consideration.

Interpretations and evaluations, then, are not completely arbitrary, since every interpretation and evaluation is concerned both with the ethical *absolutum* of the person and given fullness of the meaning of human realities. Reality admits of various interpretations and evaluations, but not of arbitrary interpretations and evaluations. It follows that attempts at interpretation and evaluation are amenable to discussion and dialog with one another, since they must always deal with the same nonarbitrary kernel of reality. This dialogic interplay is precisely the universal or worldwide discussion about ethically correct action and behavior.

As a consequence, Christian and ecclesiastical faith and the official ethical teaching of the Catholic Church cannot eliminate the possibility of a plurality of ethical interpretations and evaluations. For the potential acceptance or nonacceptance of ecclesiastical faith and official church teaching is the outcome fundamentally, although not chronologically, of the interpretation and evaluation of human circumstances that are de facto possible for the group or individual. It is true, on the other hand, that the faith and the church's simultaneous acceptance of these interpretations give their own necessary light to our ethical interpretation and evaluation of human circumstances.

Potential divergences in the interpretation and evaluation of reality and correspondingly divergent ethical systems do not exclude the possibility that we may arrive at the same outcome concerning individual concrete ethical norms and solutions to problems. The reason for this possible convergence of interpretations lies in the ethical *absolutum* and reality that is common to all. But one should not deceive oneself: a common outcome to the search for ethical truth, discovered and formulated on the basis of divergent reflection, does not exclude understanding that the common solution to the problem is, at least in part, ultimately and most deeply different on both sides.

PLURAL SYSTEMS OF MORALITY

In concrete life, the ethical *absolutum* must come into effect in ethical systems, principles, norms, and imperatives. As Thomas Aquinas would say: "General ethical statements are less useful, because the actions concern the concrete reality"; and concrete norms are thus "more true" (because their contents are richer) than the most general ethical *abstracta*.[7] But the more concrete, and therefore "more useful" and "truer" statements are human constructions, something that for Thomas is *a ratione constitutum* or, as he says in another passage, an *ordo quem ratio considerando facit* (an order that the practical reason creates in its reflection), unlike the metaphysical order that the theoretical reason does not create, but only reflects on (*considerat*).[8]

The question arises how the one ethical *absolutum* is preserved in concrete human constructions. Can they be something necessary (and in this sense an *absolutum*), or are they—in view of the enormous variety and mutability of persons—conditional and varied expressions of the one ethical absolute as seen in various human cultures, the character of individual persons, and the mutability of human realities? If so, then, the various concrete constructions deriving from persons themselves correspond not to a unified *absolutum* that possesses the same unconditional quality for all but to the necessary pluralism of ethical constructions. Nothing else can be the case among contingent and historical persons. It is necessarily true, therefore, that not one absolute ethics of correct conduct exists but various ethics exist as the forms through which various persons give expression to the one ethical *absolutum*.

In the first place, we must bear in mind that the person, in the various periods and cultures of its development, is always in the stage of learning. What one knows about the person and the world is always greatly limited. When we construct ethical proposals for the person, we must always bear in mind that our knowledge of the total reality of the person is always extremely defective. This situation is precisely the one in which we find ourselves today. As knowledge increases or as plausible hypotheses are formed, one may possibly be required to revise earlier interpretations and ethical insights, judgments, and convictions. The new knowledge that one gains about the possibility of intervention in reality, whether in the technological world, in bioethics and human reproduction, in recent medical, psychological, and sociological knowledge about marriage and sexuality, or in the realm of interpersonal, national and international relationships, has the possibility of determining a new reflection on what hitherto counted as ethically insightful and defensible.

Such knowledge even today is very different among different peoples and groups, but an inner necessity is reflected in the development of simultaneously diverse understandings of morality over the whole world. It is possible that these diverse understandings are not only subjectively but also objectively correct, for morality is concerned, not with an abstract ideal world but with the world known to the human person, that is, with the world as the person knows it. In the worldwide sphere of human reality, an ethical consciousness cannot possibly exist that is at once concrete in its presentation and identical in its universality. There cannot exist any obligation on the part of humanity to produce such a consciousness.

We must add to these reflections the observation that even identical knowledge of human reality cannot complete a univocal interpretation, and still less a univocal evaluation. Interpretations and evaluations depend largely on one's previous intellectual and emotional inheritance and on the image of humankind and the world that are influenced by this inheritance.

Neither nature nor material circumstances display a univocal and exclusive interpretation and evaluation of themselves; while they are certainly relevant to possible interpretations and evaluations (and thus do not permit total arbitrariness), they themselves cannot compel one necessary interpretation and evaluation. Rather, these interpretations or evaluations are to be found in persons who exist with their various intellectual concepts and attitudes. Various perspectives vis-à-vis the same realities and their active realization are completely possible and exist in fact. It follows that no concretely unambiguous, unconditional *absolutum* exists that can compel the person in ethical dialog.

We arrive at the same result when we reflect on a person's ethical development and growth. While there exists even in small children a reaction to their environment and to the conduct of the persons linked to them, no one sees an ethical judgment in their reactions. The education of children and youth has a determinative influence in keeping with the meaning of education. To a large extent, children begin by seeing no problem in the ethical contents of their education, which they absorb and interiorize. This acceptance is a first beginning of the development of one's own ethical convictions. Here, the parents and the family are the educators, but also the church, religion, school, and the social milieu. Even educators, however, are extremely diverse persons; they do not mediate (or only in part) a universal ethical consciousness. Therefore, the initial conditions for the child and the young person are completely diverse. The ethical codes that are impressed on them are necessarily one-sided and incomplete.

Human beings will never be completely able to overcome and neutralize their ethical beginning; thus their ethical consciousness is necessarily diverse. One of the conditions determining how deep this diversity goes, though not the only condition, is the greater or lesser diversity of the beginning. This diversity does not exclude the possibility that the person, as he or she matures, is also capable of dissent and autonomous judgment and is perhaps even strongly inclined to construct an ethical conviction that is, at least in part, one's own. This attempt can be a serious endeavor or a superficial attitude. The conviction will depend to a certain extent on the more or less strong influence of one's milieu, as it slowly takes form. Lawrence Kohlberg concluded in his well-known psychological researches that a full ethical maturity and ethical autonomous independence cannot be attained before the beginning of the fourth decade of one's life and will never be attained in most cases.

It follows that an individual's concrete ethical consciousness not only displays diversities that can affect fundamental ethical attitudes or normative ethical convictions, but also a diverse understanding of more or less common ethical attitudes and normative convictions. All this consciousness is the outcome of an inherited or acquired fundamental image of the person and the world, a fundamental human or religious faith, and a richness of interpreted and evaluated life experience.

This individual image of the person and world is also fundamentally important in explicit theoretical reflection, perhaps most especially in philosophical and theological reflection on the ethical system constructed by the group or oneself or on the particular judgments about concrete ethical problems made by the group or oneself. It is true that human dignity is more and more understood as the decisive element in the image of the person and world. In one, though as yet a vague, sense, this element is something unconditional (an *absolutum*). But one must ask how human dignity is understood: in a Kantian sense, or in the sense of the theology of creation and redemption? And what are the concrete human values that are covered and protected in various world views by means of the accepted value of "human dignity"? The differences may perhaps be proposed in a system that is coherent in itself and humanly satisfactory, but the systems are diverse.

One theory that is maintained by some even today suggests that various images of the person and the ethical constructions and solutions to problems connected with these images can be read as part of the reality of the person and his or her world, in the sense of an ethical natural law or of an order of creation. But this "reading" takes place along the path of human interpretation and evaluation that are only partly identical and can scarcely compel conviction, despite reasonings that are supposed to be plausible once it is conceded that they possess only a moral certainty.

The ability to accept the ethical insights and norms that are presented as objectively correct depends on the intellectual and emotional openness or lack of openness of individuals and groups. It is not the reason as such that thinks and comes to ethical insights; rather, it is the person with particular dispositions who undertakes to reason and to arrive at an ethical judgment. For many believing Catholics, the officially-proposed sexual ethics and the ethics of human reproduction appear indubitably correct—thanks to this disposition of confidence in the church's leadership. Other believing Catholics cannot acknowledge this ethics of sexuality and reproduction—thanks to their reflection on sexuality and reproduction which in turn sees other and more plausible possibilities for interpreting and evaluating the natural *datum* that is human sexuality and reproduction.

What is presented as "ethical natural law," and therefore as the order of creation and God's will, is always, and necessarily, an attempt at interpretation, evaluation, and ethical judgment that cannot be simply "read off" from nature and the heart. Therefore, it always retains the character of an attempt, and does not generally compel one to see in it absolutely the one possible attempt and unconditional judgment that always holds true. One may and should understand ethical solutions and norms of natural law, as long as one holds them to be correct, as one's own interpretation of God's creator will, and one should follow them in conscience. Concrete solutions and norms of this kind, however, should not be proclaimed simply and unambiguously as the "will of God," but as competent human or ecclesiastical judgments. It is wrong to demand absolute obedience to them for this reason, namely, that well-founded and competent doubts about these solutions and norms arise, thanks to one's own competence or to that of others, and such doubts are widely expressed.

CONCRETE: ABSOLUTE OBLIGATION?

An ethical *absolutum*, something unconditional, does exist, and in some way every human person is conscious of it: "Do good and avoid evil." This principle is valid as an *absolutum* in every sphere of life: it is the good as respect for every being who has human dignity, the good as justice and fairness, the good as chastity and as reproduction in a manner worthy of the person.

The further question is whether unconditional, that is, absolute, *concrete* ethical insights and statements exist in these areas of life to tell us with universal binding force the one correct form of conduct in every case. In the area of justice, do we know what "belongs" to the other or to a community? In the area of sexuality and of reproduction, do we know what is correct and worthy behavior?

On the one hand, there is neither total relativism nor radical pluralism; human reality in its plurality is a determinate *datum*, as is the practical reason that interprets and evaluates reality and makes ethical judgments. Precisely for this reason, there is no place for total arbitrariness, total relativism, or radical pluralism. De facto, these "isms" do not exist in the human world, despite numerous and profound differences in ethical judgments. V. Cathrein's idea of the unity of the ethical consciousness was not simply false.

On the other hand, we have already seen that human reality cannot compel the practical reason of multiple persons to arrive at one single and completely identical interpretation and ethical evaluation of human reality. The reason, after all, is created and finite, and each person has his or her particular experience and emotional conditioning. It is, however, comprehensible that one group or society with a particular history, experience of life, and interpretation of life should find similar answers to ethical questions; this commonalty is true also of religious societies and churches. It means that individual persons are not solitary islands when they undertake the ethical judgment of conduct; rather, they accept to a greater or lesser extent the ethos of their society. They cannot do anything else; they need the help of such a common ethos. Even if they believe that they may or must distance themselves from this ethos in individual areas to attain mature autonomy in a particular period of life, they nevertheless remain bound in some way to the original ethos.

For the individual or group, the original or corrected ethos can be the only possibility for an ethical interpretation and evaluation of particular realities of life. This ethos is, for them, the concrete and unconditionally binding translation of the ethical *absolutum* "Do good and avoid evil." Were more than one interpretation and judgment to appear to someone to be simultaneously possible, he or she would not capitulate even then to arbitrariness but would be required to live the ethical *absolutum* by translating it into the area of concrete interpretative possibilities that has already been discerned.

Does Catholic moral theology, that is, theological ethics, back up these reflections? Moral theology is a scholarly activity commissioned to bring current problems in the realm of morality nearer to their solution. But precisely because these problems are in the realm of morality—in the realm of what is personally good and ethically correct, this theology is never more than an attempt and a human endeavor. It follows that the results in moral theology will not always and everywhere be the same: it cannot be univocal.

Nevertheless, there is no discrepancy of theories and opinions within Catholic moral theology about the one ethical *absolutum* and its tautological and therefore equally absolute translations into the various areas of life. The translation of the ethical *absolutum* into the *material plurality* of human reality is, however, a different matter.

Yet even here, moral theology believes that it can construct valid ethical systems, which do not, however, attain a higher degree of certainty than that of being "morally certain." And it is for this reason, that several systems exist that are mutually contradictory. The history of Catholic moral theology is familiar with such mutually contradictory attempts at the solution of concrete problems of moral rightness; and moral theologians have never, in any century, held the same opinions about everything. It is clear that these many attempts do not contradict ethical statements of the Christian revelation, or binding understandings of a long and diverse Christian tradition.

Catholic moral theology has an immense influence, above all within the sphere of the church and among believing Christians, but also outside this sphere. It bears the great responsibility of offering positive and useful help to persons in the realm of ethics, while not presenting anything as absolutely obligatory unless it can be plausibly demonstrated as such. Catholic moral theology should therefore be modest and avoid portraying itself as too absolute within or outside its own ecclesiastical community, especially when it encounters ethical convictions held in good faith that cannot be reconciled with its own preliminary convictions.

For a long time, moral theology has been struggling with another problem. Tradition directs it to use teleological arguments in most areas of life to arrive at ethical outcomes. That is, moral theology evaluates the (premoral) good and ill implied in various attempts at solutions and reflects at the same time on the possibility of demanding a particular solution within the human and individual reality of the one who acts. How, for example, is a marriage to be consummated or lived if everything indicates that the couple's children will have a negative genetic inheritance?

In other areas of life, tradition urges moral theology to arrive at ethical outcomes through deontological rather than teleological arguments; for example, in questions about medical ethics, sexuality, and truthfulness, moral theology has believed that an unambiguous and unique, correct instruction for conduct was inscribed by the Creator on nature, which precisely because it was unique, was universal and obligatory with no exceptions. It was customary to call any form of conduct that contradicted this understanding (held as the only correct understanding) an *intrinsice malum*, or, intrinsically bad moral act.

Here, therefore, one had an unconditional quality (*absolutum*) of ethical rightness or falseness. This theory was broadly accepted in Catholic moral theology, and by Kant and Fichte, although not by the rest of Christianity, and certainly not by the rest of ethics worldwide. Today, even within Catholic moral theology, a broad skepticism prevails vis-à-vis such an "absolutum of ethical rightness" in particular areas of life. The tendency now is to see in this formulation of the absolute a naturalistic fallacy (i.e., the supposed discovery of *ethical* imperatives in the data of *nature*) and the denial of the plurality of interpretation.[9]

The authority of the Catholic Church's magisterium is essentially different from that of scholarly moral theology, and its responsibility is obviously greater. No doubt the magisterium teaches the one ethical *absolutum* and its somewhat tautological translations into the various realms of human life. But it also attributes to itself the competence of being able to issue authoritative statements about correct and incorrect conduct in the realm of contingent and manifold human reality. That is, the magisterium holds that it can exclude nonunanimous interpretations, evaluations, and ethical judgments of human reality; and instead determine a universally valid and unconditional *absolutum* in the judgment of concrete questions. Its statements are without doubt official, authentic, and authoritative, but they do not claim always to be infallible.

The latter fact does not absolutely exclude a plural interpretation, evaluation, and ethical judgment, although the church's magisterium is presented with high authority imposed by means of sanctions. We are therefore left with the question: by what authority can and does the magisterium reject absolutely divergent ethical statements, for example, of Christian groups and persons from essentially different cultures who want to be Christians, that is, those who come from Asia, Africa, or South America? The doctrine upheld by the magisterium seems to presuppose or imply a centuries-old interpretation, or a specifically "western" interpretation of human reality.

There is, however, a more fundamental question. Does the Catholic Church, under the assistance of the Holy Spirit, believe that it can and must proclaim a morality dealing with various areas of life that is absolutely valid in the same way for the whole world and for all human persons? Even a hermeneutical reading of the Bible or of ecclesiastical tradition does not give sufficient help here. We say only that if the church wishes to be credible, it may not permit itself a metaphysical or naturalistic fallacy. These problems are visible in the church today and must be made the object of serious reflection.

NOTES

1. V. Cathrein, *Die Einheit des sittlichen Bewusstseins*, 3 vols., Freiburg i. Br. 1914.
2. D. Mieth, *Moral und Erfahrung. Beiträge zur theologisch-ethischen Hermeneutik*, Freiburg i. Ue/Freiburg i. Br. 1977, 54.
3. G. J. Hughes, "Is Ethics One or Many?" in *Catholic Perspectives on Medical Morals. Foundational Issues*, ed. E. D. Pellegrino, J. P. Langan, and J. C. Harvey, Dordrecht 1989, 173-196.
4. See the instructive essay by K. Demmer, "Erwägungen zum '*intrinsice malum*,'" *Gregorianum* 68 (1987): 613-637.
5. I. Kant, *Grundlegung zur Metaphysik der Sitten* (Philos. Bibl., 41, 1971), BA 128.
6. See B. Schüller, "Sittliche Forderung und Erkenntnis Gottes. Überlegungen zu einer alten Kontroverse," *Gregorianum* 59 (1978): 5-37.
7. Thomas Aquinas, *Summa theologiae* II-II. Prologue (hereafter S.T.); In Nic.Eth.II.8.
8. S.T.I-II.94.1; and In Nic.Eth.I.1.
9. Teleologically, however, it is possible to establish an *intrinsice malum*, if one excludes the alteration of the object through ethically relevant circumstances; thus, for example, it is never permissible to kill someone only in order to do a favor for a third person.

2

Natural Law or Naturalistic Fallacy?

In recent years, the Catholic Church has frequently taken an official position on ethical questions. Many Christians and non-Christians welcome such decisive statements; others are simply unable to understand one or other of them and hold contrary positions to be the only possible, and therefore correct, positions. Earlier and more recent statements are greeted similarly; the reception of the encyclical *Humanae Vitae* (1968) and the declaration on certain questions of sexual ethics, *Persona Humana* (1975), were not different from the reception of more recent statements about the pastoral problems of homosexual persons (1986) and the acute problems of modern bioethics, especially *in vitro* fertilization, *Donum Vitae* (1987). The question is this: how does the official church—in the absence of a particular revelation about such concrete questions of humanity—know that its solutions are correct, and how do others know that their solutions, which differ from the official statements, are correct?

There may be various answers to this question, but are there perhaps also different and contradictory systems at the basis of these mutually contradictory solutions? The title of this chapter draws attention to this question. We cannot exclude a priori that the same persons will solve certain questions by using one particular system, and not even think of this system when they have to solve other questions. Part of the task of moral theologians is not to leave the official church alone in such questions for to do so would prevent its moral teaching from being sufficiently justified and nonpositivistically grounded.[1]

INTRODUCTION TO THE PROBLEM

1. In his famous discourse to Italian midwives in 1951, Pope Pius XII expressed a position on various questions of the ethics of matrimony.[2] His theme, inter alia, was the morally right carrying out of the marital act and—as a particular problem—what is possible in practice for a marriage from which, in all probability, the children will inherit defects. The Pope sees the generation of children as the primary goal of the marital act and of marriage as a whole. Accordingly, he rejects the practice of the marital act using contraceptives, that is, "artificial methods," but not the total avoidance of the generation of children in such a marriage—provided that this avoidance takes place, for example, by having intercourse during the infertile period.

The exclusion of procreation from the marital act is rejected, but not the exclusion of procreation from the realization (even the sexual realization) of the marriage. What is the source of this distinction? It is clear that two different ethical arguments are the source of the Pope's two statements. In the first case, the "nature" of sexuality itself indicates to the discerning human person the form that the individual *act* must take in accordance with this nature (and the will of the Creator); in the second case, right conduct in married life as a whole is found through human "rational consideration" of the positive and negative values implied in the various possible solutions to the problem.

Attention is sometimes drawn today to a parallel question.[3] Why does traditional moral theology, still upheld as official, hold that the "immature" act of masturbation is absolutely impermissible from an ethical point of view and always a "grave" disorder (*Persona Humana*) when, under certain circumstances, the killing of a person is seen as morally justifiable within society as a whole? This difference is at first sight astonishing; does the difference between these two moral judgments not presuppose two different manners of ethical argument? In another parallel: although killing is not unjustified in all circumstances, a false statement is always unjustified (always, without distinction, this falsehood is called a "lie").

In keeping with a long tradition, Thomas Aquinas believed that the procreation and education of children was the goal of human sexuality and its actualization. From this he deduced that an *act* of sexuality is morally permissible only in the form of the union of man and woman "in accordance with nature." Only this act is sexual conduct *secundum naturam*, which nature Thomas understood in Ulpian's sense as the nature that is common to humans and beasts. And precisely because it is natural, it is also *secundum rationem* in human terms. But it is not the *nature* of sexuality (as Thomas understands it) that determines whether such a union of man and woman presupposes monogamous and indissoluble marriage; this union must be discovered through the intervention of reason, a weighing of the arguments pro and con. The conclusion is that monogamous and indissoluble marriage is *secundum rationem* (and not just *secundum naturam*) the *condicio sine qua non* of the repeated union of man and woman, and thus of every sexual actualization.[4] Both forms of moral rightness are considered by Thomas to belong to the order that is determined by the nature of the human person endowed with reason, the so-called moral natural law or the "ratio practica."

2. We know today that both forms of argument—from nature and from reason, though each in its own realm—have always existed in Christian moral theology. Some hold that a mistake is concealed in this double form of argument, and that it must be corrected. Others, however, hold that it is a mistake to solve all ethical problems in the same way, by means of the same system, but this idea would mean that both systems are justified in their own realm (and only there).[5]

The solution of this problem has several consequences. If, for example, the official church uses now one system and now the other in its statements on moral theology as, for example, in the case of Pius XII, does it not thereby lose its credibility, as some believe? If natural law moral problems are solved on the basis of what exists in nature (e.g., the given nature of sexuality or language) or on the basis of rational insight into particular data of nature, while other ethical questions find their solution exclusively through a rational reflection and consideration of the whole complex of elements contained in an action, and both ways of arriving at an ethical solution are understood to be in keeping with "natural law" (in the sense of "human moral self-understanding"), then the question arises of the justification of such a difference. Does the nature (or essence) of the human person itself justify this difference, or is it possible that we have here a partially false interpretation of human reality?

This question does not involve only the credibility of the church's official moral teaching, but also the much more significant question whether mistaken reasonings without a proper justification and the imposition of corresponding requirements may impose on the faithful—and have sometimes imposed—moral burdens that have no justification in the essence of being Christian and therefore make the path to salvation unjustifiably harder.

3. The fundamental question posed here has been asked for a long time outside Catholic moral theology. David Hume sensed the difficulty involved in the claim that one can truly deduce conclusions for the dynamic reality of an obligation from what exists (and therefore from what exists in nature) as a static reality of being.[6] This difficulty implies the impossibility of drawing conclusions from what the person is to what he or she should do, not only in a general sense but also, for example, in the realm of human sexuality or language. One cannot deduce a particular ethical obligation from the givenness of human sexuality and its supposed finality, or from the givenness of human language and its supposed finality, in order thus to arrive at ethical natural law. G. E. Moore identifies a naturalistic fallacy in the deduction or justification of "ought" from "is," or of obligation from being.[7]

Other writers would speak, in other areas, of a metaphysical or even theological fallacy (is-ought).[8] In fact, the only thing that we can grasp from the givenness of nature (e.g., of sexuality) is what it is, how it functions, and what its natural goal is (perhaps a goal reached in a variety of ways). By itself, therefore, nature discloses only its being to us, not an ethical obligation. Thus, the question of how we "should" make use of what is given in nature in a human and rational way is exclusively an ethical question that must be solved by human reason; it is a question of interpreting and evaluating of the relevance of nature for human reality as a whole.

This consideration excludes as superfluous the double attempt at a solution that we find, for example, in Pius XII and Thomas Aquinas. The study of what is given in natures does not, as such, permit us to recognize any moral obligation, and the attempt to deduce a moral obligation from this source alone is revealed as a naturalistic fallacy. But, even if nature has nothing direct to say about moral obligation in terms of its actualization, it is nevertheless relevant for the rational interpretation and evaluation of the given, and thus for an ethical judgment about its realization in a way that is humanly right and therefore morally justifiable.

A moral judgment about right ethical conduct cannot be deduced from what is given in nature, but can be found through human, rational, evaluative reflection within human reality as a whole. Only in this way can we avoid a naturalistic fallacy and find the true meaning of the "natural law." Ethical natural law—this well-known terminology will be used here, instead of *humanum, recta ratio,* and similar terms to draw attention terminologically to the difference between this idea and the naturalistic fallacy—does not mean an understanding of "what exists in nature," but the insight and evaluative judgment of human reason (itself a given in nature and creation) with a view to right conduct in the given human, personal world.

These considerations raise a fundamental question: can it be excluded a priori that thinkers will, in the course of time, find solutions to ethical questions that earlier generations did not see? Further, why do many well-intentioned Catholics, Catholic theologians, and their contemporaries find themselves unable to agree with individual decisions of the church on moral questions, when they interpret and evaluate reality in a human manner? Is it the case that they lack insight? Archbishop Quinn of San Francisco drew attention at the 1980 Synod of Bishops to the problem that for many Catholics, the justification of the thesis of *Humanae Vitae* is simply not convincing. The bishops assembled in the Synod, and later the pope, formulated the corresponding requirement that a search must be made for better argumentation.

This introduction leads to the question of what is genuinely natural law, and what is only a naturalistic fallacy. This question has fundamental significance for normative moral theology and for the search for moral truths in the question of right ethical conduct.

NATURALISTIC FALLACY OR NATURAL LAW?

Historically, both methods of argument mentioned here have existed side-by-side in Christian moral theology. The first, however, was restricted to only a few determined areas of life, for example, false statements (lies), sexuality, and the disposition of one's body and life. Moreover, it was never used in the context of the "absolute" value of personal moral *goodness* as opposed to morally *right conduct* or with regard to right conduct vis-à-vis God as the "absolute" value, or with regard to statements that are obvious ("be good") or tautological ("do not kill without justification"). These boundaries indicate the area that will be considered next. The justification of the moral rightness of concrete human conduct in a world with only "relative" values is our question.

We are agreed that only rational human insight into the created reality of the person and the world can ground a "natural law" solution to the problems of the ethical rightness of behavior. (For the Christian, this insight is also illumined by the gospel.)

We are also agreed that in many, indeed in most, areas of human reality, a moral solution will be found, not on the basis of an individual act but through a process of understanding, pondering, evaluating, and judging the various human goods or values involved in a particular kind of conduct as a whole (the word "human" means that these goods or values are understood in their relationship to the human person). This conduct may concern the problems of an individual's interpersonal and societal relationships or the worldwide problems of humanity.

On the other hand, is the question whether individual acts that can be described in their natural reality, that is, in isolation from other circumstances, and the data that also come into play necessarily or de facto in the actualization of these acts, can be judged to be morally right or false. Many theologians in the past and in our time have accepted this possibility, and have thereby accepted a double form of argument in the realm of the moral natural law.

If the ground of this positive answer is widely questioned today, it is because it is believed to contain a fallacy. That is, this kind of argument does not lead to an answer in the sense of the natural moral law. Its outcome can only be a non-natural law and hence a normative moral statement that in this way lacks sufficient justification.

The problematic of this question and its consequences, can be demonstrated in the previous example of masturbation or killing. If it is said that masturbation, as a solitary actualization of sexuality, is not only false but immoral based on the essence of human sexuality and on the nature of the act itself, then it goes without saying that no goal or circumstance, however important, can justify such an actualization of sexuality, not the pleasure, relaxation, proof that a man is capable of marriage, or the intention to make a marriage fruitful through any kind of artificial fertilization. If, on the other hand, the moral permissibility of killing is judged on the basis of its significance in the whole context of human and social reality, then the justification of an act of killing, although it is more significant than a solitary sexual act, is not to be excluded a priori, without any exception, and under all conceivable circumstances; and in fact this judgment has prevailed in the ethics of the past and the present.

This reflection calls for an additional consideration. If one wishes to make an ethical judgment about an individual human reality on the basis of its givenness in nature, one must bear the following facts in mind. First, in the past, neither the whole reality of the human person (from the emergence of humankind to its total development in the future) nor its individual elements (e.g., the enormous powers of the cosmos, the inconceivable possibilities of human biology and genetics, the full reality of human sexuality considered biologically, physiologically, psychologically, and sociologically) was known as it is today (even if our knowledge is, in part, only hypothetical); and we cannot yet guess what the future will bring to light. If one wishes to make an objective judgment today, then one cannot take what Augustine or the philosophers of the Middle Ages knew about sexuality as the exclusive basis of a moral reflection.

Second, we never simply "have" nature (or that which is given in nature). Although human societies and individuals know "nature," they do so always as something that has already been interpreted in some way. Our moral judgments are made, therefore, on the basis of an interpretation of what we know and it is possible that our interpretation can be mistaken, or that it can change. For example, although for many centuries, the natural finality of sexuality was seen to lie exclusively in the maintenance or continuance of the human race, a more recent tendency, even in the Catholic Church, is to recognize a double finality, and finally to accept the thesis of the natural coherence of both finalities in the actualization of sexuality. Thus, we argue on the basis of nature as it is interpreted, and not simply on the basis of nature itself.

Third, together with the interpretation of natural realities, there is always also a human evaluation (i.e., an evaluation in relation to persons), whether of individual realities as such, or in their relationship to other realities in the whole of one's reality. These evaluations can be more or else different in different groups, societies, and periods of time, but also in individual persons, and they can change. Indeed it is clear that they do change. But our evaluations are the necessary basis of our moral judgments about right conduct.

If one takes account of these three facts, then one must reckon with differences and change in the formation of opinions, for example, in the judgment of particular grounds for the justification of killing. It is abundantly obvious that this is now the case. In the case of masturbation, parallel considerations must have their place if our argument is truly a consideration of natural law. And in that case, the act as such will be disclosed as only an immature actualization, not as an act that automatically discloses a moral judgment or "moral natural law." Presumably, without reflecting on what we were doing, we have always (rightly or wrongly) reflected on additional elements in our efforts to make ethical evaluations. Examples can make this difference between ethical natural law and the naturalistic fallacy clear.

(A) In many ethics, every false statement, without exception, has been condemned as impermissible in itself, and therefore called a "lie," an unjustified false statement. The justification for this view was the fact that the false statement always contradicts what the speaker really takes to be the case, and therefore contradicts his or her reality. The presupposition for this statement is the reality called "human speech," the single natural finality of which is the communication to others of what one holds to be the case. One can, however, question whether this interpretation of human speech is the only interpretation possible. Without doubt, the nature of speech is a phenomenon of communication. But this phenomenon includes more than a communication of what one is thinking. For example, the refusal of an answer is also a use of human speech, although one may call it a "deficient" use; an enthusiastic or depressed soliloquy is likewise a deficient possibility of human speech, which is given in nature.

A false statement made to preserve a secret (which can perhaps be a duty) is also a use—indeed, a very important and natural use of human speech. Thus, although human speech belongs fundamentally to the realm of communication between human persons, it has more than one natural finality. The decisive question from the moral point of view, in the case of a false statement, is what use one makes of it; that is, one must consider whether the human good intended is so significant that it justifies the social evil of a false statement. If and only if the use of human speech were to be understood exclusively as the communication of what one holds to be the case would the false statement be unjustified in every case, and a lie, a *locutio contra mentem* in the traditional sense.

Various authors have pointed this out in recent years, including A. Vermeersch in 1920.[9] It follows that it is wrong to identify the lie and the false statement, or to speak of a "logic of human speech as an impersonal finality inherent in things," which is the basis of "fidelity to a given *ordo rationis* of human nature and of the truth of the human person," and therefore to "the will of God as Creator and fundamental ground of the ethical order."[10] Such thinking is a naturalistic fallacy—not a consideration of natural law.

(B) Some have believed it possible to read the ethical obligations of the person with respect to sexuality in the natural reality of human sexuality and its finality interpreted in this way; that is, as corresponding exclusively to the natural (not artificially manipulated) union of man and woman in marriage. The natural givenness of human sexuality, however, offers several other possible uses, and indeed sometimes a frequent or even exclusive inclination and impulse to actualize them. Today we know that human sexuality also offers the (doubtless not ideal) *in vitro* fertilization. It also offers homosexual conduct and, in some cases, only this form of interpersonal sexual relationship, no matter how deficient. And, it offers the immature and highly defective form of masturbation, among other possibilities. The nature of human sexuality does not proclaim what is humanly and therefore ethically justifiable or unjustifiable behavior, and it would be a clear naturalistic fallacy to attempt to read these norms in the nature of human sexuality.

Without doubt, the ideal realization of sexuality in marriage can be discovered through fully human evaluation, but it can scarcely be shown to be a universal law. This means that it can scarcely provide a decisive criterion against deficient forms of sexuality, such as homosexuality or the immature sexuality of the young person. For it is not only the fully mature and ideal sexuality that exists. In this context, therefore, one cannot simply appeal to the first chapters of Genesis, which speak of the mature sexuality of the adult women and men and nothing else. It follows that it is reasonable persons who must discover what, along with the fully mature and ideal form, is right or wrong in the realm of human sexuality, what truly or indeed best serves humanity, taking into account all the values or disvalues of the various forms of conduct in human sexuality as a whole.

This reflection must consider not only the natural character of human sexuality and its relevance for ethically right behavior, but also its significance in human reality as a whole. The outcome is, then, the attempt to answer the question of right sexual self-realization in terms of natural law. Wherever, because of a naturalistic fallacy, it was believed that an absolute answer allowing no exceptions existed, this question has scarcely been investigated. In such cases, there are few, if any, pointers to a genuine natural law reflection, especially when in practice the false conclusion has been given positive sanction in the society. There has also been scarcely any reflection on whether the answer of natural law would be identical with the norm that has been sanctioned.

(C) The disposition over the body and life of a human person (and indeed over whether procreation occurs or not in the union of man and woman) is widely understood as the exclusive right of God and, therefore, as outside our personal control. God's sovereignty embraces not only these realities, however, but all created reality. God's universal sovereignty is transcendent, not merely in the world, and is not, therefore, in competition with human rights. It follows that it is a fallacy to say that only God, not persons, may make decisions about the realities named here. If one wishes (and rightly) not to call this a naturalistic fallacy, one may call it metaphysical or theological. One cannot therefore deduce, from God's relationship to creation, what the obligation of the human person is in these areas or in the realm of creation as a whole.

The rational person, society, or humanity as a whole, can only attempt to discover the solution of natural law, taking into account all the values and disvalues that are involved in particular forms of behavior. One should not forget here that human reason too belongs decisively to the being, and in this sense, to the nature of the person created by God. We may not give the task back to God with the intention of blaming God for consequences that per se could be avoided. That would be contrary to creation.[11]

What, then, can we take to be the reason for the fallacies indicated here, that is, for non-natural norms? B. Lonergan drew attention years ago to the distinction (valid for moral theologians too) between the "classicist" and the "historicist" self-understanding of the human person. The classicist self-understanding conceives of the human person and his or her various components as a series of created, static, and thus definitively ordered temporal facts. In an ethical context, this understanding means that one must conform to the given facts in one's conduct, and that they are to be seen as the expression of an a priori ethical requirement. The historicist self-understanding of the human person sees the task of the human person as self-realization in accordance with a project that develops in God-given human autonomy, that is, along the path of human reason and insight, carried out in the present with a view to the future.

The classicist self-understanding of the human person sees the divine *lex aeterna* as inscribed once for all on created human realities, while the historicist self-understanding conceives human reason as a specific and decisive element of the "human" reality deriving from the Creator, which can and must take responsibility for the human future as the image of God, not only in passive acceptance, but also through an active planning that takes thought for the future.

Whatever human reason correctly recognizes as a universal norm, general indication, or requirement determined by a particular situation is in fact a participation in the divine *lex aeterna*, and therefore is in each case contained within it. A classical understanding of natural law is basically a "positivist" understanding of natural law (a static law "written on nature"), and precisely does not offer genuine natural law as the living and active creaturely participation in God's eternal wisdom. The *lex aeterna*, on the other hand, is "written on the heart," that is, on reason (Rom 2:15).

Christian moral theologians have always known that *most* of the moral norms and judgments termed "natural law" are not reached by reading moral norms into individual facts of nature as such, along the path of a naturalistic fallacy. Apart from the few areas of life discussed in the preceding paragraphs, insights and judgments of natural law have been acquired in another way. Even Cardinal Ratzinger, who tends to be hostile to what some people, Americans above all, call proportionalism, holds on this point that "the attempt to establish a proportion between the good and the evil results of an act we are reflecting on is rather a judgment of common sense that we are generally accustomed to make. Even the principle of totality and the whole tradition, with regard to the consideration of the circumstances of behavior, imply the concept of proportionality, and—I believe—not without good success."[12]

To this we should add the point that in the principle repeatedly applied for several hundred years in the case of actions with a double effect, attention is paid explicitly to the proportionality of the double effect of a particular act. In the broad areas of human conduct, the question of the significance and value of an action has always been posed while taking all its components into account—precisely in order to establish whether it represents, as a whole, a value or a disvalue for the individual person, society, or humanity. This reflection, however is not written on the "nature" of particular forms of action considered in isolation but is found in a rational reflection or intuition (Ratzinger's "common sense") of the whole human person as developing in history.[13]

Moral judgment is a case, then, of human interpretation, evaluation, and corresponding ethical judgment of human forms of conduct. It belongs to the being of the created human person that one can err in such reflections and intuitions. Nevertheless, this reflective search is the only possible and justified way for persons to seek ethical norms and judgments in accordance with the natural law (illumined by the gospel); the other way of the naturalistic fallacy is fundamentally closed. The way of searching in accordance with natural law will, as we have indicated, often arrive at norms that—unlike the supposed norms of a naturalistic fallacy—can only claim a general validity, which is not universal or without exceptions, if they are truly to claim objectivity.[14] Nevertheless, such universally valid norms without exceptions are not excluded by this way of searching, as can be seen from the formulation of such norms. We shall come back to this point later.

THE NATURAL LAW OF THE INTEGRAL RIGHTNESS OF HUMAN CONDUCT

1. If one seeks to identify ethical right human conduct but cannot find it along the path of a naturalistic fallacy, then we must examine somewhat more closely the true reality of what is called "moral natural law" as the "norm" of human rightness in worldly conduct—precisely in order to show clearly the difference between this "moral natural law" and a norm of conduct that comes from a naturalistic fallacy. Note once more that we are not concerned here with norms of personal moral goodness, or with norms that are formal rather than concrete, for example, to be "good," "just," or "chaste," or with tautological norms, for example, "do not commit murder" (it is wrong to kill unjustly), "do not lie" (do not make false statements without justification). Rather, we are concerned with norms that state in material concreteness what is humanly justifiable and therefore morally right conduct and behavior in various areas, and what is not. Note also that the facts of nature do not declare this morality (i.e., one cannot read it in the facts of nature), but they remain relevant for arriving at valid ethical statements about concrete, worldly conduct.

A concrete action is always complex in the sense that it always contains various elements that must be considered in a human manner (i.e., taking into account the human nature of the person). It is not simply the significance of one or many of the human elements that must be interpreted but also, and above all, the human significance of the conduct as a whole. Therefore, the concern is not simply the realization of individual elements but the realization of the person as such *through* the realization of the entire complex of the multiple elements of a concrete action. Such conduct is the outcome both of the past that lies behind the action and thus is known, and of the future (personal, social, or global) that is the outcome of the present action to the extent that it is foreseeable here and now.

The interpreting and evaluating reason has the task of examining the entire human significance and value of concrete actions and behavior, and hence also of judging their moral rightness. What traditionally has been called *recta ratio*, or the correct judgment of the reason, now takes as natural law the various elements of a complex reality that is to be judged ethically, and sets them "in proportion," thus enabling the reason to make its judgment about the moral rightness of concrete conduct. There is, accordingly, no *quantitative* mathematical calculation of the plurality of *qualitatively* different elements involved in the action in question, together with its positive (and negative) values: such a calculation would be quite impossible in view of the diversity of such elements and values. There is, however, an act of understanding and evaluating by *the person as a whole*—an act that is often not the product of reflection but of common sense—that humanity has always believed and shown itself to be capable of. If humanity has considered itself capable of this sensible act in most of the areas of human conduct, without doubt or contradiction—because one sees that it is the only way possible to make an ethical judgment—then it is not easy to see why it cannot behave likewise in those few areas in which it was mistakenly held that one could and must operate with a naturalistic fallacy.

A central problem faces the person who seeks to make judgments in accordance with natural law. That is, the person who aims at personal moral goodness, who must make a judgment about the moral rightness of actual conduct, faces the problem of human evaluation with regard to the *entirety* of the act's positive (and negative) values, which are qualitatively so various. The literature of moral theology has repeatedly pointed out that this problematic requires a deeper reflection; even those authors who hold such an evaluation to be both unavoidable and possible admit this need. The desire is for a method that can be described and applied securely, a method that in this sense would be a criterion of evaluation.

(A) Without doubt, it is not a case of human evaluation in the sense of utilitarianism, for utilitarianism has as its criterion the great increase of human happiness possible for the greatest number of persons. Such a criterion pays insufficient attention to higher cultural and intellectual values; it can and must sacrifice the individual and his or her interests and rights to the interest of the greater number, at least in certain circumstances. The values in question here are not only material, but include other values of the person: for example, personality, culture, spirituality, justice (in the sense of the *iustum* that is to be determined in each particular case), appropriate fairness between persons (to be discovered in each case), and the acceptance of a religious faith (with all possible consequences), among others.

Thus, the highly desirable method or criterion for considering and evaluating presumably cannot be found, precisely because of the qualitative variety of values. Evaluation is an original human activity that cannot be reduced to other activities that have already been carried out. Nevertheless, one can compare a particular evaluation with another that has already been made, or with the evaluation of other persons or groups, to draw inspiration from them. In the moral theology of the past, it was customary, lacking a method of evaluation, to proceed casuistically in the tract about the right ordering of love. Right consideration and evaluation were introduced by various examples of the consideration and comparison of qualitatively different values. The treatment of the principle of the action with a double effect was similar: one established several formal criteria that were to be observed in order to make the task of establishing the correct "proportion" of the two effects through consideration and evaluation easier, and to provide a degree of certainty.

(B) Such an act of evaluation almost never begins absolutely from scratch. The new evaluation draws on evaluations that have been handed down or accepted in a society, or have already been carried out by individuals or groups. It is thus that the new evaluation is original. Since evaluations and, correspondingly,judgments about ethically right conduct are always carried out by persons who are the subjects of the evaluations, it is inevitable that the intellectual or religious world views of the subjects who make the evaluations enter into them. Besides this, since one cannot demonstrate values but only establish them intellectually, it is quite possible that some of the evaluations implied, for example, in the Instruction *Donum Vitae* (1987) can be accepted by its authors but not by all readers of the document, in the same way. Note, too, that *Gaudium et Spes* (43) accepted the possibility that believing and conscientious Catholics may come to various evaluations and arrive at various judgments in contemporary questions about humanity or moral rightness.

This variety has nothing to do with (arbitrary) *subjectivism*, but with the necessarily subjective act of evaluation that must be determined by the subject. This does not exclude the possibility of a genuine evaluation by several persons in a group or in a society, who arrive at the same result. The objectivity of the act of evaluation lies, not in freedom from determination by the subject, but in the seriousness of the endeavor, in the light of evaluations that have already been carried out and observed elsewhere, to be guided in one's own act by the entirety of the human reality that is under evaluation. This reality must be interpreted in a human and Christian way; and it is anything but a mere "good intention."

PROPORTIONALISM—ANOTHER NAME FOR NATURAL LAW?

1. Up to this point, because of the terminological parallel to the "naturalistic fallacy," the human (and Christian) way of establishing the moral rightness of real human behavior has been termed "in keeping with natural law." Recently, especially in North America, the name "proportionalism" has been given to this understanding of the natural law.[15] What is the point of this name? There is good reason to avoid the terminology of "natural law," which is easily misunderstood today; thereafter, it is per se unimportant how one names the reality that is meant, whether as *ratio recta*, human moral self-understanding, the natural ethical law, or something else. Why not "proportionalism"?

For years, I myself have frequently sought to avoid the terminology of "natural law," and have used other formulations, although I have never used the terminology of proportionalism (or even consequentialism) though others have, on occasion, attributed these positions to me. These names are possible in my opinion, only if certain conditions are presupposed: (1) that every statement that is revealed as a naturalistic fallacy remains excluded from such a natural law; (2) that one is careful, in the discussion about the moral rightness of categorical behavior, not to let statements about personal moral goodness slip into the discussion, confusing these statements about personal moral goodness with statements about the moral rightness of behavior, or compiling a mixed list of both; (3) that one correctly understands and attends to the distinction between values or goods that are moral and those that are premoral, that is, not moral, but human and therefore morally relevant to the evaluation of an action; and (4) that one does not confuse or mix norms of right categorical behavior with analytical, tautological, or formal norms, thus including them in the problem that concerns us here—the rightness of concrete categorical norms of behavior.

The nonobservance of these conditions amounts to an *ignorantia elenchi*, and renders the discussion meaningless. Nevertheless, such an *ignorantia elenchi* is sometimes seen in the discussion of the natural law (now called proportionalism). I think, for example, among those who write in English, of such parties to the discussion as G. Grisez, J. Finnis, P. Quay, J. Connery, W. May, and B. Kiely. The chief opponent of these various misunderstandings in the literature is doubtless R. A. McCormick.[16] L. Sowle Cahill, E. Vacek, and others may also be mentioned.

2. Various, or variously nuanced, attempts at a "natural law without the naturalistic fallacy" have been presented recently. In Catholic moral theology, it was first P. Knauer and then B. Schüller (to a greater degree and in a different way) who suggested analytical evaluation of the effects of a categorical act.[17] Already in 1958, G. E. M. Anscombe had attacked a normative method, which she called consequentialism, that looked only to the effects of an action.[18] The one-sided concentration on an analytical evaluation of effects or consequences with a view to establishing norms of moral rightness does have practical disadvantages: (a) it makes it easy to overlook the fact that the action itself (and not only its effects or consequences) can also be called an "effect" (with its own relevance for moral rightness) that proceeds from the subject who acts, and must itself be included in the determination of the moral rightness of the action as a whole; (b) it contains the subjectivist temptation, when actions are evaluated, to think of the intentions[19] of the effects rather than of the effects themselves. At the same time, no distinction is made between personal moral goodness (intention) and the moral goodness of the behavior itself; and (c) there is a danger that this approach may approximate utilitarianism, or be understood in a utilitarian way. Such misunderstandings arise again and again in the discussion of the natural law that is now often called proportionialism.

To avoid such misunderstandings, those who uphold our understanding of the natural law (especially those who write in English) have replaced the terminology of consequentialism with the terminology of proportionalism. Nonetheless, it frequently happens in the discussion that the natural law teaching that calls itself proportionalism is falsely equated with consequentialism or even with utilitarianism.[20] The term "proportionalism" for natural law in the sense set out here has, however, given rise to yet another specific contradiction in moral theological discussion. A few examples follow.

(A) The understanding of natural law set out here, which many call proportionalism, is not seldom misunderstood to be an attempt to relativize the norms of the moral rightness of conduct, which are understood (because of the naturalistic fallacy) to be universal or absolute. That is, this interpretation may be taken as an attempt to identify exceptions to the norms, or as an attempt to consider the entirety of an action under certain circumstances as the justification of its individual elements (which perhaps bear a moral judgment in themselves, independently of the whole). This way of looking at the matter presupposes that a solution has already been found to the whole problem of arriving at norms or judgments, the very problem that was to be assisted by the reflection of natural law (proportionalism). But this solution, as has already been said, involves a naturalistic fallacy. It attributes a moral rightness to the parts of an action that are independent of the whole (e.g., in cases of false statement, masturbation, and similar situations). But the partial elements of a whole action, since they are *human* good or evil, positive or negative values, are not only ontic or purely natural, and thus morally neutral elements; therefore, they cannot determine any moral judgment about the rightness of the whole.[21] Rather, they are human realities that must be taken into account proportionally in the judgment about the rightness of the whole: in themselves, they are not moral goods or ills, moral values and disvalues, but they are morally relevant.

(B) The understanding of natural law indicated here demands a human analysis and evaluation of the various individual positive goods or negative values inherent in an action, precisely in order to discover the rightness of conduct in the world of the human person. Such an analysis of positive and negative values, goods, and ills has sometimes been declared to be impossible. Because these values or disvalues are qualitatively different, they cannot be compared and quantitatively measured. Among other reasons for this difficulty, it is impossible for anyone to see in advance and consider all possible consequences of an action. Here, of course, the moral theologians should have noted (as they always have in explanation of the principle of the double effect) that responsible behavior must pay heed to possible consequences only in accordance with their significance and to the extent that they are humanly foreseeable.

A mistaken inclination exists to understand this analysis and evaluation as an "algebraic measurement," indeed as a "Marxist and mercantilist approach to Christian morality."[22] As we have noted, however, most of the moral problems concerning the manner of analysis and evaluation have been solved—not by means of a naturalistic fallacy, but in a teleological manner—and, as even Cardinal Ratzinger agrees, solved successfully. Moreover, the solution holds true (even among the moral theologians who protest at this point) and even in the case of the principle of double effect. Clearly, perhaps with the possible exception of cases of grave conflict, we do not have a general need for a careful analysis and a corresponding comparison of the individual elements of an action. Indeed, such an analysis holds a possible danger, namely, that one may not find the path back to the wholeness of the action from the analysis of its parts. It is clear that we are able, as common sense says, to evaluate and make a moral judgment about the entirety of an action as an entirety—and this judgment implies the evaluation, comparison, and judgment of the individual elements contained within the whole.[23] *Donum Dei* (1987), the instruction on bioethics from the Congregation for the Doctrine of Faith speaks explicitly in footnote 27 and I, 5 about the acceptance of disproportioned and proportioned risks that biologists and physicians take; the evaluations and moral judgments included in such a proportionalism are therefore considered as possible and necessary.

We must turn our attention here to the word "moral." For although this analysis and evaluation is applied to premoral realities (*human* goods and ills, values and disvalues) and their "right" realization in the world, it takes place under the influence of one's personal moral attitude (and the acceptance of *moral* values inherent in this attitude) of the man or woman who applies it. One's moral attitude enters into the analysis and evaluation, which precisely (and only) thereby becomes the *moral* analysis and evaluation of the personal and moral human being. The difficulty is often argued, that this (natural law) understanding of the moral rightness of actions subordinates morality to premoral values or goods.[24] However, this difficulty shows that insufficient attention has been paid to the distinction between the moral goodness of the person and the moral rightness of actions. For such analysis and evaluation certainly do not begin with individual acts as partial elements of an action, but with the *person* who, in his or her moral goodness, seeks to realize oneself in a concrete right *action* (with its partial elements not considered as so many individual acts).

CONSEQUENCES

It has frequently been observed that individuals would be both psychologically and ethically confronted with an impossibly high demand, if they had to analyze and evaluate every value implicit in an action. But it is not only a matter for individuals; it is also a matter of the possibility of society itself to arrive at moral norms and judgments about the rightness of behavior. Clear solutions based on a naturalistic fallacy aid one both psychologically and ethically to discover unambiguous solutions that can be simply applied. In other words, because of a naturalistic fallacy, one arrives easily at absolute prohibitions and knows unambiguously what is to be done or avoided.

The question however, is whether one has considered the entirety of an action or only one aspect of it. In the latter case, it may be that one has based the moral judgment of the action one-sidedly on the consideration of an individual aspect of the action, rather than on the action in its entirety. The naturalistic fallacy leads to a yes or no that admits no exceptions because it sees only one isolated individual reality. Natural law reflection (proportionalism) does not isolate these aspects, but requires a reflection on the concrete entirety of the reality of an action. It concerns a full concrete moral reality. But this reflection does not begin from scratch: we already possess moral understandings and judgments that can help us find the right solution for problems that arise us in a particular case.

2. The objectivity of moral norms and judgments is not determined by one or other fact of nature, but by the relative significance of such facts in the entirety of human reality and conduct. Moral norms that are based on a naturalistic fallacy cannot be gradually applied in different situations; they know no *epikeia*; their negative formulas of prohibition bespeak only an *intrinsice malum*; they are applicable literally in terms of what they say. It is otherwise with the natural law that permits no naturalistic fallacy. Natural law reflections permit statements that have not yet taken into account all possibilities of self-realization (that is, "prima *facie* duties") that require a different moral judgment from the one that was previously made when a different

kind of self-realization was envisaged. And they demand such a situational judgment for the sake of the objectivity required by the moral truth in the entirety of an action.

Such a natural law recognizes a graduality of already formulated concrete norms of moral rightness, in the sense that the objective and true moral judgment must be arrived at and formulated anew in each situation. Thus, the natural law does not wholly exclude the *intrinsice malum*. For example, what has been correctly recognized *in concreto* as morally wrong is immoral because of the given reality itself, and, therefore, it is always wrong wherever this reality presents itself. Likewise, a formulation that excludes the possibility of a different realization of a particular fact, and a formulation that has been recognized as morally wrong, is a *norma universalis*, an *intrinsece malum*. For example, someone who kills a child *only* to please a third person, acts wrongly, because of the "only." This act is absolutely and always morally wrong.

The unambiguous and absolute moral norms and judgments established on the basis of a naturalistic fallacy always call the individual to fidelity vis-à-vis their requirements. They allow no exceptions and no *epikeia* with respect to the once-formulated norm in difficult situations, but they also never require anything more. They always demand personal conversions, so that, despite his or her weaknesses, a person may always take the once-recognized and formulated norm (and only this) as a guide. The formulations of the true natural law—without a naturalistic fallacy—ask about the concrete human reality in each case, and their aim is that one's conduct should always be in accordance with this reality. Conversion is not the continual turning to a norm that has been found and formulated once for all, but the always new commitment to seek (using also one's personal inheritance) the right answer to a given concrete human reality as a whole and to embrace the corresponding action itself as the answer.

NOTES

1. Cf. J. Ratzinger, "Theologie und Ethos," in K. Ulmer, *Die Verantwortung der Wissenschaft*, Bonn 1975, 46-61, at 56.

2. *Acta Apostolicae Sedis* 43 (1951), 835-854.

3. Cf., for example, L. Sowle Cahill, "Teleology, Utilitarianism, and Christian Ethics," *Theological Studies* 42 (1981): 601-629, at 611.

4. So *passim*; S.T.II-II.154.11c: "quod quidem potet esse dupliciter: uno quidem modo quia repugnat rationi rectae; quod est commune in omni vitio

luxuriae; alio modo quia etiam super hoc repugnat ipsi ordini naturalis venerei actus, qui convenit humanae speciei: quod dicitur vitium contra naturam."

5. See J. Ratzinger on the theme of proportionalism: "Epilogue," in *Moral Theology Today: Certitudes and Doubts*, St. Louis 1984, 337-346, at 343.

6. This problematic was raised for the first time by D. Hume, *A Treatise of Human Nature*, L. A. Selby-Bigges Edition. Oxford, Clarendon 1928, 469.

7. G. E. Moore, *Principia Ethica*, Cambridge 1903, 64.

8. Cf. W. K. Frankena, *Ethics*, Engelwood Cliffs, New Jersey 1963.

9. A. Vermeersch, "De mendacio et necessitatibus commercii humani," *Gregorianum* 1 (1920): 11-40 and 425-475.

10. This, however, is the deontological argument of G. Gatti, "Linguaggio e testimonianza. Un caso emblematic di fondazione deontologica della norma morale," *Salesianum* 48 (1968): 281-306.

11. On problem C, see J. Fuchs, "Das Gottesbild und die Moral innerweltlichen Handelns," *Stimmen der Zeit* 202 (1984): 363-382.

12. J. Ratzinger, "Epilogue," 343.

13. From this point of view, N. J. Rigali points once again to B. Lonergan's distinction between the classicist and the historicist self-understanding in "Artificial Birth Control: An Impasse Revisited," *Theological Studies* 47 (1986), 681-690.

14. Cf. the clear exposition by L. Sowle Cahill, "Contemporary Challenges to Exceptionless Moral Norms," in *Moral Theology Today: Certitudes and Doubts*, St. Louis 1984, 121-135, 193-209.

15. See, for example, E. Vacek, "Proportionalism: One View of the Debate," *Theological Studies* 46 (1985): 287-314, at 288; L. Sowle Cahill, "Teleology, Utilitarianism, and Christian Ethics," *Theological Studies* 42 (1981): 601-629.

16. Above all in his yearly "Notes on Moral Theology," in *Theological Studies*. Collected in R. A. McCormick, *Notes on Moral Theology 1965 through 1980*, Washington, D.C. 1981, and *Notes on Moral Theology 1981 through 1984*, Washington, D.C. 1984.

17. P. Knauer, "La détermination du bien et du mal par le principe du double effet," *Nouvelle Revue Théologique* 87 (1965): 356-376 (though several new editions with new material appeared in various languages); B. Schüller, *Die Begründung sittlicher Urteile. Typen ethischer Argumentation*, 2d ed. Düsseldorf 1980.

18. G. E. M. Anscombe, "Modern Moral Philosophy," *Philosophy* 33 (1958): 1-19.

19. Cf., for example, S. Pinckaers, "La question des actes intrinsèquement mauvais et le 'proportionalism,'" *Revue Thomiste* 82 (1982): 182-212, at 188, n3.

20. This is rightly opposed by E. Vacek, "Proportionalism: One View of the Debate," 297ff.; cf. also L. Sowle Cahill, "Teleology, Utilitarianism, and Christian Ethics."

21. In a recent article, "The Disvalue of Ontic Evil," *Theological Studies* 46 (1985): 262-286, P. Quay has characterized the human goods or ills of an action that are to be evaluated as *bonum* (or *malum*) *naturale*. Thereby, however, his position is wholly outside the continuing discussion in moral theology. An

additional factor here is that he continues to confuse the distinct problems of moral goodness and moral rightness.

22. Thus, P. M. Quay in his article, "Morality by Calculation of Values," *Theology Digest* 23 (1975): 347-364. Quay is originally a physicist, and has frequently spoken about this problematic since publishing this article. G. Grisez speaks in a similar manner using the term "technical calculation." Cf., for example, "Moral Absolutes, A Critique of the View of Josef Fuchs S.J.," *Anthropos* 1 (1985) 155-201, at 180f. B. Kiely, originally a biochemist, has likewise taken over the formulation of "algebraic measuring" in "The Impracticality of Proportionalism," *Gregorianum* 66 (1985): 655-686, at 670. E. Vacek upholds convincingly the possibility of evaluation despite qualitative differences in "Proportionalism: One View of the Debate," 302-305. Cf. L. Sowle Cahill, "Teleology, Utilitarianism, and Christian Ethics," 618: "good moral common sense never has been and is not now to be replaced in *practice* by conceptual analysis."

23. Some fear the presence of a (situational or historical) relativism in such an analysis and evaluation of the individual elements in the entirety of the action. They do not distinguish between subjectivist *relativism* and the *relativity* with regard to all the elements of an action that is required by the will to be objective. One may consult, for example, G. Grisez, "Moral Absolutes," 171. But even the human "basic good" proposed by Grisez would not be able to escape from the necessity of an analysis and evaluation in a case of conflict. The fact of their equal "originality" would not imply that they are also equally "absolute."

An observation on this article by G. Grisez: It is a long critical discussion, published in 1985, of an article of mine published fourteen years earlier in 1971, and quoted now in a slightly altered new edition of 1983 (*Personal Responsibility and Christian Morality*, Washington, D.C./Dublin). The exceedingly tardy critical review in the newly founded periodical *Anthropos* suggests that the editor and the author had other interests than a specific review of this 1971 article. Incidentally, the first page of the Grisez article summarizes the contents of my article in such a way that I do not recognize my own position, and the following pages expand the statements of the first page, without modifying them.

24. See the English-language authors cited above, and G. Gatti, "Nuove posizioni sul '"intrinsece malum" nella teologiacontemporanea,'" *Salesianum* 47 (1985): 207-229, at 225: "E'difficile pensare che questo non comporti una qualche subordinazione dell'ordine morale ai valori premorali."

3

What Responsibility?

Ethics is not exactly a rare topic today, even in public life. The urgency of the problem is felt everywhere: the meaning of responsibility for one's actions in private, communal, and public life. Above all, the question concerns the defensibility or ethical correctness of one's action and behavior. One may not even be aware that ethical quality ultimately signifies not only substantial correctness but also the deepest interior quality of those who strive sincerely to solve the problem of the ethical correctness of conduct in the world.

Immanuel Kant most strongly emphasized the interior world of the behaving subject, that is, the person as the genuine locus of ethical quality. Ethical quality is, ultimately, the correct disposition, the personal readiness to respond to everything on the wide field of concrete ethical behavior, which is larger than any mere "obligation" (notwithstanding Kant's position).

M. Weber has spoken out against such a one-sided "ethics of the disposition" (gesinnungs-ethik) especially in the field of politics.[1] For Weber, the primary question in concrete life, and above all in public life, is not ethical purity or one's personal disposition in the field of ethical ideals. Rather, the primary concern looks beyond the ethical disposition to the defensibility and responsibility of conduct in the field of given social realities. For Weber, it is absolutely necessary to do whatever is required by the defensible structuring of this society. Weber presumably gave less consideration to the fact that his thought also demands a particular ethical disposition, which he understands simply as the correct disposition. Responsibility and disposition clearly belong together, but what is defensible and in what disposition? Various answers may be given to this question.

In this discussion, the status of responsibility stands in the foreground. Responsibility is connected to the future, with what is to be done in the given circumstances, whether one thinks of what is to be done "here and now" as immediately applicable or as applying to a long-term future. This timeliness of responsibility was included in M. Weber's political ethics. The Marxist ethicist E. Bloch, on the other hand, thinks of responsibility in a more utopian manner as being concerned with the final form of society.[2] A different position is taken by H. Jonas.[3] In his studies Jonas argues against Bloch, insisting that our behavior and conduct must respond to the requirements of our contemporary circumstances. The primary point is that we must avoid every behavior that may unjustifiably damage the individual and society in the present and in the future; that is, in our lives and in the lives of those who come after us.

Responsibility: before whom, and for what? To whom or to what is one responsible? Is it perhaps to one's own self? The Hebrew Bible, the Old Testament, speaks often of the central importance of the heart as the innermost dimension of the person in the realm of ethics (and piety). Paul employs the nearly parallel concept of "conscience in the *koine* Greek of the New Testament. There is doubtless here a continuity between the conscience and the Genesis notion of the creation of the person in the image of God. The primal experience and awareness of each person is that his or her reality is ethical, and this awareness no doubt exists even when someone believes in explicit reflection that his or her existence can or must be denied. Persons know fundamentally that they owe it to themselves to be ethical in order to be truly themselves.

At the same time, it is clear that each person also bears dialogical responsibility to the other who is one's equal. And as a social being, each person is also aware of his or her responsibility to the group, the collectivity, the society. Indeed one is responsible for one's entire generation and perhaps also for future generations. Explicitly or implicitly, each person is also aware of a responsibility to the transcendent reality in which all earthly reality exists, although one may not be conscious of this responsibility. This transcendent reality is what we call "God"; as Christians, we acknowledge that this reality has revealed and communicated itself to us in Jesus Christ. Thus, Jesus Christ is a special point of reference for the responsibility of the Christian.

Further, for whom and for what do we respond? Once again, initially one bears responsibility for one's own self. Even our responsibility for much else and for other persons is always fundamentally and in principle also responsibility for our selves and for what we make of ourselves through our actions. But it is not only a question of responsibility for other persons and things: responsibility for ourselves already covers the whole area of reality. This reality may refer specifically to our intellectual and spiritual spheres, to our education and culture, to our healthy vigor and capacity to work well, our achievement in the world and our own interior progress, to those who are close to us and to the collectivity to which we belong, to our society and to humanity and its near and distant future.

As for responsibility for one's own life: what about the problem of euthanasia when the person concerned has the full use of his or her intellectual faculties? Some theologians hold that scripture or the Christian faith has an unambiguous answer to this problem, but such a view is surely mistaken.[4] Still, it is not easy to find an unambiguous answer based on human reason that has full evidential force.[5] Clearly, the need in such a case is for a responsible personal consideration of the values involved in the resolution of the problem. To a large extent, though certainly not always, this consideration of values will be carried out in dependence on solutions that have been handed down and accepted from the past.

Responsibility also presupposes ability, which H. Jonas calls "power." This ability is certainly true of our capacity vis-à-vis the individual self; it has boundaries, however, and in fact, beyond these boundaries, there is no responsibility. These boundaries are true in other areas of life as well. Many individuals have received an ability, or power in society, for example, in politics, science, or technology. Society does not, in principle, bear any responsibility (or only in an analogous sense) for feeding of the world, applying atomic power, or war and peace; rather, this responsibility ultimately and always lies with the many individuals who belong to the collectivity or society and exercise their influence on it. Individuals therefore bear high responsibility for their influence on society, that is, for the correct use—including the responsible or irresponsible failure—of their capacity. We shall come back to this point.

How are various responsibilities experienced or recognized? What is their case? What are the relevant criteria? A simple answer to this question does not and cannot exist. Therefore, we should not expect to find answers that impose themselves absolutely on the many areas of human responsibility. It is the task of contingent human power to understand, judge, and discover these answers in the pluriformity of human reality. This discovery will no doubt take place in a historical process, and it will also display differences and changes in various cultures and epochs and in various phases of an individual's life. Thus, it is the intellectual capacity of the human person that makes possible such an act of understanding, evaluating, and judging under the most various presuppositions.

The matter is the same among Christians as it is for people generally. Neither the Hebrew Bible nor the new Testament produces statements that are independent of culture and thus universal and valid for all time; nor can these statements be given by the church or its magisterium. Rather, it is the task of human beings—of the various persons who have been given the requisite intellectual capacity—to investigate what can and must count as a conviction about these responsibilities. The task is given equally to persons who think in Christian terms, in philosophical terms, or in atheistic terms. Although D. Bonhoeffer wished to establish Christ as the basis of all responsibilities in this world,[6] he had really no other possibility than his own intellectual efforts to discover these responsibilities. It is, however, also true that conditioning through intellectual leadership, through the models one follows, through shared convictions in a society, and through comparisons with a pluralistic society can influence one's manner of understanding, evaluating, and judging. Would the attempt at a pluralistic consensus—though no doubt such an idea is utopian—be an ideal?

RESPONSIBILITY AND VALUES

Responsibility means values.

Values are understood as the enrichment of the person and humanity. They are concerned with the physical reality of the person, one's life and health, and they establish the effect of the world on the person's culture, and deepen one's intellectual, moral, and religious dimensions.

On the question of responsibility, we must ask whether there exist abiding human values for which we must bear responsibility in every case. No doubt such values exist, even if they are not very numerous. It is surely recognized universally that unchecked ruthlessness vis-à-vis another person is no human value. Totally arbitrary conduct in relation to human life, in the area of sexuality, for example, is an abiding nonvalue. The same is true of total arbitrariness in communicative utterance, in the absolute refusal to let oneself be integrated into human society, and in the fundamental refusal to make a distinction between *meum* and *tuum*.

Although such statements about universal value are extremely important, they are also extremely abstract; they mediate wholly universal guidelines for concrete realization, and they can be universalized. In this perspective, human reason is not arbitrary. Thus, our values demand unconditional responsibility.

Nevertheless, universal statements about value do not characterize the values that demand concrete responsibility. Concrete acts of evaluation must take into account, not only values that can be universalized, but concrete facts at the same time; these facts, however, are not judged and evaluated universally in the same fashion. This matter is proved by examples. Is an embryo already a *homo sapiens*? Responsibility to a norm of conduct depends on the answer to this question, which is the object of debate. Another question: is a fetus a human person with rights in exactly the same way as a child after its birth? The problematic of abortion begins with the answer to this question. How do particular people view the life of the newborn, if they consider the killing of children to be justified?

How do people interpret the commandment to respect one's parents as they grow older, if they also believe that they must display this respect by exposing their parents to a certain and speedy death? How do different human beings understand the reality of sexuality, if they not only display various patterns of sexual conduct but also consider these patterns to be justified or even demanded? What is the source of the difference, held in each case to be justified, between monogamous and polygamous societies? What is the source of the difference between fundamental self-defense and fundamental rejection of the death sentence? Clearly, universalizable evaluations are applied to human facts that are judged and evaluated in various ways. The concrete evaluations that are arrived at in this way form the basis of correspondingly various responsibilities.

Do values characterize the supreme achievements of human and ethical capacity, and does responsibility mean the obligation to perform such achievements? Or, if values are high achievements, does our response to concrete values also involve the renunciation of still higher achievements that are per se possible? For example, it is possible for an extreme asceticism to bring someone to the brink of other possibilities in life and other capacities to achieve, but it does not follow that such an asceticism is a value that is responsibly to be striven for. A dying person could be artificially prevented for a long time from definitively (totally) dying; but such a supreme commitment could prove to be inhumane and thus, fundamentally, an illusory value. If so, the renunciation of artificial means would be the responsible realization of value.

Before the encyclical _Humanae Vitae_ appeared, it was repeatedly emphasized that every new human life is an additional value that must be affirmed precisely for this reason. This affirmation is not wholly false, but the encyclical, in its statements about responsible birth control, did not embrace the idea behind it, namely, that married couples are responsible for the greatest possible growth of the family. Should technology do its utmost in every case, conscious of its responsibility, even when it sees the indefensible consequences to which its action may foreseeably lead? Ought scientists, also in a value-free manner, continue their researches even if they foresee that their results will be applied in praxis in an indefensible way? Even the "capable" renunciation of the application of human capacity can be a value, indeed a value that is superior to the capacity that one renounces; and it would then be this value that must be striven for responsibly.

When we speak of responsibility for the realization of values, we must still ask the question _for whom_ or _for what_ do we bear responsibility in the realization of values? Is it for oneself, society, the future of humanity, or for someone or something else? One's own self? There is no doubt that we do have responsibility for ourselves in many things, but in certain circumstances, responsibility can urge us to strive for particular values for others rather than ourselves. Indeed, in certain circumstances such a responsible behavior can be obligatory, though at the same time, we must assume ethical responsibility for self-realization. The other can be an individual but also an institution, a group— why not also society, even the state, or humanity? In each case, it is the task of reason to discover this responsibility in the individual situation or historical epoch, a task carried out by an individual or by a community reasoning together.

Genetic technology already reflects on how its interventions can potentially cause a change in persons in distant generations. But this potential is not responsibility for the human beings of the future in the strict sense since they do not exist at all. It is, rather, responsibility for ourselves: in view of our values, how are we projecting ourselves through these interventions in the channels of inheritance? All that the human beings of the future will be able to ask themselves is what kind of conduct they would have "expected" on our part had they lived in our time.

RESPONSIBILITY: VALUE-FREE CONDITION AND CONFLICT OF VALUES

The attempt has often been made to defend the value-free condition of science, and perhaps also that of research or technology. But this discussion has also implied the freedom for a corresponding responsibility. Is it at all possible for a totally value-free human behavior, a human behavior without responsibility, to exist? Is there a science for the sake of science, that is, a science that has no meaning, relevance, or significance whatsoever for the practical self-realization of humanity—apart from the fact that science per se denotes the value of human self-realization for which responsibility must be taken? H. Jonas, among others, has held that astronomy could be considered such a value-free science—a study removed from considerations of responsibility. But can we be sure of its neutrality when we see what objectives now exist in the realm of astronomy? Modern astronomy is surely not without significant practical goals and possible consequences.

No matter what individuals decide to do, they bear the responsibility for fitting their actions to the totality of their lived reality (to which others also belong). These value-laden decisions include, for example, the meaningful career decision within the spectrum of the many possibilities that present themselves; the meaningful choice of a project of work within the sphere of one's profession; and the meaningful choice of a partner for marriage. None of these decisions is value-free in the life that the individual structures precisely through these choices, and for which, therefore, he or she bears responsibility.

Decisions are not simply value free. What one decides and achieves, to do, in technology, for example, must necessarily become the starting-point for further technical projects and achievements. Can one bear this responsibility? This necessity must be borne in mind in the initial technological project, and responsibility must be taken from the beginning. Experiments—for example, medical experiments on patients—are not value free; it is possible that the experiment will not succeed, or will produce indefensible consequences. The responsibility for the possible consequences must be considered at the very beginning of the experiment. But the free consent of the patient, which is required, is not exempt from responsibility either.

It has often been believed in the past, and is still believed, that the nature of the human person displays in many areas the boundaries of a value-free and arbitrary condition, so that the requisite positive responsibility is also not there, for example, in the spheres of health, life, human sexuality, and language. These areas are certainly not in the least value free; however, it cannot be deduced from nature itself (as from something distinct from the human being as a person) what value-conscious and responsible behavior is in these spheres, since nature does not make ethical statements and cannot do so. Thus, what one should do is not deposited in nature as though it were a divine ethical will, for the very basic reason that nature is not created as a static entity but as a historical reality subject to process. Therefore, one who prefers to think and speak in static terms commits in reality the error of presenting a human interpretation (one's own or that of "our group") and a merely human understanding—that of a particular cultural stage—as something inscribed on nature (statically understood). That is, one presents one's own static interpretations as the divine moral will imposed as a charge on human responsibility. That imposition is a naturalistic fallacy. In this sense, therefore, one cannot "sin against nature" (to recall that formulation), though one can indeed sin against nature in another sense, namely, by acting contrary to a better possibility of human ethical knowledge. That kind of sin against nature can happen in the sphere of ecology, marriage, and in the sphere of technology or genetic engineering, or elsewhere.

If concrete values and responsibilities are not made known to us unambiguously through human nature or divine revelation, they must be sought and discovered through human endeavor. As this human endeavor takes place in a pluralistic manner both historically and indeed here and now, we need not be surprised that its results, the affirmation of values and responsibilities, are not always uniform. Conflicts can and must occur and consequently lead to necessary compromises or positive statements of law. For example, in other ages, social conditions of destitution and the needs of the poor were met through more or less individual compassionate conduct. Such works of mercy still exist, and they exist today (and necessarily) in an organized form on a large scale in religious and private welfare agencies. In our overdeveloped world, however, individual efforts are no longer sufficient. Today it is also necessary for the authorities in our society to take action, which however, presupposes that taxes will be raised and in part replace the "works of mercy" of earlier ages.

Another question: when is it permissible to carry out the transplant of an organ from someone who is "dead"? It is clear that this cannot be left to the patient's doctors' awareness of responsibility; here societal agreement and societal safeguards are necessary. Harvard professors have agreed that the criterion can and must be total brain death. This decision has been generally accepted. Nevertheless, a positive human decision must still be made in this case, because even at this point of "death" the process of dying has not yet been completed; otherwise, how could one transplant "living" organs? We now have an accepted decision in our society: after brain death, we no longer count the "dying" person as still a personal human being; therefore, it is permitted under certain circumstances to intervene in what still remains of the life of the "dying" person. We have been given this decision as a directive for responsible behavior that emphasizes values.

The Christian faith needs a manifold human interpretation, which to a large extent takes place through doctrinal statements of the church's magisterium (though its statements as such are not the teaching of the Christian faith), and also in theology (which likewise is not itself the teaching of the Christian faith). Such manifold interpretations must be taken responsibly into account as human attempts at evaluation carried out under the aid of the Holy Spirit.

It follows that secular law or the intervention of the church is frequently a factor in the discovery of values and responsibilities. But not even these resources are always sufficiently able to discover everything. It has sometimes been said that virtue must discover what law cannot determine. Here "virtue" is usually understood as one's obedience to the directives of religion. There appears to lie an erroneous equation of religion and ethics in this formulation. Religion cannot simply generate ethical decisions, though religions can, in practice, solve the ethical problematic for many persons through their directives. But religious directives are not sufficient to solve the problems of ethical responsibility definitively.

The Hippocratic oath has its significance. But the medical possibilities open to doctors today are so changed that it is clear that the boundaries within which this oath can be made have burst wide open. Cosmetic surgery is not an activity that corresponds to medical goals in the sense of the Hippocratic oath, and ought therefore to have no place in the sphere of defensible medical activity. Yet it makes a decisive contribution to the well-being of particular human beings. Shouldn't it also belong to the sphere of justified medical practice? Contraceptive sterilization seems at first glance to be something that must be understood as contradicting the Hippocratic oath. But not a few partners in today's discussion insist that the total reality of persons whom the doctor is bound to serve is more complex now than it was in the world of Hippocrates.

Medical treatments and interventions require in principle the free consent of the patient or of those who represent the patient. But a public state of emergency, such as a fight against epidemics or a state of war, justifies and makes necessary compulsory medical interventions (including isolation of the sick). This necessity is often confirmed by state regulations. One should not accept the view that this involves the temporary "suspension" of "absolute prohibitions," for the individual is a priori and essentially tied down in his or her rights to the requirements of society; that is, one's individual rights are not unlimited: therefore they are not "suspended" for a period in a state of emergency.

This holds true also of the individual's personal rights to freedom, as, for example, when competent authorities in the society order a conscription for military service in war (which can in certain circumstances place the individual's life in danger) or military or civilian service in peace-time. Today, an excessively individualistic quality surfaces in the idea that the individual is obliged to give assent to such interventions because he or she receives in turn many valuable things from society; this idea fails to see the individual as essentially a social being who is per se and essentially the bearer of obligations vis-à-vis society.

What, then, is our responsibility? The question is discussed in the public sphere and also among scholars. Here we have seen how many individual questions must be posed, and still an all-embracing answer is not possible. Nevertheless, indications along the way can give a certain amount of help in understanding the problem.

NOTES

1. M. Weber, *Soziologie. Weltgeschichtliche Analysen, Politik*, 3d ed. Stuttgart 1964.

2. E. Bloch, *Das Prinzip Hoffnung*, 2 vols., Frankfurt/M. 1959.

3. H. Jonas, *Das Prinzip Verantwortung*, Frankfurt/M. 1979;*Technik, Medizin und Ethik. Zur Praktik des Prinzips Verantwortung*, Frankfurt/M. 1985.

4. On this cf. J. Fuchs, "Christlicher Glaube und Verfügung über menschliches Leben," in *Christlicher Glaube und Moral*, ed. K. Golser, Innsbruck/Vienna 1986, 14-42. English Trans.: "Christian Faith and the Disposing of Human Life," in J. Fuchs, *Christian Morality: The Word Becomes Flesh*, Dublin/Washington 1987, 62-82.

5. Ibid., 18f. (English trans., 66f.).

6. D. Bonhoeffer, *Ethik*, ed. E. Bethge, Munich 1949.

4

Structures of Sin

In an encyclical, Paul VI spoke about the "progress of the peoples";
John Paul II speaks more carefully but also more appropriately about
social development. According to his 1987 encyclical, *Sollicitudo Rei
Socialis,* this development depends, not on social systems such as capi-
talism or communism but on human and Christian solidarity. The latter, as virtuous conduct, has the power to overcome personal,
egotistical sin, which in turn is responsible for the structures of sin that
characterize the situations of injustice in our society.

At the beginning of the encyclical, John Paul II's intention is
stated: not to carry out a social analysis of today's reality so much as a
moral and theological analysis, to reach a more nuanced concept of
development (n. 4). This analysis appeals explicitly to the competence
of theologians, especially of moral theologians (n. 41), concentrating
here on the theological concept of sin seen as the cause of the structures
of injustice.

Although the concept, the "structures of sin," has had a secure
place in theological writing in recent years, this encyclical marks its
first appearance in a Roman document. It is only in the most recent
years that "social sin," the parallel concept, began to appear in Rome;
this concept, though less precise, addresses the same theme. We find it
in John Paul II's Apostolic Exhortation *Reconciliatio et Paenitentia* (2
December 1984) and in the two documents on liberation theology from
the Congregation for the Doctrine of the Faith (6 August 1984 and 22
March 1986).[1]

STRUCTURES OF SIN AND ORIGINAL STATE

The manifold structures of injustice in human society are an evil
(though not a moral evil) that not only create much suffering, but also

lead to many movements and struggles that are often turbulent and in part violent. It is customary to characterize these structures as structures of injustice in the framework of society as a whole; this judgment is correct but perhaps also inexact and insufficient, since structures of injustice exist also in individual groups within the society, and even within individuals. The latter are not only beings who aim for what is good, or even beings engaged in a neutral struggle; their struggle, too, is self-seeking and aims at what is unjust, leading therefore to injustice in society. Such strivings are not only free personal sins: they are also structures that exist a priori.

Humanity has always known of the existence of structures of injustice. Philosophically, such structures were understood as human structures that had gone wrong, with their roots in human freedom. Christian theology went further by taking into account their origin in keeping with revelation, deducing them theologically from personal sin (original sin and personal sins) and calling them structures of injustice that derive from sin.

As an example of the awareness of wrong structures deriving from freedom, we may reflect briefly on the theories of justice held by philosophers who trace our social system to a theoretical (i.e., not historically datable) *social contract*. It was necessary for such philosophers to posit a theoretically original or natural state, as the starting-point for a social contract. This original or natural state appears to them as a wholly unsatisfactory state that must therefore be overcome. Both the description of this state and a sketch of the state under the social contract show what deficiencies and faults are known to us and even attributed to the original or natural state as the starting-point for a social contract that is regarded as necessary, precisely because these structures have gone wrong.

In recent times, John Rawls has renewed and popularized this philosophy in his *Theory of Justice*.[2] To characterize the essence of the original state, which he presents as something other than a de facto natural state, Rawls simply calls it the original state; however, his ultimate aim is to work out a just fundamental structure of human society. When he constructs the human beings of the original state who must sketch for themselves a just fundamental structure of society, Rawls omits many elements of egotistical human beings as we know them, whose egotism is a defect that makes them incapable of sketching a just fundamental structure of society. Rawls is, therefore, familiar with the egotistical deficiencies in the structure of the person who de facto exists, the structures that lead one astray into injustice. And he is familiar with these deficiencies in the person in an original state: reflections of persons in this state on the requirements of a just social contract show that they, too, are aware of their reality, which is something other than ideal.

Rawls admits that this theory is not wholly independent of Immanuel Kant's suggestion of a social contract.[3] In the natural state theorized by Kant, human beings already live in various groupings and social structures. Within this society, however, many contradictory individual interests arise, leading to dissatisfaction, conflicts, and violence. In order to eliminate the appalling results of the obvious deficiencies and structures of injustice in the natural state, Kant holds that it is necessary to have a social contract, which, although it would not alter the existing legal relationships, would transpose them from the unsatisfactory realm of private law in which they exist with their negative consequences into a system of public law, that is, into a "civic state" that provides for distributive justice.

The utilitarian philosophers, unlike Rawls and Kant, thought of the natural state as the starting-point for a necessary social contract. Thomas Hobbes, for example, held that egotism and egotistical conduct were dominant in this state.[4] Thus, the deficient structure of injustice in persons and society generates the struggle of all against each other, and the social contract is necessary to resist this struggle.

Christian theology has naturally always known about the deficient structure of justice in persons and their socialization without, however, seeing the original condition thus presupposed to be a state already characterized by egotism and injustice. In the revelation of the Hebrew Bible, this state is presented as an epoch prior to the egotistic and unjust condition of humanity; it is human sin that introduces the dramatic change.

It was not only Christianity, under the influence of the Hebrew Bible, that held this view; Stoic philosophers of antiquity were likewise familiar with a primitive but innocent state of justice prior to the situation of injustice that now seems to belong to human beings. Cicero, for example, sketches such a state by eliminating from it everything that is lamented as evil in the person in the egotistic situation of injustice. The cause of the dramatic change from one state to the other is human guilt.

On the basis of the Hebrew Bible, Christianity derives the origin of humanity's egotistic condition of injustice from sin, as it is understood theologically. The order of marriage and family, socialization in the state, and authority would also have existed in a sinless original state (*status antelapsarius*). Coercion, repression, and punishment (in the state and the family) presuppose, not the sinless human being, but the one who strives egotistically (*status postlapsarius*), and can be justified in so doing, because in humanity's sin-determined state of injustice, social life is in practice impossible without the occasional application of such means.[5]

In the writings of the early Church, two institutions play a particular role: slavery and private property.[6] Both were considered to be justified, within certain limitations, but both are typical institutions of humanity after the Fall. In a society conceived as sinless, all would have been equal, and there would have been no private property.

The fact of slavery, without which the society and economy of the first Christian centuries seemed absolutely unthinkable because the free human being had developed an extremely negative attitude to work, is often attributed to sin by the early Christians and justified on the basis of this sin because it (sin) had come to characterize humanity. A fundamental source of this reflection is the account in Genesis of Ham's sinful behavior vis-à-vis his father Noah, when Noah is drunk and lies naked in his tent. Ham and his descendants are subsequently cursed by Noah: "Cursed by Canaan. A slave of slaves shall he be to his brothers" (Gen 9:25). Ham is here called the ancestor of Canaan, and this account is seen as the beginning of slavery, which is thereby thought to be justified.

Early Church writers held various understandings of the sinful process of development begun by Ham with slavery as its justified outcome. Thus, slavery is a penance for sins committed (i.e., sins that continue Ham's sin), slavery frightens one from committing further sins, or slavery is a measure that prevents one from sinning.[7] Even in the Middle Ages, Thomas Aquinas theorized that the justification of slavery, which did not exist in the original state before sin, was a necessity, in the present condition of humankind. Less capable human beings must be led by those more capable.[8]

Private property also presupposes humanity's sinful state since everything would have been held in common in a sinless natural state and in the graced original state. In a later period, Thomas Aquinas also justified private property by the fact that sinful human beings administer the goods at their disposal better if they have private property as well as common property.[9]

STRUCTURES OF SIN AND SIN

Christian theologians generally deduce the social structures of injustice from sin, understood morally and theologically. Independently of an interpretation of original sin, one can speak (with Karl Rahner) of our situation of freedom as originally determined by guilt as a quality that is present and inherent in the history of our freedom from the outset. This guilt is evident and has, as its various consequences, the structures of sin in human reality.

First, the individual human being, as person and as acting subject, displays structures of sin, as do various small (and smallest) groupings and social entities. The individual, both privately and within the context of socialization, is from the outset of life under the influence of one's milieu, but ultimately also of one's own sins. Therefore, one is inclined in various ways to sin and to be part of sin's injustice—this inclination is how persons are structured. This structure of sin in the human person manifests itself first in personal sins and thereby also in its consequences for human society.

Second, we must point to the *objective* realities of sin in human society, which manifest sin and the structures of sin. When the early church speaks of the various measures of coercion that are justified in the context of the state and smaller groups, and even in the (extended) family, indeed even within marriage; they are aware that such measures are manifestations of a situation that ultimately comes from sin. Since humanity does not exist outside the situation determined by sin, and is in absolute need of such coercive measures if it is to be assured of at least some kind of ordered survival, these measures are justified in the eyes of the early church, even if they are determined by sin.

The same is true of slavery and private property, though they bear the mark of sin on their foreheads. The early church did not reflect on today's question whether one should call these sinful institutions or institutionalized sins. Such objectivizations belong to natural law (*jus gentium*), not to a natural law that derives from an original state but one that is determined by humankind's sinful situation that is therefore (as it was formerly held) required and justified.

A great deal of what is characterized as natural law in traditional and contemporary law and moral theology is genuinely natural law but only under the sign of the humanity that lives in sin. Only thus is it possible under particular circumstances to distinguish justified false statements from sinful lies, and only thus can the conscious accomplishment of something evil be justified correctly, either in keeping with the familiar principle of the action with double effect, or through a teleological evaluation of goods. And, finally, it is only thus that it is possible to justify economic practices that appear at first sight to mock all justice, that is, when they have to count as generally-accepted "rules of discourse" about mutual exchange and an equally mutual indemnification. No one who participates in economic life can withdraw from these rules at least within certain limits.

Some theologians have wished to understand this natural law as a natural law of compromise. The American moral theologian Charles Curran's theology of compromise is an especially well-known example of this school. There is in fact no difficulty in calling such norms and modes of conduct natural law *tout court*, since they are in accord with practical reason as it performs in the only existing human reality, even if this de facto reality is determined by sin.

Third, we must consider what are today called *situations of injustice* in human society on the international and national levels. Various human goods, for example, economic goods, opportunities in society, and cultural goods, are often distributed in a disproportion so excessive that they contradict their own goal, that of being available in principle to all. This contradiction is an evil of human society (in a premoral sense of evil). It is an injustice not yet understood as moral, though it is often derived from personal unrighteousness understood in the ethical sense, that is, from sin. It is, therefore, not to be justified. We have here a situation in our society that is seen to be unjustly determined by sin and therefore to be an unjust structure of sin. It is a genuine evil, absolutely incapable of being justified, and this judgment implies an ethical duty to overcome such structures.

In general, it is not customary in today's discussion about the structures of injustice as structures of sin to refer to so-called original sin; this reference is scarcely ever made, since it would amount to an attempt to illuminate the obscurity of the structures of injustice by means of a still greater obscurity, the mystery of original sin. Rather, reference is generally made to personal sins that count as the origin of the structures of sin. Sin is understood morally and theologically as the cause of the structures of injustice; consequently, if these are to be overcome, it will be above all through the repentance of the sinful person— one who lives unjustly must change into the just person who lives in solidarity.

The encyclical *Sollicitudo rei Socialis* sees injustice or sin, to lie above all in the "lust for profit" and the "thirst for power" (n. 37f.). Clearly, the thought here is of situations of injustice in human society as a whole, although such situations exist by analogy at all times and places in interpersonal relationships and in the significant and less significant events of daily life. The subject of the encyclical, however, is primarily the problematic of the Third World, of the tensions, especially economic tension, between North and South; and of the division between social imperialisms and blocs, above all those in East and West; and, finally, of the "idolatry" of money, ideology, class, and technology. Nevertheless, the encyclical also considers the Fourth World (n. 14, note 31; n.16f.), and the situations of injustice within individual groups or states, in both the First and the Third Worlds.

The sin of unrighteousness leaves man unaffected and cold in the face of inequality and injustice. We hear that "it is the property of whoever has acquired it lawfully." And we are told that those who invoke this principle do not hesitate to generate new and deeper situations of injustice in their own personal interest and in the interest of groups or nations. They have no intention, or an insufficient intention, of reducing the existing situations of injustice in the way and to the extent that it is possible; indeed, they seek rather to strengthen and exploit these situations without further concern, in their own interest.

It is, however, possible in situations of injustice and sin to generate stable personal and societal attitudes through the effect of custom over a long period; then, injustice and sin can no longer be perceived as what they are; and the same can be true of long developments in society. The effect of being born into, or entering, a social environment that thinks and evaluates in an unjust manner is that eventually one cannot recognize injustice. This blindness can also happen in the history of individuals. The task of those who see and know (i.e., of churches, politicians, and other experts) is to awaken human sensitivity to justice and injustice and to personal righteousness and unrighteousness.

Within this context of the "structures of sin and sin," we must also look explicitly at the danger that accompanies this dialog about the structures of sin, that is, about sin as the cause of these structures of injustice. The danger is that we will forget that great inequalities and deep structures of injustice can have other causes than sinful conduct. Appalling societal conditions can also be the result of error and ignorance; they may even be attributed to human persons who have indeed done what is ethically wrong, but who were acting, nevertheless, out of fully selfless love."[10]

One may think, for example, of those in distress after catastrophes of nature and similar disasters, of underdeveloped human groups that live closed in on themselves and separated from "developed" groups, or of the fate of those who by nature or insufficient education are less gifted than others, less capable, or less rich in imagination and energy. There are those who are disabled in various ways, and those who are unacquainted with positive relationships in society. Not all people are de facto equal. One may also think of the great dangers and evils that are inherent in the growth of population, without being limited exclusively to the problems and evils of overpopulation, but considering also the negative effects of a rapidly diminishing population.

It may indeed be that behind these and many other human fates stands sin as the cause or as one of the causes (and perhaps stemming from some place and time unknown to us). But to use a well-known example in the scholarly literature, is it truly certain that a homosexual, who is not accepted socially in his relatively small world, and is thus decisively handicapped in his advancement; is so homosexually oriented because of a sinful refusal of the human affection and rich emotional love that was offered in the first years of life? Or is there a lack of human affection and solidarity in human fate that is not determined by sin? Only then would the guilt involved in refusing solidarity make the remaining structures of injustice—those that were not determined by sin—structures of sin.

When one speaks of structures of injustice as structures of sin, one should not overlook the fact or the possibility that the sin need not lie exclusively on the side of those who are unaffected by the evil of injustice. Not only the "haves," but also the "have-nots" can be the sinful cause (at least in part) of the existing structures. In the case of individuals who are in need and in the case of particular asocial groups, organized peoples, and governments, there exists a fatalistic lack of concern and care, a lack of willingness to work and to help themselves, in the expectation that others, the "haves," will come to their aid and take responsibility for overcoming their situation. Such an attitude and such conduct can also be sinful in the sense that sin is the cause of deficient structures not being overcome. Even in the Third World, fourth worlds exist that are determined by sin. In such cases, how is solidarity to be practiced?

It has become customary to speak of structures of injustice as social sins or structures of sin, but too little attention has been paid here to the notion that the structures of injustice also generate sin and consequently produce further structures of sin. A lack of sensitivity to ethical rightness and goodness often develops from living in structures of injustice, which is difficult to overcome. Not only are many, often appalling failures—or compensatory acts—committed by those who suffer deficiency; many antisocial and often unjust mutual relationships also develop among those who live side by side in distress. Indeed, measures of self-help, for example, dealing in drugs, can damage innocent third parties in a grave way. We must acknowledge, therefore, not only the justified protest against injustice and those who are (or at any rate seem to be) the cause of the injustice, but also conduct full of hatred and crime that cannot be justified in any way. Situations of injustice derive to a large extent from sin; in their turn, they often generate attitudes and forms of conduct that are sin.

OVERCOMING THE STRUCTURES OF INJUSTICE

We must overcome the structures of injustice that govern the lives of many in human society. It is of secondary importance whether these structures derive from sin, that is, whether or not they are "structures of sin," for often their derivation cannot be determined with precision.

Wherever ethical unrighteousness and sin are at work, we must question not only the structures but also the persons who consciously cause, strengthen, or prevent the destruction of such structures. This obligation to overcome the structures of injustice affects the individual qua individual and the individual in his or her share of responsibility and work, for example, in economics or politics. Moral unrighteousness and sin always affect the individual as a person, but they also affect the individual in the context within which he or she bears responsibility with others.

What is required is the ethical *goodness* of one who is concerned to destroy the structures of injustice and change them into righteous— into ethically *right* structures. What is required is human and Christian solidarity with the disadvantaged; not solidarity in the sense of a voluntary commitment to common experience in the class struggle but in the sense of a committed respect for the common dignity and fundamental rights of all, including above all the dignity and rights of the socially disadvantaged. Such a solidarity demands a change in attitude from those who do or have done injustice in sin. They must turn from lust for profit and thirst for power. In Christian terms, we call such a change repentance.

But even if the existing structures of injustice do not derive from the sins of this or that individual, the requirement remains for ethical and Christian solidarity with those who suffer under structures of injustice. This requirement is repentance in an analogous sense: repentance from being closed in on one's own interests and blind to the justified claims of the disadvantaged. Such a solidarity is not something we are born with; one's ego must be forced to discover it.

Such repentance can be extremely difficult, and still it remains a requirement to be accomplished, even when it is in principle already accomplished in a person's innermost attitude. Above all, this repentance must advance from being an interior and virtuous attitude to become an active struggle to overcome the structures of injustice within the realm of what is concretely possible. One's attitude to life must change, and not merely one's private and public commitment to less unjust societal structures.

The formulation "to less unjust societal structures" acknowledges that a completely just structuring of society remains a wish that cannot be fulfilled in practice, while at the same time it is possible to make some effort (often only a limited effort) to improve the structures. Charitable donations are one, very limited, way to change the unjust situation. To alter the situation itself as a structure is only possible one step at a time. Indeed the attempt at a total transformation often makes the situation worse; many Latin American countries and many Latin American businesses have already experienced this lesson in their complicated relationships with their more powerful and richer partners.

In the meantime, we are faced with the necessity of working with injustice and of cooperating with these structures to a certain extent. Such cooperation is a requirement of having an effective will to alter the structures of injustice. Our task is not to pursue an ideal or a better situation that is impossible here and now; rather, we must accomplish a prudent—and in a certain sense "compromised"—realization of the best that is possible here and now. At the same time, we may never be content with only that which is concretely attainable or only that which we have already attained.

The structures of society ought to be righteous: they ought to be right. Such a "rightness" of the structures presupposes a certain measure of ethical *goodness* in persons who are active in society. But such a goodness may not rest on its own laurels, for then it would not be goodness. It must fight for the *rightness* of societal structures. Nevertheless, the full ethical goodness of the person and the full rightness of societal structures stand, according to Christian conviction and teaching (and according to the witness of experience) under the law of the eschatological reservation. In other words, full goodness and rightness will never be fully attained while this earth lasts. Universal love and solidarity, likewise, will never be so universal that they will change this earth to a totally righteous paradise. Not even the committed struggle against the structures of injustice and sin will ever be a total victory. The only requirement that has an absolute claim on us is that we strive, in every situation, to do whatever is concretely the best thing possible.

NOTES

1. To indicate the intellectual background in which the encyclical *Sollicitudo rei Socialis* is at home, I note that both Paul VI and John Paul II had used the formula "structures of sin" in the discourses in the Latin American context at Medellín (1968) and Puebla (1979). And in a discourse on 5 November 1986, John Paul II gave a cautions hint that "perhaps" the term "structures of sin" could be justified.

2. J. Rawls, *A Theory of Justice*, 5th ed. Cambridge, Massachusetts, 1971.

3. I. Kant, *Metaphysik der Sitten*, Hamburg 1966.

4. T. Hobbes, German translation: *Vom Menschen—vom Bürger*, Hamburg 1977.

5. See, among others, O. Schilling, *Naturrecht und Staat nach der Lehre der alten Kirche*, Paderborn 1914, and *Die Staats—und Soziallehre des hl. Thomas von Aquin*, 2d ed. Munich 1930. Cf. also J. Fuchs, *Lex naturae. Zur Theologie des Naturrechts*, Düsseldorf 1955, pp. 81-103. On the whole question, cf. J. Fuchs, "The 'Sin of the World' and Normative Morality" in *Personal Responsibility and Christian Morality*, Washington, D.C. 1983, 153-175.

6. R. Klein, "Die frühe Kirche unde die Sklaverei," in *Römische Quartalschrift* 80 (1985): 259-283.

7. Ibid., p. 260: the statements of the leading bishops "were so various, in keeping with the social origin, education, and social insight of each one, that it is not possible to identify a common suggestion of a solution."

8. S.T.II-II.57.3.ad2.; I-II.94.5.ad3.

9. S.T.II-II.66.2.

10. B. Schüller, *Die Begründung sittlicher Urteile. Typen ethischer Argumentation in der katholischen Moraltheologie*, Düsseldorf 1973, 162.

5

"Soul" and "Ensoulment"

The concept of "soul" and "ensoulment" is frequently found in biological and anthropological discussions about the origins of human life. It is also a problem in the field of philosophical and theological anthropology.[1] And since the question is interdisciplinary, I cannot avoid dealing briefly with two areas that must be presupposed: first, how do I understand what biology says about the becoming of *human* individuals; second, how do I understand the becoming of the individual *person*?

AN INTERPRETATION OF THE STATEMENTS OF CONTEMPORARY BIOLOGY

Considerations about the soul and ensoulment play a necessary role in the interpretation of contemporary biology. Not all biologists, however, understand their science in the same way. I shall set forth briefly what I believe I can learn from biology, and how I interpret what I have learned.

1. The results of biology.

Considered from a biological point of view, male and female cells are specific to the genus, that is, to "human life." They bear in themselves the possibility intended by nature, namely, to be brought together through help external to themselves—for example, through personal sexual union, artificial insemination, or *in vitro* fertilization. Once these cells have been brought together, the possibility and the tendency exist for male sperm to penetrate the female ovum. From their union follows an interaction of the cells that can, ultimately, after a period of twenty-four or thirty-six hours, lead to their fusion.

Biologically considered, the zygote that thus comes into being is an individual life, genetically distinct from its parents but genus-specific: it is human life. It has an inner tendency to develop its own genetic information and to appropriate and develop exogenous (i.e., epigenetic) informational resources. Since this cell division leads initially to totipotent cells that can develop or be developed into additional genetically similar zygotes, the process of the cell's individualization is not yet complete. However, in the space of about fourteen days, the possibility of plural totipotent cells is excluded, and a definitive *individualization* of the zygote is attained.

Thanks to the nidation of the young embryo in a womb, it has the possibility to develop through additional genetic and epigenetic differentiation of its genetic riches, including its already-acquired epigenetic riches. In six to eight weeks, it develops the many organs of a human being, above all the brain with the cerebrum. Thereby, the possibility inherent in the zygote, that it will one day be born as a particular human person, is fully realized: it has been individualized; it has attained full differentiation. The further development of the fetus needs only *growth* (though admittedly a growth that is influenced epigenetically). If it comes to birth, the newborn will continue to develop, given favorable conditions; and, with the presupposition of interpersonal relatedness, it will arrive at the personal actualization of its individual and specifically differentiated possibilities.

2. An Interpretation and its Problems.

The zygote contains within itself a genus-specific and genetically specified living principle that has the inherent tendency leading to its ultimate birth as a personal human being. But it is not absolutely preconditioned: in fact, only a very few zygotes reach birth as their endpoint. Their development takes place in various phases. The young embryo requires a qualitatively unambiguous biological individualization through nidation in a womb to receive epigenetic information and for the qualitative development of the organs that make full human activity possible.

In my opinion, it is impossible to overlook a qualitative difference between the zygote and the newborn human being. While the zygote does indeed initiate a path that leads to the goal, it cannot go along this path alone. It initiates a particular process that it does indeed endeavor to continue, but this process is not a qualitatively linear continuum. Although the human being that is one day going to be born is indeed initiated in the zygote, this human being is not contained in the zygote—other than its genetic determination.

One may rightly doubt the correctness of the statement often heard, that the human being one day to be born is already present in the zygote. In accordance with this doubt, one would have to pose the question of what phases have to be gone through before one can speak, not only of a potential personal human being (i.e., one to be realized in the future) but of an actual human being already existing in reality.

As is well known, utterly contradictory answers are given to this question. The two extremes are the following: the first (about which doubts have just been expressed) holds that the zygote is already the fully personal human being, needing only the development of its already present personal reality; the other maintains that the only personal human being is one who can intellectually and freely make active decisions in society and act accordingly (sleep and other discontinuities remaining united as a continuum in the "ego").

Two other answers express this same idea in different terms: the first holds that it is anthropologically impossible to speak of existing personal life until biological individualization has been fully accomplished, that is, as long as the totipotent cells of the zygote are still divisible, since a divisible person is a nonsensical concept. The other holds that one cannot speak of actually existing personal life as long as not even the organs (above all the cerebrum), which are the necessary instruments of later personal activity, have developed, that is, before a period of six to eight weeks. Still another theory says that the proof that the fetus is at least from this point a person is already seen from the fact that active personal existence in society would not be able to develop through interpersonal encounter after birth, unless the newborn were not already a person and, precisely for this reason, capable of being aroused interpersonally to adopt personal conduct.

On the basis of these reflections, it is possible to ask an ethical question: granted that all the phases of the individual becoming of the human person are entrusted to our care and responsibility, do we owe the same care and same protection to the various phases of this process in their greater or lesser closeness to the definitive personal stage? And therefore to the cells as such, before their fusion, and indeed both before and after a possible sexual union, since these phases, too, would surely come under the same heading? Or do we owe this care and responsibility solely to the entire process of the personal coming into being of the human person, whether we consider this process to be personal or prescind from the question of its personal character?

Precisely these questions generate the problem of human personal existence in its relationship to the human soul and its ensoulment.

EXISTENCE AS A PERSON

Existence as a person means existing human life, or more precisely, individual human existence, that is, existing as "one in body and soul," according to *Gaudium et Spes.* This text from the Second Vatican Council does not say when this union occurs in the process of the human coming into being. In an argument that goes somewhat deeper, a person is described as an individual that is capable of (determined for) intellectually characterized behavior (F. Böckle). This formula can be equally applicable to the human being that has grown to the point of actual intellectual behavior, to the newborn, or even to the fetus that has developed to the point of being an organism.

One frequently hears the formula that a person is the "autonomy and self-possession of a human subject in knowing and free relatedness" to God (K. Rahner). This formulation could be understood restrictively to apply only to the human person who has matured to the point of adult intellectual activity. However, it was surely not meant to be so restricted. Personal existence means therefore the intellectual capacity of the human person, which is oriented to the free self-realization of a subject in a given bodily nature.

Because of the intellectual capacity of the person, human personal existence means created participation (through human nature) in the intellect of God and is thereby necessarily bestowed by God in freedom—precisely with a view to the intellectual and free realization of the human reality of the earth.

Theologically speaking, God wills the personal human being to exist and chooses the human as a privileged partner in the free realization of the human world in the Spirit and name of God—and also to be the privileged "I" of God's special love. It is precisely in love that God wills the personal human being.

The question thus arises, what is the reality and the significance of soul and of ensoulment in the being who is "one in body and soul" and, precisely thereby, a person.

SOUL AND ENSOULMENT IN THEOLOGICAL AND
OFFICIAL CHURCH TEACHING

Within Christianity, the concept of soul has repeatedly been, and still is, an object of dispute. This dispute concerns not only the concept of an "immortal soul," which is important for eschatology; it applies also to the questions of whence the soul comes and how is the human individual ensouled? How is the human individual made "one in body and soul"? In this latter question, we find various statements and nuances in Christian theology and in official church teaching.

Theology.

Origen (and the Priscillianists) held that a preexistent soul was poured into the body generated by the parents, but the official church condemned this dualism (cf. Denziger 403, 456). Other theologians quite correctly argued against this theory, saying that the parents generate not only the body, but also a human being (generationism). But then arises the problem of how a spiritual soul can come from human generative power. Therefore, the dominant opinion arose that God directly creates the spiritual soul and places it in the body that has been generated with the purpose of receiving it. This opinion became the "theologically certain" teaching (Denziger, 361f, 685, 1440, 2015, 3896).

According to Thomas Aquinas, however, the insertion of the soul takes place only when the generated body, or as it was then understood, the menstrual blood of the woman that had been given form by the male sperm, is sufficiently disposed for it. It follows, then, that the generated embryo already has its own life before its ensoulment from a spiritual being (*De pot.* 3.12). Against this theory, Albert the Great taught simultaneous ensoulment, namely, the coincidence of individual human life and ensoulment. Since the end of the nineteenth century, it has been understood that the zygote comes into being through the fusion of male and female cells and thus has a life of its own; and if this life is personal life, then the soul is its form-giving principle.

More recently, it is not the question of where the soul comes from that has become the problem for theologians, but the so-called ensoulment. How is it possible to combine the two statements that while a human being generates a human being, only God can create the spiritual soul? The fundamental answer lies in the principle that God acts as the transcendental cause, not in the manner proper to creaturely causes (*causa secunda*).

With this notion as his starting-point, Karl Rahner constructed a solution: the parents are the cause of the whole human being, for the body in simple human causality and for the soul through a self-transcendence of the human cause that God has given the human being as a basic possibility. That is, God as the divine dynamic is transcendent; but God, as the possibility of human self-transcendence, is immanent to the created human being. Accordingly, it is not possible to speak of an additional ensoulment by God of a body generated by the parents; rather it is the parents—transcending themselves through the divine dynamic that is always present in them—who are the whole cause of human life. Rahner's solution has found much recognition and little contradiction.

The Official Teaching of the Church.

Through the centuries, the Catholic Church has understood the human person in keeping with the schema of spirit-body, body-soul (Denziger 800, 3002). The soul is higher than the body (Denziger 815), it is *anima intellectiva* (Denziger 657) or spirit (Denziger 2766, 282; *Gaudium et Spes* 14) that is directly created by God *ex nihilo* (Denziger 3896). Therefore, the soul does not belong to the divine substance (Denziger 201), nor has it had any existence of its own prior to the body (Denziger 403, 456).

According to the Council of Vienne, it is the *forma corporis* (Denziger 209), the vital principle of human life (Denziger 2833). The instruction of the Congregation for the Doctrine of the Faith on questions of eschatology (17 May 1979) understands the soul to be the "I" of the human person. In *Gaudium et Spes* 14, the Second Vatican Council to a certain extent superseded, or at least made clearer, the body-soul schema by seeing the personal human being as "one in body and soul."

In the Catholic Church, one often hears that the human person is from the outset a human person, a body with a soul, "one in body and soul." The beginning was and is widely understood to be the act of intercourse; it was not and is not so widely known that the conception of a new "human being," the fusion of the cells, may take one or two days after sexual union, and can also occur through artificial insemination or through *in vitro* fertilization.

Thomas Aquinas's idea that the ensoulment of the zygote by the spiritual soul takes place forty days (and in the case of girls, eighty days) after the zygote comes into existence has never been officially condemned. For Thomas, the killing of the fetus before the ensoulment was morally impermissible; nevertheless, it was not the killing of a human being with the consequent ecclesiastical punishment of excommunication. In canon law, Thomas's opinion held good until 1869, with the exception of the years 1588-1591 (J. Connery).

The Congregation for the Doctrine of the Faith published a statement about abortion in 1974, calling for the protection of newly generated life from the point of conception. The statement explicitly emphasized that it did not intend to pronounce on the correctness or incorrectness of the customary justification for this requirement, namely, that the newly generated life is a human unity of body and soul from the moment of conception. Rather, the statement's condemnation of any intervention vis-à-vis newly generated life has a purely tutorial character.

One may not intervene against the life that has been conceived, because of the possibility that it is already the life of a human being with a soul. The 1987 instruction, *Donum Vitae*, of the same Congregation is likewise very careful in its formulations: it does not assert the personal human existence of the newly conceived life, but only requires—here, too, in a tutorial perspective—that it be treated *as though* it were the life of a personal human being.

AN ANTHROPOLOGICAL REFLECTION ABOUT SOUL AND ENSOULMENT

Christian faith tells us that God has a relationship of particular love toward the personal human being, that is, to the human unity of body and soul, but faith itself does not offer any theory about the essence of this unity. Here I shall take these various theological and official church statements as my starting-point for an anthropological reflection on the soul and on the problem of ensoulment.

The soul.

The soul may be understood in a variety of different ways: as spiritual nature, as autonomy, as self-consciousness, as freedom. It would, however, be an impermissible dualism to conceive of the soul as something existing in its own right that is also joined to something else—something bodily—which likewise exists in its own right. It is only the personal human being, "one in body and soul" that exists in its own right. The soul—along with the body, is a *principle* of existence, the innermost foundation of something that exists, the personal human being.

Because the soul is spiritual, it is of a higher quality than the other principle of existence, the bodily principle. It is the "vital form" of the body, which precisely for this reason is not only a material, but also a human body. It is therefore surely more correct to see the personal human being that is "one in body and soul"—and not just the soul—as the "I" of the human being, as the object of God's grace and love. This unity, however, is from the soul as the spiritual principle of human life.

Because of the unity "in body and soul," the spiritual soul moves and acts exclusively in the dimension of the body's space and time. In this sense, both soul and body mutually coexist though they are distinguished from one another as principles of existence of the personal human being. (The question of the immortality of the soul and resurrection, which is thereby posed and which is absolutely urgent in theology, does not bear on the problem that concerns us here and will therefore be left to one side.)

Ensoulment.

How does one understand the unity of body and soul? Reference has always been made to the act of sexual union, in which the human being generates a human being, that is, "one in body and soul." But two difficulties present themselves: first, the act of sexual union is not an act of generation in the strict sense of the word; second, it is not clear how human generation can be the generation of a spiritual soul.

First, the act of sexual union is an act carried out between two persons. In the ideal case, it is above all the expression and nurturing of interpersonal love, the giving and receiving of oneself, and it is this, even when generation is naturally or otherwise excluded from the act. It is absolutely impossible for this act of sexual union to be the act of generation in the true sense, since conception (the fusion of the cells) takes place at a significantly later time. In the best of cases, therefore, this union can only contribute to generation by predisposing the appropriate circumstances. This contribution, however, can now be replaced by technology. Still, technology is a substitution that can only be effected by a human person. It is not possible, despite what apologists against *in vitro* fertilization sometimes claim, to make new life by technological means.

Second, generation takes place through the fusion of two human gametes. But the human being is "one in body and soul." How can the biological fusion of two gametes generate the spiritual principle of existence, the soul? The traditional and correct answer is that it only happens through God's communication of a share in God's own spiritual nature. This doctrine is true because it is through the spiritual nature of the soul that God directs grace and love to the human being who is "one in body and soul." Theologians have asked, must God now give the soul, "in addition" to the bodily principle, existence?

We have already indicated Karl Rahner's solution to this problem. From the very beginning, God has given the human being the innate possibility of self-transcendence. The question of the body's ensoulment therefore becomes superfluous. In concrete terms: the possibility given by God, of self-transcendence to become "one in body and soul," is encoded in human cells, or better, in the bearer of those cells. The manner of empowering a fusion of the gametes—through sexual intercourse, artificial insemination, or *in vitro* fertilization—has therefore no significance for the becoming of the personal human being. The process of becoming, with its various stages, results from the cells' encodification. Their self-transcendence to the spiritual nature, that is, to the soul, belongs to this process. Thus, it is fundamentally irrelevant whether we are capable of discerning with greater or lesser exactness the stage and moment of the person's becoming, that is, the uniting of body and soul. It is, however, possible to understand this attempt at a solution, which has been presented here as acceptable, in three various ways.

1. Because of the God given possibility of self-transcendence, the personal human being, "one in body and soul," is generated in the fusion of cells. That which is generated thus develops under the direction of the soul in accordance with the inner possibilities of the zygote. This understanding leaves us with the problem of how the soul can be responsible for the direction of its development, when it is not yet individualized and therefore does not yet seem to exist. The soul, it would seem, does not exist before the indivisibility of the person or while there is the possibility, present in a first period of the cell division, that twins can be formed, that totipotent cells can break off and recombine.

Problems are also posed by the lack of organic development in the first weeks without which the activity of body and soul is not possible.

2. The following reflection has also been offered: in the fusion of the gametes, the unity of body and soul, whereby the soul is "the form of the body," is generated. The soul directs the process of development forward to the further individualization of the human reality that has been generated, and thus forms its body. It has also been suggested that we understand the process of development as such to be the soul. The problem left by these attempts at a solution is that the soul that works toward further individualization is logically not yet an individuum—a person, or "one in body and soul."

3. The following attempt seems to be preferable: through the fusion of the gametes, a dynamic process comes into being in what has been newly generated that makes for the becoming and the birth of a bodily spiritual human being. The process demonstrates qualitatively distinct stages: full individualization (the exclusion of the division into totipotent cells); nidation in a womb; the development of the organs required for intellectual personal activity; birth; and the awakening of personal consciousness in interpersonal encounters. However, it is not possible biologically or philosophically and theologically to determine unambiguously the precise point at which that which is to be, actually is a personal human being, "one in body and soul." The *terminus ante quem* seems to be indicated to some extent by the unfinished period in which the division into totipotent cells is still possible, that is, before full biological individualization has taken place. The period before the formation of the organs could also be such an indication.

THE SOUL AND THE FUNDAMENTAL VALUE OF HUMAN LIFE

It is commonplace to speak of the dignity and value of human life. But what value is attached to the soul in this remark? Dignity and value are not infrequently called "ethical dignity" and "ethical value." These terms do not mean that these realities are in themselves ethical, in the proper sense of this word, but that they require a particular ethical conduct: protection. The question, then, is what protection is, or is not, owed to generated life? Such a question arises independently of the question whether the generated life already has a spiritual soul of its own.

Soul as human value.

The soul is a spiritual principle of existence and a created participation in the reality of the one who is wholly spiritual, namely, God. One occasionally comes across the question whether the soul has an "infinite" value; such a question has, of course, no meaning, because the soul must count as created: God alone—the Creator—is infinite. The attempt, therefore, to base the defense of personal life, the defense of the "one in body and soul," on an infinite value of the soul is a mistake—no matter how the soul is conceived. The dignity and value of the created soul are communicated to the body in the personal unity of body and soul. The human being as a whole, the "one in body and soul," is the one called by God through grace to a particular relationship and love; therein lies its highest dignity.

A fundamental dignity is, without doubt, proper to every stage of human life from its beginning. This assertion is particularly the case, if one understands the zygote as actualized human existence—as "one in body and soul." If one does not believe this interpretation, if one considers the zygote only as the possibility of an actual human existence, then one must pose the differentiating question whether the *same* dignity belongs to the incompletely individualized zygote that is not yet "one in body and soul" as to the embryo implanted in the womb, and perhaps also whether its dignity is the same as that of the fetus that is differentiated with the cerebrum as an organism. And is its dignity straightforwardly the same as that of the newborn, or as that of the human person that is self-consciously and freely realized in human society? Finally, is there a distinction between the dignity of the last two stages—although the interpersonal development of the newborn is scarcely understandable if the newborn is not already a person ("one in body and soul")?

These questions are asked today; they must be heard, and their solutions pondered. It is relatively easy to think that a defense of the human cell is not obligatory in precisely the same way as a defense of the gametes; the latter, because of an act of sexual union, are looking for one another. If so, then the defense of the zygote that ultimately comes into existence through the fusion of the gametes is more strongly obligatory. The difficulty really begins when I am asked to grasp that the biologically not-yet-fully individualized embryo should receive the same personal defense as the one who is "one in body and soul." And it may be even more difficult to think this way about the embryo that has not yet developed as an organism.

In this perspective, it is not correct—despite a common practice—to speak without difficulty of an embryo's personal right to defense as a personal human being, since it has perhaps not yet made the stage of transcendence to a spiritual soul. Our difficulty does not exclude the possibility of demanding from the moral perspective—as do the Vatican documents that have been cited—that such defense be given to the embryo "tutorialistically" (because of the uncertainty of our knowledge about its reality). In the same way, it is not appropriate to claim that the embryo's stages of development benefit from an actual supernatural relation of partnership with God.

The dignity and value of the soul, even of the human being who is a person in the full sense, is not infinite; nor is the soul ethical in the strict sense of that word, though it is in the highest degree ethically relevant, that is, it requires our ethical evaluation. But the life of the personal human being—"one in body and soul"—is not itself the highest human value; otherwise, how would it have been possible in lengthy Christian tradition to permit the sacrifice of this value in particular circumstances for the sake of other, clearly higher values, or even to destroy this value by killing it? The life of body and spirit is not the highest human value, but it is the most fundamental human value. Without it, there can be no other personal human values. If these reflections hold, then we face once again the question of the extent to which the various stages of the development of human life need and deserve protection: the cells, the gametes, nonindividualized zygotes, undifferentiated embryos. If it is the case that these stages do not possess the status of the personal human being who is "one in body and soul," then what interventions are ethically defensible in certain circumstances?

Ethical reflections.

Our ethical reflections on the problem of the "soul and human life" are correct to take as their starting point the human person, a unity of body and soul, acting intellectually and freely; the life of this human being has a right to the greatest protection possible. In reflection, the attempt is made to extend this protection to the various stages in the process of becoming bodily and spiritual human life—not only to the newborn or even to the organically developed embryo but likewise to the zygote or even to the union of the gametes resulting from personal sexual union. Thus, the fully developed personal human being is counted as present in some sense in the various stages of its development—although this is a presence only "in the making," as "potential" human life, or as human life that is becoming "one in body and soul."

The formulations that have just been used formally imply that some stages of the process of becoming a human person have not yet reached the status of personal human existence. It is therefore necessary to state more clearly whether those formulations of the stages of the process are to be understood merely as a development in the sense of the further growth of the person or as a development in the sense of the person's becoming "one body and soul." The latter is the goal of the process that begins with the fusion of the gametes. In this case, one must ask whether before the definitive individualization (or before the formation of the organs), the justification for an intervention in something that is not yet a unity of body and soul must absolutely follow the same conditions as intervention in the life of a human being acting personally—who already is "one in body and soul." Naturally, one has to reflect on these relationships.

As has already been pointed out, the reflection presented here as valid for centuries in the Catholic Church, has not been explicitly rejected even in the last decades by the Congregation for the Doctrine of the Faith (despite changes in the biological sciences). Theoretically, even the official teaching office of the church does not exclude the possibility that the experiment with the embryo is not subject to the same strict conditions as those applied to disposing over a human life that is more than potential. This statement has a different sound, however, from the frequent formulations customary in official, though mostly secondary, documents.

The tutioristic path is followed in official teaching; in face of the uncertainties that have been set out here; this path takes the absolute form of a "never," although a clear "no" in the case of certainly existing personal life has never taken the form of the absolute "never." Therefore, in the face of the tutioristic solution, it is necessary to assert with some force, a reflection that is in keeping with the tradition of moral theology: what is to be done in case of a conflict between the protection of a personal life "in body and soul" that only perhaps exists (the embryo) and the protection of other urgent, important, and certain values? Is it not possible that under certain circumstances, the scales will tip in favor of the second of the conflicting possibilities?[2] There would be no contradiction involved in this principle if the political authority, acting for important political and pedagogical reasons, were to require a protection that is perhaps not absolutely required ethically.

NOTES

1. This chapter was originally a lecture prepared for an international and interdisciplinary workshop on "Human Life—Human Personhood," F.I.A.M.C. Bio-Medical Ethics Centre, Bombay, 7-9 December 1988.
2. Of highest interest in this regard is R. McCormick, "The Removal of a Fetus Probably Dead to Save the Life of the Mother," Ph.D. dissertation, Gregorian Institute, Rome 1957.

PART 2

Historicity and the Moral Absolute

6

Historicity and Moral Norm

INTRODUCTION TO THE PROBLEM

1. The world of the human being is, for us as personal subjects, a world that is an object. It exists in space and time; that is, while always being itself, the world is not always itself in the same way, nor is it an ensemble of elements that is always the same. The world is in a permanent state of evolution and change. In this sense, it has a "history" of its own—a "natural history"—whether one thinks of the world and the universe as a whole, or of their innumerable individual elements. In this sense, river and mountains have their own history, and so, for example, do the various species of animals (in their biological, psychological, and sociological existence), and individual beings in their individuality.

The person, as he or she considers the world as object, discovers that the person, too, is part of this objective world. One must consider oneself and the effects of one's actions in the same way as one considers other realities—including other persons. The person, too, has a natural history: as humanity, as a group or individual, and as a concrete activity. Self-defense of the group, "mother-love," and other self-related acts are not only phenomena of personal morality, but also of subpersonal elements, as in many animals. One may think not only of the biological and physiological aspects but also, for example, of psychological and sociological aspects and of the teachings of the behavioral sciences of recent times.

2. The human being discovers and experiences the self as historical in another sense, namely, as person and subject. This means first of all that one perceives and experiences oneself as capable of reflection, free initiative, responsibility, and moral conscience. Such an experience

is an absolutely original reality that is not reducible to any other element of reality; that is, it is independent of the problematic of a possible philosophical explanation of this self. And this understanding applies also to the other persons to whom one is related.

As a personal subject, the human being has a different history from "natural history," that is, from the history of the world as object. As humanity and society, and as a personal individual, the person not only has a history but is constitutively historical. As a subject that is essentially historical and moral, the person is always oneself: free, responsible, the origin of one's own decisions, and interpersonal. But the human subject is also oneself in a way that is always different. One's self-expression occurs in the multiplicity of the time that goes by and in the space of the world as objects that are given to one. While always oneself, the human being lives and unfolds as person and subject of one's own continuous self-development in the multiple particularities of time and space.

The complex reality of personal decisions and activities in the world are not the subject's self; they are a continuous and various succession of active personal developments of the world as object. The subject as such is present in them as their source; one develops oneself in developing the world (that includes oneself) as object. As a consequence of the subject's historicity, the personal human being is, on the one hand, always oneself; on the other hand, in one's multiple self-expressions in time and space, one continually specifies and changes not only something in the objective world but truly the self itself as subject and person—and the richness of being precisely this human person. For this reason, continuous self-expression in the history of one's life never becomes a simple repetition. Since the human being must continue to realize oneself personally—as responsible person-spirit-body-world at a determinate point in time and space, the human person as subject is continually confronted with the necessity to discern what to do and how to decide.

3. This historicity and individuality generate a problem. With the passing of time and one's life, the person remains the same subject, remains precisely this particular human being with characteristic specificity; indeed, it is because one has lived one's own history and become precisely this person that one now stands at this precise point. And from this point on, the person must live his or her own history, changing oneself by changing the world. Since the person is called to live responsibly, the truth that one must seek and live is not merely the truth of being a person; it is not being this specific person or the truth

of one's own historical becoming that counts. It is also the history of this truth in the fullness of its moment-by-moment concrete reality. This call to the individual is an indispensable and exceedingly difficult call. But the individual, society, and humanity have already prepared themselves for this inalienable and difficult duty. They have already discovered and formulated moral norms that will facilitate the discovery of moral truth in the concrete case and facilitate life together in society. Such norms explain the behavior that can be expected of individuals in human society. But moral norms understood in this way are necessarily characterized as being rather general. Their intention is to help but they cannot provide *sic et simpliciter* concrete moral truth for all moments of the individual's life or even the truth for a particular community or society in the course of history.

4. What problems can arise? Is it certain that a particular norm can sufficiently consider all elements of an individual's concrete problem? Is it certain that all moral norms inherited in a society sufficiently consider today's reality in its partial changes? Is it certain that new generations necessarily possess the ability to evaluate and judge human realities in the same way as preceding generations? As human beings are partially different in their self-perception, interpretations, and evaluations, it appears certain that new generations will partially change their way of proceeding in these matters with the passing of time. Finally, can it be true that the human person is a historical being, while his moral norms are not historical at all?[1]

THE HUMAN PERSON AS A "MORAL" AND "HISTORICAL" BEING

1. Before we discuss moral norms directly, it is necessary to continue reflecting on the historicity and correlative morality of the person as subject. From this point of view, the human person is not subject to change. But since the person is a subject in the continuous flow of time that characterizes the world as object, a historical and mutable character also belongs to the essence of one's immutability in this world. We leave aside here any evaluation of the human being and humanity; our interest is rather the self-perception of the person that belongs to our own experience.

A person is always aware of one's own identity as a subject, although one is never at a zero point from which to begin history. At every moment, he or she is aware of the past, of decisions already made, of a self-realization that has already begun, of a history of one's own that has already been formed. This past, however, instead of bringing one to a halt in the here and now, brings one to a decision about how to continue this history into the future, which begins precisely in the passage from the past to the future.

The project toward the future—as a decision about the immediate next step in one's own history and as a project that exceeds the next step (as is always the case, at least in some manner)—seeks to realize afresh the history that is past and to integrate it in future history in a new way. Thus, in the historical life of the human person, the subject is always present, although the fullness of this history is never grasped so long as one remains a subject in history. But the self-realization of the person as a historical person, that is, living one's own history, brings the subject ever nearer to being oneself in history and hence to the fullness of being a subject and person that is constitutively historical.

The historicity of the human person as subject has its own special importance when we see that the human being as subject and person always perceives oneself (I do not say, "recognizes oneself" in a reflexive or explicitly accepted way) as a moral being (moral conscience), that is, as a being who is always aware of having the moral duty of one's own self-development in history. This duty means that one's development must have the "truth" proper to each of its concrete moments; it cannot be simply arbitrary. It follows that self-projection—and one's own history that has been lived toward the future—requires a serious discernment and will to choose the path that this discernment identifies. Only thus will the history lived by the personal subject be a true self-development.

The "future" that the human person projects and lives is distinguished from one's definitive "future," which is not determinedly oneself; one can and must await this future and receive it from that which is definitive. The human subject perceives that the definitive "future" is part of the absolute mystery on which depends also, in the same sense, the fact that one is a historical and moral person and perceives oneself as such. The Christian calls this mystery God—the God who in Jesus Christ and the Holy Spirit calls us to the realization of our history and toward our future in human history and beyond, in the future that is promised.

2. Our historical existence in time becomes real in our particular space; it is this space that is often called "human nature" although it is

not a nature that can be understood in an individualistic sense. It is essentially interpersonal and worldly (i.e., essentially in relation to other persons and to the subhuman world). The person perceives this space or nature as a given: in bringing it to realization one realizes one's personal history in time. The space of nature—like an extension of one's own being as subject and person—offers one the rich possibility of the construction of a human world; however, because of its "human" meanings (for the person or for humanity), it also sets limits to our realization of the construction of the human person and the world. In this sense, it must be said that the human person, to the extent that one perceives one's self to be a moral being, also perceives the duty to "live" the human person as world, that is, to "create" in one's history a world of the human person that is truly a development of the world, and to mark it with the sign of the historical self who operates in the space of the human person as world.

I have said that the reality "given" to the human being can be called "nature"; theologically, it can also be called "creation." But we must always bear in mind that this nature, or creation (we will call it nature-creation), was not given to us "from the beginning" in exactly the state in which we find it today. Rather, it was given and created as a reality that bears in itself the possibility of evolving and of being developed in order to become the human reality that presents itself to us today. We do not know the zero point from which it started, or the possibilities that it holds for our future. But we know that it is the person who took and takes the initiative in forming the given nature-creation, as it was in periods long ago, and as it presents itself today.

In this sense, it is correct to say that although we know that the nature-creation of the human being is the world, we know very little about it. The future will discover more. Metaphysical reflection on the being of the self as world offers us fundamental knowledge, but very few facts. There is, then, the danger that we may wish to call "metaphysical" whatever displays itself to us (perhaps only de facto) as a seemingly "permanent" human reality. Accordingly, it is the reality of nature-creation as it exists today that has been given to us, together with the charge of interpreting it, evaluating it, and developing it correspondingly.

But we do not see the reality of nature-creation, as it exists in a simply "objective" vision, that is, as it exists de facto. We always see this reality as it has already been interpreted by us. Such interpretations are subject to the influence of the history of our ways of interpreting nature-creation, which history is not without the influence of our human environment and society and—we do not forget—our faith and ecclesial community.

Just as the nature-creation given to us has always already been interpreted by us, so it has also already been evaluated by us in its ensemble and individual elements. How the reality of the person as world is evaluated clearly depends on how nature-creation is interpreted, but we do not start from a zero point of evaluation. Rather, the evaluation emerges from a living relationship with the personal history of the human interpretations and evaluations of nature-creation— and this relationship is influenced by faith and concrete society.

3. When we think about the problem of moral norms in this context, some relevant ones already become clear; the person as subject is a historical and moral being, self-realized in the realization of nature-creation. But nature-creation also has a continuous history of its own, so that we never encounter it in a purely "objective" manner; we have always already interpreted and evaluated it. Only if we can also consider the human person in this way will it be possible to perceive and formulate moral norms; it is only in this way that we can grasp how moral norms are to be understood.

HISTORICITY OF MORAL RIGHTNESS

1. The historicity of the person concerns the subject as a person and the human realization of the world as object (nature-creation). Normative morality has always stood for the right realization of the subject (person) and for the right realization of the object (nature-creation). On the other hand, the distinction has not always been made in a systematic way; indeed, the two aspects have not seldom been confused, even to the extent that the discussion was no longer clear.

The right realization of the subject or person is usually (or at least very frequently) called "moral goodness," or simply personal "morality," because only the subject or person as such, and one's own attitudes and free decisions, can be called "moral" in the narrow sense of the word. With respect to morality as such, one can speak only of personal moral goodness—or its negation, that is, of moral badness or immorality.

2. The right realization of the world or object (nature-creation), to distinguish it from personal moral goodness, is usually called "moral

correctness—righteousness or rightness"; it bespeaks the appropriate or inappropriate realization, on the part of the personal human being, of the world as object, as nature-creation. The greater number of moral norms speak of this rightness as human conduct. The distinction between the moral goodness of the person and the person's moral rightness in conduct—although in the strict sense of the word, only the person can be moral—does not mean that the two distinct realities are separate or without an intrinsic mutual relationship. In fact, the rightness of human conduct is accepted and assumed in human conduct by personal morality, that is, by the moral goodness of the subject-person. Personal morality, precisely because it is goodness, seeks to become incarnate in right realizations of the world-object; that is, as it always wishes what is good, it wishes also the good of the world-object. The first moral principle is *bonum faciendum, malum vitandum.*

The concept of moral goodness has remained basically the same throughout the history of moral theology. One must, for example, aim to realize oneself, to do good, and to follow one's conscience, among other things. The same cannot be said of the moral rightness of conduct, which has been a problem historically. It is true that the rightness of conduct depends on moral goodness, on whether or not one is ready to accept it. In this sense, one is said to be "open" and tries not to close one's eyes to correct solutions to moral problems. But rightness itself depends rather heavily on the reality of the world-object, considered as a "human" world, that is, as the world of the human person.

3. Concerning this last point, humanity has not always had, and does not have today, the same solutions. The realities of the world change to a certain extent; the results of science may be well-founded for the moment, but they, too, are only hypothetical and may possibly change. The human interpretations of the facts that have evolved in history are not necessarily identical; nor are the evaluations of various data always the same, since they also depend on which vision of the human world (*Weltanschauung*) one freely assumes. All these elements belong to the "given" reality, and moral judgment about the rightness of their human realization must take them into account, or lose its objectivity.

4. The judgment about the rightness of human conduct is not per se a "moral" judgment or a moral norm. Rather, it is a response to a question that is "neutral" from the moral point of view: which realization of reality is humanly appropriate or inappropriate? Such a judgment is a judgment of "moral" rightness, for the sole reason that

morality, in the strict sense of the word (i.e., as the goodness of the human person) demands a realization of the world-object that is not arbitrary, but right. Thus, the moral norms of the right realization of the world-object are called "moral" because the requirement of (personal) morality and the judgment about right conduct (a morally neutral judgment) coincide in the same subject-person.

If one thinks of the possible variability of the many elements that make up the world-object and must be taken into consideration in the formulation of norms of moral rightness, one will see that not all norms can be materially and completely the same for all circumstances and times. A moral theologian likes to formulate this consideration as follows: *the* moral rightness does not exist.[2] Anyone who would appeal to an "eternal law," with regard to the norms of moral rightness, must understand that it contains all the concrete solutions for right conduct in a world that is variable.

5. Given these explanations, it is evident that the problem indicated in the title "historicity and Moral Norm" refers primarily to the norms of moral rightness in conduct in the world-object. It is interesting to note that this theme therefore refers to norms that can be called "moral" only by analogy, and it is superfluous to say that "moral norms" are here understood in the sense of moral rightness unless the text or the context make it clear that the opposite is the case.

NORMS OF MORAL RIGHTNESS

1. The human person is constitutively historical, but the world-object is historical, in another sense. The question is this: how can the historical human person be responsive to permanent norms of right conduct in the world? To reply to this question, we must first ask what precisely is the object of the norms of moral rightness.

Although we do not wish to enter here into an evaluation of humankind and thus into the origins of the problem of judgments and norms of moral rightness, a brief reflection may nevertheless be useful. In the course of their self-evolution (thanks to the creation of God) toward full humanness, persons, like other beings of creation, will certainly have had experience of their own behavior and will have learned rules of conduct. The more one becomes "spirit," the more one also helps "nature" to become "culture." In its development as a "spiritual being," the person perceives slowly and increasingly that such norms as one has discovered are "moral"; that is, they are not left to individual, arbitrary decision.

There are, for example, norms of social, family, and sexual conduct. Thus, to take the last area first, the person senses in some way that he or she is a cultural being and soon discovers and establishes "taboos" that are to be observed. That various peoples have identified many and various "taboos," or moral rules, in this area is well known. Even today, for example, one finds in vast and well-civilized populations of Asia the taboo that forbids one ever to touch the genitals, even for urination.

Thus, norms are formed, in a more or less conscious manner, based on the knowledge, interpretation, and evaluation of "facts" (nature) and lived "experiences." Frequently, the "elites" of society will intervene to formulate norms that are to be observed in a community or society. But new knowledge or experiences, or new methods of interpreting and evaluating realities, can also intervene and result in the formulation of new norms partially distinct from those that existed previously. The historical person is confronted not only with the historically changing reality of the nonhuman world, but also with norms that seek in various ways to interpret and morally judge the rightness of the human realization of reality. The human person who seeks a judgment and a moral norm for right behavior always finds oneself before the continuing judgments and norms of one's community and society. Despite this, it remains a personal task to discover one's own norms and correct judgments, in the light of this historical continuity of moral norms.

2. How are the moral norms of rightness, thus arrived at, to be justified? The answer is by means of a hermeneutical reading of concrete reality. The results of such a reading are called, in the long history of moral theology, norms of the "moral natural law." The more difficult question, still much discussed today, concerns how this hermeneutical reading is to be done, and one of the traditional answers is that nature itself teaches us right conduct. The Stoics gave this answer in their ethics, which considered nature in a pantheistic way to be divine. Christianity does not consider nature pantheistically but understands it as having been created by God the creator and thus as being only human. Nevertheless, Christian philosophers and theologians often hold that nature does in many ways show us morally correct conduct.

When in fact, nature-creation does speak to us, it tells us only what it is and how it functions on its own. In other words, the Creator shows us what is divinely willed to exist, and how it functions, but not how the Creator wills the human being qua person to use this existing reality. The person, created as a rational and prudent being must interpret, evaluate, and judge the realization of nature from the moral point of view. This given reality is not nature considered in the abstract and ahistorically. It is not, for example, abstract sexuality, uninterpreted human life, or theoretically false statements that must be evaluated, interpreted, and consequently judged morally. Rather, it is nature itself as it is concretely realized in the ensemble of concrete reality that we must consider, and such reality consists not only of one determined element (e.g., a particular sexual activity), but also of various other elements that are real or to be expected as consequences. It follows that what is to be interpreted, evaluated, and judged, not by nature but by the rational and prudent person, is the ensemble of the various realities that constitute a concrete activity as a human act.

In some matters, the reflection we have just made is observed; in other matters, it is believed that one can read the moral norm of right conduct directly from nature. In 1951, Pius XII held his famous discourse to the Italian midwives on matrimonial questions.[3] He spoke, among other things, of contraception using "artificial" means and of the possible uses of matrimony from which only a sick child was to be expected. Pius XII holds that procreation is the principal natural goal of the conjugal act, that is, of matrimony itself. Nevertheless, though he considers an artificially contraceptive act absolutely illicit, he does not judge a totally infertile use of matrimony (with nonartificial means and for proportionally important reasons) in this way. What is the reason for this difference?

Nature intends a conjugal act that is procreative and, at the same time, unitive; therefore, the conclusion is drawn that a person also has the moral duty to observe this tendency in conjugal life. With respect to children as the fruit of conjugal life, however, nature does not display an unambiguous tendency; therefore, marriage partners morally can and must determine, freely and prudently, from the condition of their conjugal life as a whole, the number of children they will have. In the first case, it is held that nature speaks morally; in the second case, that nature does not so speak. If, in the second case, it is left to the rational and prudent person to find a good solution in the ensemble of conjugal life, why are there not parallel moral methods for the first case? Here there is just one difficulty: The idea that the word "natural" predicated of the individual act is understood, not only in the physical sense, but also in the moral sense, is a naturalistic fallacy.

There exists a sexuality that is "natural" in the full sense of the word, and a sexuality that is rather "deficient," for example, an immature sexuality (masturbation), an exclusively homosexual sexuality (neither procreative nor unitive), and a unitive sexuality that can also be procreative only by means of *in vitro* fertilization. Such existing types of sexuality do not per se tells us the right manner of their realization. Not nature itself but the person reasoning prudently must interpret, evaluate, and judge this matter.

To carry the reflection further, it is important to note that traditionally, within the sphere of marriage, various "imperfect" sexual activities (e.g., sex without orgasm) are not excluded from a moral point of view, although such imperfect sexual activities are not procreative and therefore not natural in the same way as the "natural" conjugal act. In the same way, a conjugal act that is known in advance to be sterile and nonprocreative is usually morally acceptable. Therefore, it would seem that nature itself offers various types of sexual activity but it does not tell us whether these are morally acceptable or not. It is not nature that tells us what is acceptable but the person who reflects on the facts, interprets them, and judges them from the moral point of view—from within the entire scope of what it means to be a person.

Therefore, the moral norms of the right conduct share the historicity of the person and the person's world. Nature itself and its individual elements do not teach morality. Nature is not free of change, nor may it be considered in the abstract, or only through individual natural elements; it must be considered in the entirety of a concrete reality. Thus, only the person as one who is rational, prudent, and essentially historical—can and must make moral judgments about a concrete reality—about the nature or creation that has taken concrete form in history.

3. The hermeneutical reading of nature-creation in the abstract and as concrete reality has its own history in the history of the person-subject who seeks norms and moral judgments about correct behavior. This hermeneutic is not carried out without a relationship to the normative indications that have been discovered hitherto in the history of the person. There is, thus, a continuity between the moral norms of the past and the norms of the present. But the specificity of what is normative in the present must also take account of the specific discontinuity

between norms in the past and in the present. It is only thus that the hermeneutical or historical reading of nature-creation and concrete reality can be valid, because it is also a hermeneutical reading of norms inherited from the past.

As Christians, we are aware that this reading of nature-creation and the concrete reality is also carried out in the light of faith, the scriptures, revelation, and the teaching of the church's magisterium. Not that these Christian realities tell us in a simple manner the morality of correct behavior in this world; rather, they give us a Christian ethos, and norms of correct behavior that were believed at certain periods to be compatible with the faith. They give us a specific vision of the person and the world that makes it easier to attempt to discern valid moral norms of rightness. Thus, there exists a strong historical continuity in our vision of what is normative for moral rightness.

But even the Christian scriptures, revelation, and the magisterium share in the historicity of the human. Even the reading, therefore, of these normative sources must be hermeneutical, if we wish to find genuine help in them as we seek a view of moral rightness for today. A reading that is basically fundamentalist will not help.

As for the scriptures: First, we need an exegesis that is scientifically exact: what are we really being told in the sacred texts? One may, for example, think of the recent document of the Congregation for the Doctrine of the Faith on homosexuality. In this document, we find a reading of the scriptures that is not only different from the document *Persona Humana* (1975) of the same Congregation (in which there was no reference to the "classical" biblical story of Sodom); there is also a failure to indicate that serious exegetical problems beset the interpretation of other texts, including Rom 1, and that the text of Gen 1 and 2 has nothing to do with the problem of homosexuality.

Second, it seems that it is wrong to look in the scriptures in a fundamentalist way for formal divine revelations of categorical norms of moral rightness—given the nature of divine revelation and the nature of historical and contingent norms. Categorical norms of moral rightness do not exist in full independence of their genesis in our moral conscience.

Third, one must consider what the various biblical authors wished to say to their particular historical situation, how they understood the conditions of the human world, and what were the convictions of their culture. Fourth, one must see whether their moral statements intend to be a true moral teaching or only an exhortation (paraenesis) in which the moral contents are presupposed (and in this sense accepted, but not taught).

Fifth, I do not see how it is possible to think of a "force of inspiration" that confers a special authority on each and all statements of scripture (as some theologians have written). If St. Paul states that his advice is only his own (although he speaks as a Christian and as an apostle), inspiration does not alter the fact, affirmed by the apostle himself, that what he says is only advice—and this advice was specifically for his contemporaries.

With respect to the norms formulated during the history of Christian moral theology, that is, in Christian tradition, our observations must be similar. We must observe what is truly affirmed for a well-determined historical situation, under what historical conditions, and in keeping with the moral convictions of the particular period or cultural tendency. And similar questions arise with regard to documents and decisions of the magisterium, which are likewise historically conditioned by certain presuppositions and convictions.

4. After these refections on the historicity of the moral norms of right conduct, we can ask what is meant by the frequently affirmed objectivity of the norms of moral rightness. A negative reply is that objectivity does not derive from formal revelation, tradition, or the authentic documents of the magisterium. A positive reply is that if the norms of moral rightness derive from a process of knowledge, evaluation, and judgment, then it must be admitted that they are determined not only by the elements of the world-object, but also by elements of the judging subject that necessarily enter into this process.

For example, the subject cannot recognize a norm that according to one's self-understanding and interpretation requires more than is humanly "realizable" ("zumutbar," to use K. Demmer's term), even by one who is simultaneously sinful and redeemed. The subject cannot make a moral judgment without involving his or her understanding of the self and world, and the possibilities one has, that are likewise conditioned historically, of evaluating these realities.

Not all values are always actual. The facts and experience of a particular culture and civilization, and the evaluation of its realities, enter into a concrete judgment that becomes objectively normative for such a reality. It follows that an ideal intuition is not, ipso facto, a moral norm. Rather, the norm must say what the ideal can require and intends to require—in view of the objectivity and subjectivity of the reality in which the abstract ideal is involved and in which therefore it must be realized. It is only in this way that a norm is truly objective—whether it is discerned by society or by a single person. This objectivity does not prohibit a reflexive control of the norm, nor does it prohibit a comparison with different norms, to see which of them is nearest to the ideal and to concrete reality. Understood in this way, the various norms are part of the eternal law, in that it implies all that the realization of the ideal must be in its various concrete instances and in the world-object given the datum of the created human person.

The concept of "objectivity" set out here differs from the usual concept of "objectivity"; the latter is accustomed to call any norm "objective" if it is generally accepted in a society, for example, in the Catholic Church, or proposed by a competent authority, for example, by the church's magisterium. But such norms, considered objective in this sense, can not only be inadequate or formulated in an inadequate manner, but can sometimes even be shown to be partially or totally "erroneous," whether by competent persons or by a general rethinking in later periods. There will necessarily always be fresh endeavors to bring the hitherto accepted norms to a greater objectivity.

These considerations were confirmed in the Second Vatican Council. In *Gaudium et Spes*, a formulation finally reached after great struggle says that the moral norms of matrimonial life must come from criteria taken *ex personae eiusdemque actuum natura*, (i.e., from the person and not only from the nature of the acts). Further, the Council admitted that faithful and truly responsible Christians may yet reach different conclusions about moral rightness and that even pastors do not always have sufficient answers to new moral questions (*Gaudium et Spes* 43). Finally, it considered that the richness of various cultures is needed to fully manifest human nature and its myriad paths to the truth(44), which seems to include the moral truths that correspond to the various elements of such cultures.

This understanding of the objectivity of the moral norms of right behavior raises another problem. What does it mean to assert that certain moral norms accepted or taught in society (e.g., in the church), or the opinions of particular groups or persons, or that certain judgments of conscience can be potentially "erroneous"? The problem is this: can one say that such norms, opinions, or judgments express precisely the objective moral truth of concrete reality? But to speak about an "erroneous" conscience and judgments reflects the opposite reality, namely, that such judgments are not in conformity with the judgments generally accepted in a society, and clearly considered to be true.

THE FUNCTION OF THE NORMS OF MORAL RIGHTNESS

1. Norms of moral rightness seek to grasp and express the moral truth or truths about the reality of the human world in order to help both individuals and society. It may seem that such norms are discerned and formulated precisely to resolve the problems of being the persons we are. But then it would also appear that these norms are fixed only for today and are, in this sense, static. They ought, however, to be capable of being normative for the essentially historical and changing human reality, which does not give the person a "today" or any quiet moment of total stasis.

How do the norms of moral rightness serve the historical person, and how do they function for such a service? Some theologians consider such norms as laws that are simply to be applied, especially in the case of norms formulated negatively; other theologians see such norms as the expression of a reflection made prior to experience (and therefore as abstract). While such norms are certainly useful, they do not refer formally and exactly to the truth of each concrete reality. For the moment, however, let us leave this difference between the two types of theologians.

2. Experience shows us that persons generally live comfortably within the norms of moral rightness, both as individuals and as society. This comfort depends on the fact that although the human person is historically changing, this change is neither total, nor continually and explicitly observable. Nevertheless, historical changes, both in the reality of the world-object and in personal interpretation and evaluation, exist, and the person is in some way aware of this fact. Application of the norms is therefore not a univocal process but requires a hermeneutical reading that takes account of the concrete here and now to discern precisely what the norms are fundamentally saying about this concrete reality. That is, norms must be applied "analogically," and in this sense, too, they have a historical character.[4]

Since the norms of rightness are essentially human judgments, and therefore historical, existential doubts can arise. Therefore, if everything is historical and changing—even if not totally—problems remain. If some norms were formulated for realities fundamentally different from the realities that exist today, or with a different understanding of these realities, the question arises whether a norm formulated in this way can be helpful or "valid." Should it not be replaced by another norm?

If problems previously unknown arise today because of new knowledge—for example, in the fields of embryology or genetics—can these problems be resolved by means of principles or norms that were established without this knowledge, that is, by norms that were not truly formulated for our new problems? If norms of rightness are frequently formulated in an inadequate manner without taking account of certain realities, and if they are seemingly unable to give a sufficient answer to our problems—although the norm literally claims to be the solution of the problem—then ought we not reformulate the norm, at least in part, to make it more adequate? This reformulation would require as some propose (e.g., Virt and Demmer), reinstating the virtue of *epikeia* in moral theology.

A similar problem could arise in the case of a single person and in cases commonly in doubt, or in questions that are seriously discussed by those who are "competent." It is conceivable, not only in particular cultures different from "ours" but also in "subcultures" within our more general culture, that there are convictions and visions of the world that—to the extent that they exist—are consequently the foundation of certain "objective" moral norms. That is, behavior in response to these convictions corresponds objectively to the reality of the world for these cultures, and therefore must be respected as such, although at the same time they are not acceptable for the rest of us.[5]

When, therefore, we have serious doubts with regard to certain proposed or inherited norms and whether they are genuinely helpful to us, we must undertake a serious hermeneutical reading of the norms in question. If, for example, it is clear that the intention has been to read the norm "into the nature of things," that is, if it is a clear case of a naturalistic fallacy, the norm is not useful and must be reformulated or newly justified. If, on the other hand, a norm was justified, not by a naturalistic fallacy but "teleologically," it may be that we must check the evaluation of the various elements involved in the norm. As has just been shown, the cases vary.

Similar problems are reflected in certain formulations that were proposed long ago and recently. Thomas Aquinas, for example, requires a hermeneutical reading of the norms rather than an unconditional application, when he says that concrete norms, unlike general principles, *valent ut in pluribus* (and not more). It may be that the principle *praesumptio cedit veritati*, with its origin in law, does not apply in moral questions: if a *praesumptio* that was made at the outset can be falsified, then one must review the norm. Modern English-speaking ethics has introduced the concept of prima facie duties; this concept does not mean that these obligations formulate evident norms but that difficulties and doubts that can be demonstrated in concrete applications demand a new reading of inadequately formulated norms. That is, our reading must take account of all elements relevant for the solution of a moral problem.

We must consider in this regard the intention of authors such as G. Martelet, D. Capone, and P. Chirico.[6] These authors accept the full validity of the norms (or documents) that are the church's official teaching on human sexuality, but require in various ways that the application *in concreto* of such norms should also take account of other elements in the concrete human reality—elements that are likewise morally relevant to the effort to arrive at a "true" application. These authors are basically recommending a hermeneutical reading of the accepted norms in a more concrete context. Fundamentally, the accepted norms have been formulated in a manner that is not totally adequate, insofar as they make a valid judgment about a single element of a reality that is much more complex.

When L. Kohlberg discussed the progress of moral maturity in the life of individuals, he saw the apex of personal moral maturity to lie in the ability to find solutions for one's conduct in increasing independence from "moral authorities," that is, in the person's becoming more oneself in moral judgment. Does not this growth imply that the serious hermeneutical reading of moral norms must be ever more important and decisive?

Briefly: the person is a historical being—together with the world—and not excluding one's moral norms of right conduct. Thus, moral norms, if adequately understood, are not in tension with the historicity of the person; rather, there is continuity and discontinuity in both.

NOTES

1. See A. Auer, "Die Erfahrung der Geschichtlichkeit und die Krise der Moral," *Theol. Quartalschrift* 149 (1961): 4-22, and "Die normative Kraft des Faktischen. Die Begegnung von Ethik und Sozialempirie," in *Begegnung* (Festschrift H. Fries), ed. A. Seckler, Graz/Vienna/Cologne 1972, 615-632. W. Kerber, ed., *Sittliche Normen. Zum Problem ihrer allgemeinen und unwandelbaren Geltung*, Düsseldorf 1982. K. Demmer, *Deuten und Handeln. Grundlagen und Grundfragen der Fundamentalmoral*, Freiburg i. Ue./Freiburg i. Br. 1985, and

"Christi vestigia sequentes, eiusque imagini conformes" (LG 40). Appunti ti teologia morale (ad uso privato degli studenti), Rome 1986. S. Bastianel, *Autonomia morale del credente*, Brescia 1980. G. B. Sala, "L'imperativo morale e la storicità dell'uomo": *La Civiltà Cattolica* 2957, 1 September 1973, 361-377. R. M. McInerny, "Truth in Ethics, Historicity and Natural Law": *Proceedings of the American Philosophical Association*, Washington, D.C. 43 (1969): 71-82.

2. K. Demmer, *Deuten und Handeln*.

3. Discourse of 29.10.1951: *Acta Apostolicae Sedis* 43 (1951), 835-854.

4. Cf. J. Fuchs, "Moral Truth between Objectivism and Subjectivism," in *Christian Ethics in a Secular Arena*, Washington, D.C./Dublin 1984, 29-47.

5. On this problematic, see also J. Fuchs, "The Sin of the World and Normative Morality," *Moral Responsibility and Christian Morality*, Washington, D.C./Dublin, 1983, 153-175.

6. G. Martelet, *Amour conjugal et renouveau conciliaire*, Paris 1967 (cf. discourse of Paul VI on 31.7.1968). D. Capone, "La Humanae Vitae nel ministero sacerdotale," *Lateranum* 44 (1978): 195-227, and references there to the article on homosexuality. P. Chirico, "Morality in General and Birth Control in Particular," *Chicago Studies* 48 (1969): 125-143, and "Tension, Morality and Birth Control," *Theological Studies* 28 (1967): 258-285.

7

Innovative Morality

In 1975, Enrico Chiavacci, professor of moral theology at the archiepis-copal seminary in Florence, published an essay in the Italian edition of *Communio* (22) entitled, "Ethos cristiano ed etica cristiana" ("Christian ethos and Christian ethics"). In this essay Chiavacci distinguishes between two kinds of ethics: (1) ethics as a system of moral commands and (2) ethics as a system that actively searches for moral commands. In the first system, new research into moral questions must, at all costs, avoid one thing: coming into conflict with the commands of the ethical system. This system presupposes both the knowledge of "Being," and the a priori possibility of "deducing" ethical norms from Being (the "ethical ideal").

On the other hand, the kind of ethics that actively searches for moral commands involves the obligation to recognize, in each case, valid norms and concrete answers as God's will. This search must be based on the data of divine revelation (which is Jesus himself, not his individual acts and words), and the use of human reason, although this involves the danger, posited by the very fact of being created, that one may err. Clearly, Chiavacci wants to distinguish between a static morality of commands that are definitively laid down in advance and a morality of responsibility, which not only demands keeping a command, but also the responsible search for God's will that has not been already communicated on every point and in advance.

It is in this sense that theologians have begun to speak recently of an *innovative moral theology*. Whether one is attempting to find solutions to serious human problems, observing acknowledged norms in a way that is correct here and now, or discovering the interior attitude that is concretely appropriate in the action that is acknowledged to be

God's will—in all of these, there is an individual, innovative element that plays a role in full ethical action and self-realization.

A MORALITY ALREADY IN EXISTENCE?

The opinion that ethical norms are already in existence and that therefore they only need to be accepted, submitted to, and realized in people's lives, *without further ado*, is widespread today. This opinion is held by many Christian people, by many priests, and—I fear—also by a number of moral theologians. Many documents that come from the church's magisterium can also be read in this way. However, the extent to which these norms are "already in existence" is in many ways an open question. What norms are we to think about? The "revealed" norms from the Hebrew Bible or the New Testament, or the norms given by "natural law" through creation and therefore from God, which are simply "to be read" in the creation? Or are we to think about the norms proposed by the magisterium of the Catholic Church? If these norms are already in existence, then the only duty incumbent upon all Christians is to adhere to them in their daily lives. This means that they cannot pose superfluous or critical questions about the justification of these norms, or set out independently on a search for new or additional norms, ones that would at least be different from those that already exist.

While morality, and the establishment of its norms, is certainly not an arbitrary "no-man's-land," this does not mean that morality is carried on among people who merely receive commands and are obedient subordinates. If we understand the world as God's redeemed creation, then everything that exists has the Creator as its ultimate, fundamental source. In this sense, then, it is possible to understand a life consciously, intentionally lived in accordance with what is understood as the valid norm, as a life lived in fidelity and obedience. This obedience does not mean, however, that the fundamental source of what can be seen as valid has imposed itself on us as something that has value and that has allowed us to know it precisely as such. Both the human person and human society are God's image precisely because they can grasp and comprehend what can or must be seen as valid, and they can do so on their own initiative. In this sense, their morality is not only received or imposed, but also autonomous and always innovative. Of course, this autonomy does not exclude the particular help given by the shining light of the gospel. We must develop this idea further.

The basic principle of every moral system is to do good and avoid evil (*malum morale*) and, as far as possible, every human ill (as a *malum non morale*). But even this basic principle is a primary and inescapable human experience and insight. Thus, it is a moral innovation of the ethical subject him- or herself, and not simply the adoption of a norm that is already in existence somewhere else, imposed and discovered to exist in this form. One aspect of this innovative insight is that this basic ethical principle has value and is therefore to be applied in many areas of life—for example, in justice, truthfulness, and chastity. The true meaning of this fundamental principle becomes clearer and more concrete when it is applied. What also becomes clear is that an ethical innovation is taking place. The reason for this innovation is that while people share a fundamental understanding of the ultimate meaning of justice, truthfulness, and chastity, there are nuances in the way each person grasps them. Thus, even the most general norms fundamentally have only an analogous, not a univocal, validity. But precisely for this reason they can and must be simultaneously universally valid and innovative.

The problem, however, is what form of behavior and realization of the world and oneself are correct when applied, for example, to justice, truthfulness, and chastity. On the other hand, a total arbitrariness is excluded here because human reality is a given that is already in existence. Therefore it demands a response in human behavior that corresponds to this reality. But on the other hand, reality itself does not give any unambiguous directive about how human positive and negative values are to be established in the various areas of reality. Because of their history and correspondingly different understanding of the person and the world, various areas of culture and various individuals will to some extent assess these values differently—and innovatively.

It would clearly be fallacious to maintain that what we have said so far has consequences for the discovery of ethical norms, *except* where someone holds concrete ethical norms of behavior as revealed by God, or sees them as demanded by nature itself (created by God) as it already exists (in its present stage of development). Therefore, on the basis of historical and personal development as well as through exchanging opinions with contemporaries, it is important to determine how a person or society can interpret and evaluate the realities that exist. This development means that the discovery of concrete moral norms and modes of correct behavior is necessarily innovative. One must not expect that the result of human and Christian ethical searching will lead to total uniformity. Rather, it will be partly pluralistic (cf. *Gaudium et Spes* 43). The innovative recognition or insight into concrete ethical norms of behavior or ethical imperatives is possible only in a hermeneutical process of seeking and finding what is required in each individual case. This process is not possible simply by the uncritical adoption of already existing norms or directives.

We have already mentioned the fundamental ethical principle that is intelligible to us and has absolute validity: one must aim at the *bonum* and do it, while avoiding the *malum*. Historically, moral theologians have appealed to Thomas Aquinas for this principle, so let us reflect on Thomas for a few moments. Translation into several modern languages shows that we are inclined to understand the term *malum* as that which is personally, ethically evil. But while this understanding is indeed fundamentally present in Thomas and is part of a long tradition, it is not unambiguous and precise. For Thomas, *bonum* and *malum* can mean both a person's ethical goodness or badness, and the ethical correctness or incorrectness of a person's conduct. And while these two ought to coincide, they do not always do so. When Thomas speaks of *bonum* and *malum* the problem at issue is correct or incorrect action and behavior. This problem is multifaceted and concerns the innovative search and discovery for the correct structuring of human reality, human life in space and time, and the world of the human person.

A mistaken innovative ethical solution introduces an evil into the human world that is not personal-ethical evil. Thomas has no great problems in the area of personal morality: the mistaken conscience, on the basis of incorrect innovative judgment, "excuses" the person who, with a good conscience, follows a mistaken innovative judgment in his or her decision and action. In the area of action, however, the incorrect innovative judgment remains the cause of the evil that is brought into the world by the action. Alongside personal morality there also stands the evil of the incorrect act (a *malum*). This is why Thomas, though calling such a person "excused" personally, does not call the person "good." We would prefer to say that the mistaken innovative judgment concerning the correctness of the action and its consequences does not diminish the personal goodness of the one who acts.

It is well known that Thomas maintains that the innovative recognition in the realm of ethically correct behavior manifests itself as a recognition of "consequences" (*conclusiones*) from natural "inclinations" (*inclinationes*) that every human person discovers in him- or her-self. What Thomas is referring to is the inclination toward the three goods of (1) the "existing human"; (2) human "existence as animal," and (3) "specific human existence" (*ad bonum secundum naturam rationis, quae est sibi propria*).[1] The innovative search of practical reason corresponds to the third good. Thomas emphasizes, however, that the world of the human person in which this searching takes place is a contingent world. Because of this contingency, the concrete consequences (*conclusiones*) drawn from the fundamental inclinations are not *logical* inferences but new pieces of knowledge, innovations.

Thus, in the case of norms, they cannot be compared either to the universality of the natural inclinations, or to the total universal validity of the first ethical principles. The ethical innovations of conduct's ethical correctness give us neither ethical norms of conduct that have absolute universal validity (*valent ut in pluribus*), nor concrete consequences that have more than a *morally* certain normative character. This does not mean that the innovative products of practical reason cannot be a genuine participation in the "eternal law of God"—though only "in some manner" (*aliqualiter*), only created—but this is possible only via created practical reason.

This reading of Aquinas is clearly not in keeping with an ethical "integralism" that many Christians so urgently long for today. Nor, however, is it in keeping with a radical ethical "pluralism," although Thomas does not argue strongly against the possible justification for such a multifaceted ethical pluralism. In his own century, Thomas was not familiar with pluralism to any great extent. However, it is something that we encounter today in a variety of forms, for example, in the cultures of Asia, Africa, and Latin America, as well as in Christian societies or societies influenced by Christianity.

Thomas would presumably agree, at least in principle, with the formulation of the German moral theologian, Dietmar Mieth.[2] According to Mieth, theological ethics knows only one metaethical principle: that the human person is capable of morality, or the one insight of natural law that one must do what is good and avoid what is evil. Everything else requires empirical mediation.

The English moral philosopher Gerard J. Hughes recently wrote an essay "Is Ethics One or Many?".[3] What he says about the inherent necessity for an ethical pluralism is also in keeping with Thomas Aquinas's fundamental reflection that moral theology is necessarily innovative.

IS MORALITY ALWAYS TO BE SOUGHT ANEW?

A moral system may and must call itself innovative, if what it says does not exclusively mean the adoption of something that already exists. It must have its own innovative element; something that is not already contained in what exists but derives from the person making the ethical decision even if it is only the judgment that an ethical answer that already exists is the *correct* answer, in concreto, to the person's problem. Nevertheless, the ethical answer that already exists would still be stated in rather general terms. It would not be a precise and explicit statement relating to the present, concrete situation. Such a statement is an innovative act of the person who comes to know, and who decides.

But this innovative activity goes deeper. Not only does it determine that an already existing answer is correct (or incorrect) in the here and now. It also experiences the correct (or incorrect) answer now simply as such, but in the mode and "color" of the nuanced particularity of the individual or societal situation, and in the contextualized givenness of the person who wants to appropriate the answer that already exists. Thus, the already existing answer that is appropriated receives—innovatively—a final nuance and meaningfulness that it did not have in the abstract, already existing formulation that was appropriated. In other words, the human person who decides or acts takes, in every instance, an innovative step beyond the statement of the already existing and appropriated norm. One's ethical decision and ethical conduct are never only the execution of a norm. They are more than formal acts.

This statement raises a further and perhaps more significant question. Is it possible that it is not only right and necessary to step beyond what is stated by an ethical norm or answer, but also—in spite of its clear formulation—to understand it as insufficient or irrelevant for the concrete reality with which one needs to cope? Hermeneutically speaking, is it not possible that I might seek a concrete answer in an already existing norm with an expectant attitude and thus receive a light from that norm that perhaps de facto never dawned on me before? But is it not also possible on the basis of my present situation that I must consider this light inadequate because it does not take into account particular data in my present situation? In this case, would not adopting the existing norm as a sufficient answer necessarily fail to answer the concrete problem?

Aquinas had cautious reservations vis-à-vis concrete norms of conduct, as well as the custom (which is slowly becoming established in today's moral theology) of speaking about *epikeia* even in the case of already existing ethical norms of conduct. Presumably his reservations have the following intent: It is possible (in a hermeneutical circle) that the norm I wish to follow in making a concrete decision does in fact enlighten me, and yet is not able to give me the answer I seek because it does not encompass the totality of my ethical question with all its particularities. Then it becomes clear that I must be innovative, that is, I must give the already existing norm the meaning and content that it does not yet have in its abstract formulation, but which it has precisely and objectively for me and my problem. I have the right and, on occasion, the duty to be innovative.

Of course, we always have already existing norms. We have adopted these norms from some source—for example, family, society, church, organizations, friendships. We are certain of them or, at any rate, we consider them plausible. But perhaps without daring to yield to the temptation, we also doubt them, either in their general formulation or in their capacity to adequately address a concrete situation. We can and must live with such ethical norms. A complete system of compelling ethical proofs does not exist. The so-called application of already existing ethical norms is in each case an authentic innovative act. Another aspect of our innovative ethical capacity is that we have to cope adequately with the problems that arise in our daily lives, that is, not necessarily on the basis of compelling proofs. At times, however, doubts, contrary arguments, and the influence of one's social milieu can become so significant that in the case of individual ethical norms innovation in substance may, or even must, be considered justified. It is not possible to exclude these cases absolutely.

A MORALITY FOR EACH INDIVIDUAL?

On the one hand, these reflections lead to the realization that there is no totally prefabricated ethics for the concrete human person and Christian. On the other hand, an abstractly prefabricated ethics can have significance for the genuine ethics of a society or individual. In some sense, each individual and society ultimately has a morality of its own. Certainly this morality is concerned with what is universally human or seen as normative in a particular society. But because of individual or societal fundamental options and the need to make totally concrete decisions, this morality is also concerned with what such "prefabricated" ethical data cannot satisfactorily address in a concrete, here-and-now, situation.

In other words, it is impossible to receive the complete ethical answer to ethical questions from already existing norms and answers. What is ethically good and correct for an individual or a particular society can never be determined completely by already existing and general ethical statements. In each case (within the totality of human and Christian ethics), it is the individual and the concrete society whose ethical order must be innovatively established and discovered. It is this "ethical truth" that is the ultimately decisive question. The ethical truth of each individual and each concrete society can only be found innovatively.

The question here is not only "what" is to be done. Equally important is the question: It is to be done "as what"; that is, what meaning does it have within an individual's life history and particular understanding of life and the world? This answer can differ from person to person and from group to group, but it belongs essentially to the question of "ethical truth." What is understood with moral certainty to be a requirement has to have value for us as the absolute call of God.

For example, marriage partners with their different personalities must understand what a particular word or gesture is capable of signifying in their relationship. A celibate life is an already existing lifestyle. But what can or must be appropriate for the individual celibate life is not set forth in advance with universal validity. Generally speaking, there are no fixed rules that govern a student's majoring in a certain subject (e.g., law, geophysics, nursing); one has to discover innovatively in what sense choosing a certain major is morally justifiable.

Seen in this perspective every genuinely human and Christian moral system is largely a morality of open options and decisions. "Open" here does not mean "totally arbitrary." It means, rather, not totally formed by already existing norms. "Open" means that the human (and Christian) person who acts is entrusted with the task to search responsibly and discover the correct innovation. The well-known formula: "What is not forbidden or commanded is permitted or left to one's arbitrary choice," is not correct. It ought to read: "No normative authority (myself included) has as yet made a clear or sufficient statement about the problem under discussion." The burden of responsibly discovering correct conduct rests on the shoulders of the one who makes the decision to act. Therefore, a *novum*, an innovation, is involved. And it is involved not only in the interpretation of already existing norms, but also in the search for a decision that has not been explicitly formulated in advance. In the strict sense, the attempt to discover the correct innovation is a moral task.

This ethical task, however, is often not reflected upon in addressing difficult—be they large or small—political or social problems, for example, nuclear power, space exploration, biotechnology. Usually one speaks of moral tasks more or less exclusively within the context of the private and personal sphere. However, the ethical character of these political and social problems is being seen and expressed more often today. In the United States, for example, there are ethical associations, institutes, and presidential commissions that deal with biological questions, business ethics, and other concerns. But the requirement for ethical innovation includes the total sphere of daily life and living: the encounter with others, behavior in traffic, family obligations, and daily business practices, among others.

The most general directives in these areas are known. What is needed is the eye that grasps the reality and its many large and small problems, the corresponding interpretation and evaluation, and the objective (not subjectivist) ethical answer, that is, ethical innovation in daily life. Often there is no explicit reflection on this constant claim for ethical innovation, but in certain circumstances, one becomes explicitly aware of it. It is always an innovation that has its roots in a historical context. It would be incorrect to call this whole realm of morality "subjective," as opposed to what is "objective." Ultimately, every search for objectively correct solutions to problems is carried out by persons who ought to aim at objectivity.

We have indicated that in each individual instance, a person needs to embark on the innovative search for the necessary decision. However, we cannot forget the teaching of Christian theology and the Christian spiritual tradition that God's Spirit is intimately close to us in such a search. Nor can we forget that tradition also teaches us that God's Spirit—at least on occasion—can mediate the answer that is sought through inspiration (although not in a way that one observes). Nor should we forget that God's Spirit can make its individual divine will known through inspiration in a way that cannot be deduced from the data of the situation. Here we think above all of the experiences of the great mystics. About the middle of this century—in the heyday of so-called situation ethics—there was much discussion in moral theology that revolved around the question: "What, precisely, does God want from me personally, and how do I recognize it?"

During this time, Karl Rahner attempted to answer the question on the basis of Ignatius of Loyola and Martin Heidegger. In his *Christian Existential Ethics*, Rahner claimed that it was absolutely impossible to replace the individual person—even, and precisely, in the presence of God.[4] In claiming this, Rahner took up a position that was clearly far from the theology of the Middle Ages. In his opinion medieval theology aimed all too one-sidedly at a sufficient understanding of the human person and his or her morality on the basis of alleged universally valid knowledge and statements (including moral statements). In his understanding of the person, Rahner reckons with the possibility of an individual will of God not only for mystics who have received special graces but—in the normal case—for every individual.[5]

Rahner does not want to exclude the possibility that a valid solution to the problem can be found by means of a good interpretation of the data of the situation. But he maintains that in many cases, it is ultimately the existential experience of the divine will for the individual that provides the answer to the person who seeks. The question is how God lets us know the individual will of God. As we have already said, the concrete and individual data at our disposal and our interpretation of that data have their place as a matter of course. But these data and interpretations alone do not manifest the "individual will of God" as such. Rahner maintains that the discernment of spirits (subject to theological and psychological criteria) provide this possibility. Perhaps today, we would prefer to say the discernment of the tendencies that can be perceived in ourselves. The Christian tradition teaches that what comes from God's Spirit can be distinguished in principle from what comes from other tendencies that press on us.

Rahner, however, is more specific. He refers to the Spiritual Exercises of Ignatius. Again, the concern here is with an "existential knowing" of the human person in relation to God as that person engages in the ethical search. This "existential knowing," however, points to a "fundamental evidential character" at the base of our discernment of the spirits (and hence of our knowing the individual will of God).[6] This "fundamental evidential character" consists in the experience of "objectless consolation," that is, in the fullness of God's love that is experienced without any specific object or thus in "emptiness." Rahner, with Ignatius, maintains that one can find the confirmation of a concrete object of choice if one places it into the "pure openness of the transcendence toward God that has become the theme of one's existence" (B. Fraling). It seems that Ignatius often proceeded in this way, and his Spiritual Exercises direct others to do likewise.

Regardless of the position one might take on Rahner's theory, even in the process he envisions, we have a creaturely experience of a congruence between objectless "consolation" (experience of God's love) and the readiness to make a concrete choice. This experience can awaken courage, power, and greater readiness. But can it give absolute certainty that one has discovered the individual will of God? Even great saints and mystics have thought it possible, and yet erred in individual questions. Presumably many Christians have also found a good path for their lives due to an "existential act of knowing." The question is: With what certainty? Not only psychological and subjective, but also objective certainty?

My inclination would be to answer by saying that one can discover the individual will of God with a very high degree of certainty. However, it is only "moral certainty." This "moral certainty" is the only certainty of which we as creatures (even as Christian creatures) are capable. On the other hand, Rahner's exposition shows that all Christian moral theology presupposes praxis in leading the Christian life. But it is precisely under this presupposition that ethical innovation takes place.

MORALITY GUIDED BY THE BIBLE?

May (or must) moral theology also be innovative vis-à-vis the statements of the Hebrew Bible and the New Testament? For us, the Hebrew Bible and the New Testament are *Verbum Dei*, the Word of God. For Christians, the revelation is Jesus himself, the son from Nazareth and the Son of God the Father. Jesus is the *innovation* of the scriptures, the message of the reign of God and of the human person who belongs to that reign—in contrast to the human person of "this world," that is, the sinner.

Jesus brings his message into the reality of the events of the world. But his message is not abstract. Rather, it is bound up with the reality and understanding of his experience of the world at that time. The message about the relationship of God to the human person, and the human person's relationship—and ethical attitude—to God, has universal validity. But the message must be nuanced in light of the character of the individual and the particularity of a given culture or epoch. The struggle of an individual to achieve an understanding that is possible and binding is necessarily innovative and ultimately "unutterable." Furthermore, it is not entirely clear at all points what in the biblical message about God and God's ethical attitude is truly God's message, and what is historically conditioned dress for expressing this message. Coming to grips with this dilemma is also an innovative ethical experience. How, for example, do I assimilate into my own ethical attitude the God of the burning bush, Mount Sinai, or Jesus' New Testament eschatological discourses?

Concrete, categorical ethical requirements in the scriptures are requirements of a particular time and culture. Certainly this temporal element does not eliminate the possibility that many of these commands are universal human requirements. But it is up to us to discover, innovatively, those requirements that are universally human, and those that are temporally and culturally determined. Or to be more precise: What requirements can and must be valid here and now, and for me personally? Even Jesus himself, his concrete person and lifestyle, deeds, and words, belong to this realm. Following Jesus is an absolute demand, but there is not the same demand to imitate Jesus. How we—how I—imitate Jesus today must be discovered innovatively by Christian communities and individuals.

Most moral theologians today agree that even the New Testament does not contain any new or special ethical commands that exceed human (i.e., creaturely) ethical requirements. This assertion is true both of the concrete ethical requirements of the pauline corpus, and of Jesus' Sermon on the Mount. What is new is the Spirit that determines all Christian ethical conduct—for example, with regard to Jesus' position on adultery as it was legally understood and limited at that time and in terms of creation theology, and of Paul's catalog of virtues and vices. The special element in the Sermon on the Mount is the requirement that the sinful person should not selfishly limit what is intended by the commandment of scripture or the reality of the ethical natural law. Though sinful people ignore this requirement, it derives its validity from human existence as such. Jesus calls us to acknowledge the true intent of the ethical order and its divine, primal source.

What is new in the Sermon on the Mount is the horizon against which all Christian ethical conduct takes place: the reign of God that has begun with the (theologically understood) Christian power, freedom, and the Spirit of the Lord Jesus who is historically and mystically

present. New also is the theological depth of the anthropological implications of the Christian message and its ethical consequences, that is,
the deeper understanding of God's love for the human person, the dignity of each person, and the fundamental equality of this dignity in
everyone. But to establish the significance of all these new elements for
concrete Christian living, they must be interpreted. And this interpretation must be done not only by cultures and epochs, but by individual
Christians. In each instance, ethical innovation is required.

A definitive list of Christian attitudes and requirements has never
been handed to us. Heinz Schürmann once attempted to establish the
abiding validity of biblical statements and requirements.[7] He had to
admit, however, that in every case, these statements have an abiding
validity by analogy or even only in terms of a tendency, that is, a validity that needs constant innovation. The moral theology of Christians
is fundamentally—in one way or another—innovative.

NOTES

1. S.T.I-II.94.2.
2. D. Mieth, *Moral und Erfahrung. Beiträge zur theologisch-ethischen
Hermeneutik*, Freiburg i. Ue./Freiburg i. Br. 1977, 54.
3. G. J. Hughes, "Is Ethics One or Many?" in *Catholic Perspectives on
Medical Morals, Foundational Issues.* ed. by E. D. Pellegrino, J. P. Langan, and J.
C. Harvey. Dordrecht 1979, 173-196.
4. K. Rahner, *Schriften zur Theologie*, 2, Cologne/Einsiedeln/Zürich,
1955, 227f.
5. K. Rahner, *Das Dynamische in der Kirche*, Quaestiones disputatae 5.
Freiburg 1958, *passim.*
6. Ibid., 113.
7. Heinz Schürmann, "Die Frage nach der Verbindlichkeit neutesta-
mentlicher Wertungen und Weisungen," *Prinzipien christlicher Moral*, ed. J.
Ratzinger, Einsiedeln 1975, 9-39.

8

Ethical Problems in the Christian Prayer of the Psalms

INTRODUCTION

In its origins, the Book of Psalms is a book of prayers and hymns that came into being in the course of several centuries. The community or the individual prays or sings to God in the presence of God. Songs and prayer poems express a deep relatedness to the God of the people, the community, and the individual, a relatedness that permeated the entire reality of life in ancient Israel. All is praise and thanksgiving, lamentation and request, testimony and exultation declaimed in the temple, in the family, in solitary quiet.

The psalms were also declaimed in the synagogue in the time of Jesus. In the gospel narratives of the New Testament, the theology and piety of the psalms are clearly visible as well as their ethical perspectives, though they have undergone a partial change in the course of time. One may, for example, see this change in the divergent interpretations of the Sadducees and the Pharisees. But diversity did not prevent the psalms from remaining the hymns and prayers of the Jewish community, especially in the temple on Sion.

The Book of Psalms was also the book of prayers and hymns that Jesus used when he took part in singing and prayer—in the temple with his family or with the flock of his disciples—and when Christians likewise shared in this prayer in the first Christian period.[1] The fact that theological and ethical stances of certain psalms no longer wholly corresponded to the theology and ethics of their contemporaries posed no problem for the people of the first century C.E.; nor was there an obstacle in the fact that Jesus himself—to a certain extent, in the company of other Jews—had spoken of God in a different way from that of the psalms, or that the moral behavior which he proposed and expected of his disciples was not totally identical with that contained in them. In many aspects, the Jews of Jesus' time still lived the spirit of the psalms, above all the deep bond of union with God, praise, thanksgiving, and confidence in prayers of request—all based on the faithfulness of God in Israel's history, the same God who was also the God of history after Jesus Christ.

The early Christian Church also prayed and lived the Jewish psalms.[2] It is certainly an exaggeration to say that the Book of Psalms was the only book of readings for Christians. Certainly the church in the beginning and during the age of the martyrs soon began to pray hymns to Christ, that is, to develop a prayer culture of its own; there existed along with the piety of the psalms, an impassioned piety directed to Christ. But it is certain that the church had already developed a piety of the psalms by the year 200. This piety spread and began to take on a broad dominance in Christian worship, although with a decisive difference from the piety of the earliest Christian communities. These later communities developed a certain christological form of praying the psalms within their own group (as the texts of the New Testament show), which was accompanied by a conscious endeavor to arrive at a specifically Christian understanding and piety, although this took various forms and many accommodations were necessary.

This line of interpretation was maintained by the church in the following centuries; in our time, even in the new Roman breviary, a brief line at the head of each psalm suggests a Christian understanding to the one who prays. In this way, the psalms have become the chant of the monks, the spiritual or prayerful reading of those who pray the Roman breviary, and the prayer of many individual Christians. When the Katholische Bibelwerk of Stuttgart issued a paperback of the new German translation of the Holy Bible, it issued not only the New Testament, but "The New Testament and the Psalms."[3] The biblical scholar Herbert Haag expresses well the role of the psalms in Christian piety:

> The Psalms are the book of the Old Testament which was taken over with the least reservations by the Christian Church, since they were the prayerbook of Jesus and of the community of his disciples. For this reason, it was never possible to raise one's voice in criticism of the retention of the Jewish Psalms; quite to the contrary, the Church had no doubt of the correctness of its

perception that no other stance is appropriate to God's people in the new covenant than that of God's people in the old covenant— it must unceasingly come before its God as a praising people of God.[4]

Nevertheless, individual points in the psalms do present difficulties for Christian piety; these difficulties are perhaps more clearly seen and taken into consideration today than in other centuries. "Naturally, God always and everywhere, in the history of the individual and of the collectivity of humanity, has had to deal with the human person, especially in the Old Testament. But all of these encounters were, after all, basically 'attempts to draw closer'."[5] If Karl Rahner was correct in making this formulation, then the psalms, too, must be understood as "attempts to draw closer": but in this case, a living piety of the psalms in the New Testament period cannot be free of problems and difficulties.

While the fundamental note of deep union with God found in all the psalms has indeed remained basically the same, it is perceived differently in psalms that come from various centuries; these differences already existed before Jesus, but with him, and in the Christian centuries, an image of God, the person, and the world has developed that is extremely different; and these images influence the singing and praying of the psalms.

In the Constitution *Divino Afflatu*, Pope Pius X could still emphasize the abiding fundamental tenor of the psalms, though he did so in a rather one-sided manner on the basis of many texts from the early church. His text is in the new breviary as the second reading on his feast (21 August). The official general introduction to the present breviary is, however, more nuanced and speaks twice of the "difficulties" that face Christians who wish to make the text of the psalms their own. It therefore repeats the exhortation of the Second Vatican Council that Christians who make use of the Psalter should "acquire a thorough biblical education.[6] It also indicates that a few individual psalms (58, 83, and 109) and individual verses of others have not been included in the breviary, since their ethical stance makes it scarcely possible (at least psychologically) to ask Christians to make use of them. They are, nevertheless, found in other popular editions of the Psalter.

The difficulties mentioned here are of an ethical character, especially in the so-called psalms of revenge. The commentators on the Book of Psalms draw attention to the impossibility of "realizing" certain texts in the psalms. Even Romano Guardini, who praises the "wisdom of the psalms" as the "word of God," along the lines of Pius X, cannot avoid observing that their authors were, in the last analysis, not yet Christians and that we therefore cannot affirm everything in them.[7] B. Fischer has a similar formulation.[8] The same observations are found in Protestant commentators like Claus Westermann and H.-J. Kraus.[9]

The problem is not, however, limited exclusively to Psalms of revenge: H. Haag's formulation goes nearer to the heart of the issue:

> Especially in the early period, we find less prayer for spiritual goods and more prayer for temporal, material benefits. There is indeed prayer for redemption and the forgiveness of sins, for fellowship with God and for a righteous conduct in life, but the majority of the prayers which have come down to us have an apparently "worldly" content: healing from sickness, rescue from the danger of death, shelter from enemies, help in hunger and the distress of war. But in all this multiplicity, there is ultimately *one* great theme: *life*.[10]

And the life in question is our life on this side of death.

The Book of the Psalms has become the book of Christian piety. The Christian moral theologian also likes to use psalms and has much profit from doing so. But as a moral theologian, one must ask questions about the Christian character of these prayers that were written so many centuries ago by pious non-Christians. Even if one is willing to acknowledge the presence of intense emotion that is found in many psalms, one must still ask questions, for emotional intensity alone cannot explain away their ethical difficulties.

Are pious Christians who pray the psalms simply unaware of their moral difficulties? Do they simply brush aside the potential difficulties? Or can it be that the morality of the psalms has an influence on the morality and conduct of Christians? In that case, what ought to be done?

In the sections that follow we shall offer some reflections on the moral difficulties of the psalms. The numbering of the psalms used here is the Hebrew enumeration, which differs from the Latin; it is used in all modern translations.

HUMAN PERSONS BEFORE GOD

Psalms are prayers to God or speech in the presence of God. But do Christians truly pray to God in the psalms, that is, to the God whom they know from Christian revelation? This is a religious question and a question of moral conscience. Beyond doubt, Christians pray to God as they know God; but do they genuinely recognize this God as the God of whom the Psalter speaks? Yes, this God is the one in whom all the world has its existence and who gives breath to each one—life until death; this God is the one who is revealed and who is essentially monotheistic, even if not yet confessed to be the Trinity of Father, Son, and Holy Spirit. We can, however, ask whether prayer to this monotheistic God of the Psalter is perhaps simpler than prayer to the one triune God of Christianity.

And yet the Christian feels something foreign in the piety of the psalms, something that is not wholly Christian. How is the Christian to understand the God in Psalm 82 who rises up "in the assembly of the gods" and holds judgment in the circle of the "gods"; who says to these "gods," "You are gods, you all are sons of the Most High; yet now you shall die like men, fall like any of the princes"? Christians do not know this God who has other "gods" as royal courtiers. Who is the God exalted high above all "gods" (Ps 97:9) and "king" of them all (Ps 95:3), before whom the gods and idols must cast themselves to the ground (Ps 97:7)?

One may try to understand this use of speech in an anthropomorphic and metaphorical fashion. But in reality this use of speech contains more than metaphors. We have here relics of mythical ideas and faint memories of the religions of the foreign peoples among whom Israel has lived. Paul Tillich indeed believed that one should speak of a "monarchical monotheism" that developed between polytheism and monotheism in certain psalms.[11]

God's "sitting on the throne"—not only on the throne of the cherubim of the temple (e.g., Ps 99), but also and especially on the throne "in the heights" (e.g., Ps 113), "above the flood" (Ps 29:10), that is, in "heaven" surrounded by the "heavenly beings" (the "sons of the gods")—is different from the concept of God that most Christians have even if the Christian concept, too, is partly metaphorical and anthropomorphic. Even the kingdom of God, which is so frequently mentioned, is much more prominent in the psalms and intervenes in the history of humanity much more strongly than Christians generally expect it to do. Nevertheless, Christians pray the psalms to, and in the presence of, the God of Christianity. Do they perhaps overlook or not care about the specifically outmoded character of the concept of God that remains in them?

A further observation has more significance from an ethical point of view. The God-king of the Book of Psalms is unquestionably the one from whom proceed the directives, commandments, and laws in accordance with which the people of God and the individual Israelite attempted to live their "righteousness." This connection between God and the law is taken for granted. The most important concept is the commandment of fidelity to the God of the covenant, negatively the renunciation of worship of the "gods" or idols worshiped by other peoples. This renunciation involves participation in the prescribed cultic service of God and the human-ethical righteous conduct of individuals as it was understood at that period. But such a divine "act of giving the law" is hardly attested in a positive fashion—and not even the decalogue is a true exception. Psalm 19:8-10 sings:

> *The law of the Lord is perfect,*
> *reviving the soul;*
> *the testimony of the Lord is sure,*
> *making wise the simple;*
> *the precepts of the Lord are right,*
> *rejoicing the heart;*
> *the commandment of the Lord is pure,*
> *enlightening the eyes;*
> *the fear of the Lord is clean,*
> *enduring forever;*
> *the ordinances of the Lord are true,*
> *and righteous altogether.*
> *More to be desired are they than gold,*
> *even much fine gold;*
> *sweeter also than honey*
> *and drippings of the honeycomb.*

The deepest and most strongly expressed law-centered piety is found in Psalm 119.

Christian theology has a very different view of things. Under the guidance of the God who never abandons us, God's people in both testaments developed forms of worship and human-ethical conduct. In principle, these forms were largely identical, but in their details—corresponding to social and situational differences as well as to changes in mentality—they exhibit partly different modes of human life and conduct before God. To the extent that we hold ourselves obliged to regard these forms of worship and conduct as correct, God and our Christian conscience require us to put them into practice.

The question, however, is whether praying the psalms confirms many Christians in their view that everything that we acknowledge to be the expression of moral order, indeed everything that is proclaimed in a pastoral context or even by the official teaching of the church to be "God's commandment" and hence "not to be doubted," is a directive, a commandment, a law that is directly addressed to us by God. Unenlightened piety centered on the psalms would, in this case, produce a negative ethical effect that would certainly not be without importance.

On the other hand we have, for example, the profound Psalm 50, in which God renounces the many sacrifices that are prescribed in the law and, instead of appealing to directives and laws, simply requires the human person in his or her totality to praise God and God's righteousness (cf. also Pss 15 and 24). And God waits for this praise not only from those who belong to the first covenant with its laws, but from all peoples, for whom God wills to be "salvation" (Ps 67).

But, again, is "salvation" in these psalms what Christians expect it to be? In the ancient psalms, salvation is the maintenance of a person's earthly life (especially the Israelite's) and success in this life, which is exclusively the gift of God. The psalms do not distinguish between the(Christian) "salvation" of the righteous, which flows over into eternal life, and the wickedness of the evil doers that ends in damnation; these concepts are completely unknown in the Psalter. The good that one seeks who prays the psalms (for oneself and one's people) is life on earth: life in the praise of God, life in righteousness (though righteousness is also a way to win God's favor for earthly life), life with friends and without foes, life in prosperity and without sickness, life without distress, tribulation, and the danger of death.

How does the pious Christian pray Psalm 146:4: "When man breathes out his life and turns back to the earth, then all his plans are finished." Paul uses different language in 1 Cor 15:22: "As in Adam all die, so in Christ will all be made alive." In the psalms, dying is the transition to Sheol, to a continued *existence* that is somehow in the presence of God.[12] But it is a transition without participation in life; Sheol is silence and darkness, with no relationship to the world of life and God, without the temple and without God's loving favor, without distinction between the pious and the wicked. Psalm 115 expresses it thus:

Heaven belongs to the Lord,
but he has given the earth to men.
The dead can praise the Lord no more,
nor those who go down into the silence.

How do Christians pray Psalm 88:4-13, in which a lonely individual in mortal sickness laments before God and implores God for help in the face of death, that is, for deliverance from dying?

For my soul is filled with evils;
my life is on the brink of the grave.
I am reckoned as one in the tomb:
I have reached the end of my strength
like the slain lying in their graves;
like those you remember no more,
cut off, as they are, from your hand.
You have laid me in the depths of the tomb,
in places that are dark, in the depths . . .
You have taken away my friends
and made me hateful in their sight.
Imprisoned, I cannot escape . . .
Will you work your wonders for the dead?
Will the shades stand and praise you?
Will your love be told in the grave
or your faithfulness among the dead?
Will your wonders be known in the dark
or your justice in the land of oblivion?

Neither the longing for heaven nor the fear of hell motivates the praise of God and the uprightness of the pious ones in the Psalter. These responses can be motivated only by the following considerations: first, reverence for God as God; second, a genuine feeling for uprightness; and third, the hope that God will graciously continue to bestow earthly life and prosperity as the reward for the uprightness of the pious.

Deeper Christian motivations are lacking, so is Paul's reflection in the first Letter to the Corinthians, and its corresponding hope in God's favor: "If the dead are not raised, then let us eat and drink; for tomorrow we die" (15:32*b*). Kant's theory and postulates of an ethics of obligation is also lacking. Christians who pray the psalms believe and hope in more than the psalms promise; their understanding of life and death has its basis, despite the words they repeat, in a radiant faith that had already begun to spread in the time of Jesus and took on impetus above all through Jesus himself.

In the psalms, the only recourse for one striving to attain righteousness or asking for forgiveness for sins is God, who has the power to preserve us, at least for the moment, from death and the shadowy existence of Sheol as well as from other suffering and distress.[13] Suffering and distress (including that caused by the enemy) are generally (though not exclusively) understood in the psalms as the consequence and penalty of sin (one's own and other people's), not as events independent of sin, as most people today consider them. And yet, in the confrontation with suffering and distress, Christians have had broadly the same experience as the psalmists, and still have the same experience on occasion. In this case, the Christian simply prays the psalms in their literal sense, although it may be more Christian to cry out one's suffering and need in the simplicity of distress before God, entrusting oneself to God and recommending oneself to God, taking refuge there with hope and also with humility and devotion.

THE GOD WHO WORKS ALL THINGS

The one who prayed the psalms in ancient Israel had a living experience of God, but little experience of the world, and this must necessarily influence one's stance and conduct, since here one attributes directly to God who works all things, everything that happens in nature and in history, both what happens in the community and what happens in the life of the individual.[14] Even if some statements in the psalms about the God who works all things are anthropomorphisms intended to remind the one who prays that God is always graciously open to us, nevertheless the psalms seem to lack a sufficient knowledge of the natural law governing events on earth.[15]

In them, everything is God's will, God's command that things come into being, God's working. In the everyday life of the psalms, earthly secondary causes (in the reality of which God is naturally present) somehow lose their significance as autonomous mediating causes. It is not easy for us to accept the notion that everything in nature and in history—all human working and all human suffering, living, and dying—are derived immediately from God, but this notion is found in the psalms to an extraordinary degree.

The theology of divine providence—so difficult, and doubtless not yet completely formed even today—is present in the psalms in pious but also naive form. It would therefore be virtually impossible for those who first prayed the psalms to understand the observation of Thomas Aquinas that while God's providence does govern all things (even the events of nature with their secondary causes), it governs the human person in a more exalted fashion. God permits humankind to share in divine providence so that the human person can bear responsibility—individually for oneself and also for others.[16] Christian piety will doubtless not follow the text of the psalms straightforwardly at every point, but praying the psalms will perhaps cause many Christians to see God directly in many events in the same way that the pious person of the Old Testament did, and to turn directly to God.

The pious Christian is happy to join the pious person of earlier ages and to say in prayer that everything comes from God, that God created heaven and earth (Ps 115:15*b*) and that God is present to the whole of reality (Ps 139). But we tend to understand in a reductionist way the statement of Ps 104 that God has ordered everything directly and in its individual details in a great scheme. Many statements in the psalms—that God appears in the mighty events of nature, for example, in storm and thunder, on the mountains and in the sea, not only as their final cause but as their direct cause; that God likewise planned the events related in the exodus from Egypt and carried them out one by one; that God mysteriously and skillfully forms a human child in the womb of the mother (Ps 139:13; or with mythical undertones "in the depths of the earth," 139:15); that God gives children to married couples as a special gift; that the night watch of the city is not sufficient unless ultimately God's own self keeps watch over the city; that the employment of time in work is not so central, because it is the Lord who gives gifts to those who belong to God even while they sleep— these and many other statements no doubt stimulate trust in God. And, indeed, their aim in the psalms is to stimulate such a trust in God. But what is fundamentally meant here is expressed in Psalm 115:3: "He brings about whatever he pleases." This verse is intended precisely to underline the distinction between the true God and the "gods of the peoples." Christians who pray these words cannot pray them with a wholly honest conscience, if they are to understand them in the light of Psalm 115.

In the face of the frequent, serious affirmation that it depends on God alone to give or withhold the gift of life when one is in distress, or to determine whether the outcome of one's whole life is disappearance into Sheol, or whether enemies—God's own and the people's—will be hurled with the wicked out of this life and into the "pit" (Sheol), many Christians who take into account the significance of earthly secondary causes will wish to pray in a more nuanced manner. But cannot the prayer of the psalms even today influence many Christians' understanding of events on earth?

A Christian prayerbook would not have Christians complaining to God in misfortune and distress, or even accusing God because of God's wrath; they will not grumble that God has already been angry for such a long time—How long, O Lord? (Psalm 13:3). "Will the Lord then reject me forever and never again be gracious. . . . Has God forgotten his mercy, closed up his mercy in anger?" (Ps 77:8-10). But perhaps the text of the Psalter lets us hear something that does come to expression in this or a similar way in the individual Christian, and is sometimes even uttered unhesitatingly.

Christians—after Christ—read and pray with deep personal commitment to the God who can forget and forgive. Few psalms are as well known to us as Psalm 130, "Out of the depths I cry to you, O Lord." The psalms speak of one's sins (the individual's and the people's) and of the sins of one's forebears (e.g., Ps 79: 8f.). But the prayer for forgiveness by Christians is different from that in many psalms. The piety of the psalms seeks to attain or to win back God's favor in this earthly life through the forgiveness of sins, and this forgiving favor is sought so that the wicked and one's enemies—who are basically the enemies of God—cannot continue to jeer at the pious of Israel in their tribulation or defeat in war because they have been abandoned by God.

From the time of its exodus from Egypt and the war of conquest until it was settled in Canaan, Israel was continually involved in conflict with other people, who were its enemies and, ultimately, the enemies of its God. There is no doubt that victory or defeat depends on the weapons and strength of armies; but the psalms repeatedly teach us that it is ultimately God who bestows victory or inflicts defeat. How *may* Christians pray during the situation of war, and how *can* they pray? Can they, for example, make use of Psalm 33:

A king is not saved by his army,
nor a warrior preserved by his strength.

> *A vain hope for safety is the horse;*
> *despite its power it cannot save.*

May Christians, and can they, speak thus with a good conscience? Can Christians attribute a defeat in war to their "angry God"? Take, for example, Psalm 78:59-64:

> *They provoked him to anger with their high places;*
> *they moved him to jealousy with their graven images.*
> *When God heard, he was full of wrath,*
> *and he utterly rejected Israel . . .*
> *He gave his people over to the sword,*
> *and vented his wrath on his heritage.*
> *Fire devoured their young men,*
> *and their maidens had no marriage song.*
> *Their priests fell by the sword,*
> *and their widows made no lamentation.*

Can Christians, and people of this century, attribute their victories to God? Does our conscience permit us to make Psalm 44:4 our own, without omitting anything?

> *No sword of their own won the land;*
> *no arm of their own brought them victory.*
> *It was your right hand, your arm*
> *and the light of your face: for you loved them.*
> *Israel trusts in its God; everything depends on the Lord.*

Even in distress and tribulation, the ancient Israelites did not lose their hope in God—even when they believed they must cry out to God. And if for once God's anger turned against the people, yet they are certain that God's anger will be only for a certain period. "The Lord is with me, I do not fear" (Ps 118:6).

GOD'S CHOSEN PEOPLE

God's history with one chosen people is for us from the outset an unfathomable mystery; the ancient biblical understanding of this fact may perhaps contain myths that were common to the various peoples at that period. The symbiosis of religion and politics that results, the favor shown by God to precisely this one people and the exultant self-awareness of this people as it gives thanks for its history—all of this (whatever may be said in favor of a theology of salvation history) requires a great deal of faith on our part.

But this is the situation that we find, for example, in Psalms 105 and 106. We cannot do other than venerate the faithfulness of God, which is repeatedly praised in the many things that God has done for people or that are at any rate attributed to God, including much that we take to be terrible and incomprehensible. Against this background, the thankfulness of the people and of King David for the God who chooses and is faithful, is certainly holy: "happy the people whose God is the Lord" (Ps 144:15*b*).

Two points are especially surprising (although they are understandable in the perspective of ancient Israel: first, the absolute authority of the central position of Sion (Jerusalem), praised in many psalms, and of its holy temple as the dwelling of God in the midst of the people (cf. Ps 48); and second, the equally absolute promise of the never-ending duration of the clan and throne of David (cf. Pss 89:4f.; 132). We can understand these realities today in a theological and spiritual manner, but their immediate meaning in the Psalter is religious and political, and they are therefore understood in a thoroughly earthly way, although they show in the course of history that they lack earthly permanence. We can pray the psalms that refer to these realities with an honest conscience only if we manage to enter into the heart of the people of many centuries ago.

Those who belong to the chosen people, in "the inheritance of the righteous" (Ps 125:3) are in principle and should be in fact those who are morally "righteous"; we have already seen what this means ethically according to Psalms 15 and 24, and what it signifies for the piety centered on the law according to Psalm 119. Thus, the Israelites are to be distinguished from other peoples, their enemies, and the wicked. The psalmists like to appeal more than we Christians ought to do, to their personal righteousness and innocence, seeing in them a claim on God: God shall give them earthly protection and let them prosper (see, e.g., Pss 18:21-28; 71:17; 140:14).

According to the psalmists, therefore, the righteous one can be certain of God's faithfulness in this earthly life: God keeps this one alive (Ps 40), and snatches that one away from the foe (Pss 54:7; 125).

God withholds no gift from the righteous (Ps 84:12) and always grants divine protection (Ps 112). "Thus will the man be blessed who fears and reveres the Lord" (Ps 128:4); these gifts are earthly blessing. However, Christian experience does not always correspond to the prayer of the psalmists; and our requirement today that there should be "more justice" in human society has a different justification: an ethical justification.

GOD AND THE ENEMIES OF THE PEOPLE

When Israel and its psalmists consider the Lord to be the only God and their only God, it follows that all the other "gods" and the peoples who worship them must be understood as "enemies," as rivals of God and foes of God's people. The accursed symbiosis of religion and politics that resulted from this viewpoint was common to all ancient peoples. Those who are consciously "other" thereby hate God's people in some way, and thus ultimately hate God. Therefore, the psalmist prays to God: "your enemies raise a tumult: those who hate you lift up their heads" (Ps 83:3). Correspondingly, God must "hate" the others (Ps 1:5), for in reality God is the enemy of the enemies of the people. Since for the psalmists everything ends when life on earth is ended, it must be shown in earthly time—in victory or defeat—on which side God stands. Everything is attributed personally to God, and everything is understood as done in God's name: Israel is to fight and conquer the land of other peoples; it is to carry out the curse of complete destruction on the defeated peoples (it is a crime not to do so, according to Ps 106:34); and it is to hate its enemies (as God does) and take vengeance on them, which means that it must understand its wars as a divine commission.

The hatred of one's enemies, which ought to be foreign to Christians (although it is often fomented by the world's powers even today), is understood in the biblical milieu as a hatred that is required on religious and ethical grounds. We read in Ps 139: "Do I not hate those who hate you, abhor those who rise against you? I hate them with a perfect hate and they are foes to me." This hatred turns into ethically "obligatory" revenge.

Since for the psalmists, it is ultimately a question of the people's God, they pray to God to destroy their enemies—to trample them, break them to pieces, pursue them, count their guilt against them, let glowing coals, fire, and sulfur rain down upon them, hurl lightning against them, make them lick the dust of the earth, and send them down into the "pit" (Sheol); "let even their prayer become a sin" (Ps 109:7b).[17] "The just shall rejoice at the sight of vengeance; they shall bathe their feet in the blood of the wicked" (Ps 58:11).

It will not be easy for Christians at prayer to enter fully into the world of the psalmists. It is certain that they cannot simply make these texts their own—neither their spirit of hatred and vengeance, nor the fact that everything takes place in God's name or is attributed directly to God. Christians may perhaps succeed in understanding them to some extent, and in sharing the psalmist's committed stance to God and God's people. But perhaps they will also be thankful for the changes that have been made in human relationships and in the relationship between God and human beings in the course of centuries, and above all, through the spirit of Jesus Christ who has been at work for nearly two millennia.

CONCLUSION

Objectively speaking, the psalms contains enormous difficulties for the Christian who uses them in prayer. Not all Christians will be aware of these difficulties to the same extent; it is not possible here to say how far the individual at prayer is able and willing to meet the requirements of the Second Vatican Council and of the general introduction to the new breviary, namely, that one must study to prepare oneself for the use of the Psalter. Nor is it possible to say to what extent this study can help one to overcome the psychological difficulties in the attempt to appropriate the piety of the psalms. It must likewise remain an open question whether pastoral help is available today for an appropriate study.

Two reflections should not be lacking here: first, the difficulties inherent in the Psalter can present a handicap to the genuine spirit of the Christian ethos and Christian ethics, at least to some extent; second, the praying and singing of psalter, taken as a whole, was and is a wonderful act of praising God. We must not therefore be influenced too negatively by the difficulties that persist.

NOTES

1. Even if recent Jewish researchers are correct in asserting that there also existed Jewish groups at the time of Jesus who did not use the psalms in their worship in the temple, this cannot be true of all Jewish groups and the earliest Christians, since the New Testament authors reveal a living familiarity with the psalms.

2. On the historical data that follow, see B. Fischer, "Die Psalmenfrömmigkeit der Märtyrerkirche," in *Die Psalmen als Stimme der Kirche*, ed. A. Heinz, Trier 1982, 12-35. See also Alfons Deissler, *Die Psalmen*, vol 1, *Die Welt der Bibel*, Düsseldorf 1963, 22f.

3. 3d ed., 1982.

4. Herbert Haag, *Gott und Mensch in den Psalmen*, vol 28 in *Theologische Meditationen*, ed. H. Küng, Zürich/Einsiedeln/Cologne 1972, 12.

5. Karl Rahner, *Was heisst Jesus lieben?* 2d ed. Freiburg i. Br. 1982, 38f.

6. Constitution on the Liturgy, 90.

7. Romano Guardini, *Der Anfang aller Dinge. Weisheit der Psalmen*, Mainz and Paderborn, 2d ed., 123f.

8. B. Fischer, "Die Psalmenfrömmigkeit der Märtyrerkirke der Kirke," 17-20.

9. *Ausgewählte Psalmen*, trans. and ed. by Claus Westermann, Göttingen 1984, 25, 54f. H.-J. Kraus, *Theologie der Psalmen*, Neukirchen-Vluyn 1979, 25f.

10. *Gott und Mensch in den Psalmen*, 17 (my emphasis).

11. Paul Tillich, *Systematische Theologie*, I, Stuttgart 1956, 2d ed., 262.

12. Cf. Psalm 139:8: "If I climb the heavens, you are there. If I lie in the grave, you are there."

13. See, for example, Ps 50:23b: "To the one who is upright I will show my salvation" (i.e., life); Ps 116:15: "Precious in the sight of the Lord is the death of his faithful"(i.e., their being preserved from dying and from Sheol). Cf. Ps 130:3f.: "If you, O Lord, should mark our guilt, Lord, who would survive? But with you is found forgiveness: for this we revere you."

14. Cf. Herbert Haag, *Gott und Mensch in den Psalmen*, 27; Romano Guardini, *Der Anfang aller Dinge. Weisheit der Psalmen*, 25f.

15. Cf. H.-J. Kraus, *Theologie der Psalmen*, 25f.

16. S.T.I-II.91.2.

17. Compare, for example, Ps 109:6-20, from which a few verses are quoted here: May the iniquity of his fathers be remembered before the Lord, / and let not the sin of his mother be blotted out! / Let them be before the Lord continually; / and may their memory be cut off from the earth! / He loved to curse; let curses come on him! / He did not like blessing; may it be far form him! / He clothed himself with cursing as his coat, / may it soak into his body like water, / like oil into his bones!"

Ps 137:8f. is well known: "O daughter of Babylon, you devastator! / Happy shall he be who requites you / with what you have done to us! / Happy shall he be who takes your little ones / and dashes them against the rock!"

The Magisterium and Moral Theology

In mid-November, a group of twenty young Catholic journalists from roughly that many different countries were in Freiburg for a week on a study-trip. They had been in Rome in the previous week where they had also had contact with authorities in the Vatican. The Secretary of the Congregation for the Doctrine of the Faith, Archbishop Bovone, told them among other things that the Congregation's chief problem at the moment was Catholic moral theology. We are, of course, already aware of this problem, but to what extent are the endeavors of the church's magisterium with all the nervous energy they require, necessary?

INTRODUCTION

Christian life is an obligatory expression of Christian faith in God's self-communication, according to the Second Vatican Council's *Lumen Gentium*. The Christian life in this world is a life in keeping with the gospel. No doubt a moral discourse of the Christian people and the church arises in our consciousness and in the Christian proclamation. But this discourse does not contain simplistic Christian answers to all moral questions that affect us amid the myriad and changing conditions of life.

Christian faith as such does not offer perennially unchanging solutions to life's many questions, but neither does it permit arbitrary solutions. The influence of Christian faith is more fundamental than would be supposed from the concreteness of individual questions; it penetrates and animates the many individual solutions, and in this way brings its influence to bear on them.

If pastors are to offer leadership, then they too will have to banish all forms of arbitrariness from the Christian construction of life, so that it is compatible with the spirit and statements of the gospel. Pastors cannot always and definitively offer final solutions to all moral questions.

Jesus, in fact, behaved in this spirit of the gospel. He insisted on conversion from an egotistical, that is, sinful, orientation to absolute righteousness, and he resisted the selfish interpretations of moral precepts that were accepted at that time. Jesus corrected precepts of the law that came from self-seeking and hard-heartedness (e.g., the letter of divorce); he admonished trespasses against the ethical order in force at the time (e.g., unrighteousness, hard-heartedness, and adultery). But he was far from teaching a moral code of correct behavior distinct from the code that was then accepted, and even further from teaching a perennial code governing every form of correct human conduct for all periods and in all cultures. Jesus—the Son from Nazareth—could not do this in the least.

And Paul behaved in a similar spirit. While he insisted on fidelity to the proclamation of God's kingdom and to the normative conduct of this kingdom, he also promoted the ethical norms accepted in his time—so long as they did not contradict the spirit of the Lord or bear in themselves the spirit of cults and pagan behavior. Paul himself sought to solve some new ethical questions (e.g., the dissolution of a Christian marriage or a mixed marriage); however, on other questions he gave advice, and nothing more. At no time did he give immutable answers to the many concrete questions of daily life: he did not think of answering for the future.

Note that both Jesus and Paul are interested in the realm of daily living; both were exclusively interested in the concrete questions of their time. To answer individual questions, they did not outline a "Christian" morality for world history. Thus, ethical leadership (the "magisterium") began in the Christian community, in the church anchored to the concrete here and now of Christian life. But in the course of time, this focus blurred and a problem developed—the problem of the magisterium and the people and the tension between the magisterium and moral theologians.

In the remarks that follow, I shall briefly explore four themes: (1) the competence of the magisterium in questions of moral theology; (2) the meaning of magisterium, moral theology, and doctrinal commission within the church; (3) the style of the magisterium in its relationship to moral theology; and (4) the conduct of moral theologians vis-à-vis the magisterium.

THE COMPETENCE OF THE MAGISTERIUM IN QUESTIONS OF MORAL THEOLOGY

A few years ago, to the great astonishment of its readers, the Roman Jesuit periodical *La Civiltà Cattolica*, which is subject to prior censure by the Papal Secretariat of State and, in particular cases, by the Congregation for the Doctrine of the Faith, published a leading article on infallibility and infallibilism.[1] The essay rebuked the tendency to attribute a kind of quasi-infallible significance to every word of the pope; this tendency was judged to be in keeping with a further tendency to a certain Byzantinism at the papal court. Although the leading article was not signed, it had essentially one author, the ecclesiologist Giandomenico Mucci, S.J.

A few months ago, this time under his own name, the same author published a critical essay in the same periodical with the title: "The competence of the infallible magisterium."[2] Mucci regards as important the distinction made by the Council of Trent between *salutaris veritas* (the truth of salvation) and *morum disciplina* (the ordering of right conduct), both of which are the object of the church's teaching. For Trent, *mores* (ethical conduct) meant more than morality in its narrower sense; it included also Christian custom and the ethical natural law, at least in its fundamental principles. It is significant for Mucci that the *mores* are understood as having a relationship to the gospel (in the sense of revelation); for this reason, they are inspired by faith and have their ultimate origin in the gospel and profound theological reflection. This origin is true also of those *mores* that, in terms of content, have no compelling relationship to "the deposit of faith."

But while a few general moral principles are universally accepted as having been revealed and, therefore, as amenable to definition by the church as matters that are to be accepted in faith, Mucci discovers in many moral theologians—namely, in F. Sullivan and F. Böckle—the position that the majority of individual ethical norms of natural law are not revealed.[3] As their contents have to do with norms that are subject to change in the history of persons, they are not sufficiently linked to revealed truth to permit us to affirm that we could not sufficiently defend or explain revealed truth without them.

The Second Vatican Council teaches (*Lumen Gentium* 25) that the magisterium can determine that the teachings that are intimately and necessarily connected with formally revealed truths are to be held (not "believed") to be authentic and infallible. Above all, Mucci cannot see why the church's competence to give authentic and infallible teaching should exclude precisely "those particular and concrete norms of the natural law that form and as it were constitute the history of each human person as a person; it is a matter of the practical possibility of the person to discern between good and evil." Mucci thinks that the two Vatican Councils cannot have meant to exclude these norms.[4]

Many theologians agree with Mucci. Mucci seeks to introduce his ecclesiological thinking into the realm of moral theology, in which however he is not a specialist. This attempt is fundamentally praiseworthy. The two Vatican Councils connected ecclesiology and moral theology only in an inchoative manner; the same is true of dogmatic theologians, generally. F. Sullivan, an ecclesiologist whom Mucci criticizes, is the first praiseworthy exception here; his attempt in 1983 to cross specialist borders must be judged successful.

Mucci is concerned above all, and rightly, with the competence and right of the church's magisterium. But as soon as he ventures into the territory of moral theology, he is confronted by new questions. What, for example, are the conditions for the *possibility* that the magisterium can solve the manifold and extremely difficult questions related to identifying individual ethical norms in contingent situations? Can these be identified with adequate certainty, such that a problem's solution can be seen as authentic or even infallible, and proclaimed authoritatively?

Or can the magisterium—even with the help of first-class specialists—penetrate so deeply into such specific questions as economics, trade, politics, nuclear weapons, and human sexuality, among others, that it can have a greater possibility and competence than that of simply offering believers a helping hand and of making known what seems at the moment the best solution to the problems at issue? Can the magisterium impose authoritative solutions that are always binding, despite the essentially historical character and mutability of persons and the fact that earthly realities and human interpretations are subject to change? If the magisterium were to insist on the competence Mucci defends, would it not lose credibility in the course of time?

The moral theologian must also question the images of God and the human person that are presupposed in Mucci's article. Mucci holds that if God did not make authoritative and definitive answers to moral questions accessible to Christians through the magisterium, they would ultimately not be able to distinguish good from evil and would no longer be able to conduct their lives as they should. But here one has to ask whether beings made in God's own image are not already empowered by their creation to continue responsibly the work of creation in a genuinely correct way, without having to be repeatedly reminded by competent authorities. Ultimately, all Christians are in the same boat—believers and the magisterium, for the magisterium, too, is composed of believers—and in this boat, no one receives binding revelations. Even if it is true that the gospel gives light to human beings who are marked by sin, and even if the Spirit is close to everyone in the boat in various ways without, however, taking the place of human authorities—still no one is immediately and absolutely enlightened.

As far as the human construction of life and our distinction between good and evil is concerned, Mucci has too little considered the fact that his statements are ambiguous to today's moral theologians; moral theology today speaks a much more precise language. In his article, the distinction between good and evil doubtless means the distinction between what is ethically correct and what is false in the construction of life and the world. Good or evil—open or closed to salvation in Jesus Christ—are terms that can be predicated only of persons who are oriented in love and seriously attempting to discover and do what is correct. The magisterium is concerned primarily with good and evil in the personal sense and, therefore, with the salvation of the personal human being (and even the scriptures, according to the Council's Constitution *Dei Verbum*, are infallible exclusively in questions of salvation). However, the magisterium is also concerned with the earthly construction of life and the world, which is a question of salvation only in a secondary sense.

The reflections that are set forth here belong to the self-reflection from which the magisterium can never excuse itself, the self-reflection that must regulate its relationship to moral theology.

MAGISTERIUM MORAL THEOLOGY, AND DOCTRINAL COMMISSION WITHIN THE CHURCH

Norbert Rigali is professor of moral theology at the Catholic University of San Diego in California. Moral theologians are accustomed from time to time to hear his independent but never rebellious ideas. In 1988, he published an essay in the periodical *Horizons* on the theme of "Moral Theology and the Magisterium."[5]

Rigali begins with a sapiential observation: there is a time for moral-theological indoctrination and a time for critical moral-theological reflection. In accordance with their different tasks and methods, he distinguishes the pastoral ecclesiastical magisterium and scientific moral theology. While these two institutions are to be distinguished and not confused with one another, they are also complementary and interrelated. If some Catholics think that moral theology has built itself into a second magisterium, then they are truly drawing attention to an unjustified state of affairs. For Rigali, however, the autonomy of moral theology and occasional discrepancies vis-à-vis the magisterium do not by themselves signify "another" magisterium; rather, they are a sign of vitality within moral theology as opposed to a lamentable lack of autonomous activity.

What is moral theology?

The starting-point for the distinction that Rigali makes between the magisterium and moral theology is clearly the thesis of Y. Congar and A. Dulles, namely, that the Middle Ages understood the magisterium as a pastoral ministry in the church, as distinguished from the nonpastoral (Rigali says nonclerical) ministry, which is the scientific task of moral theologians.

For Rigali, the moral theologian is a believing Christian; he or she stands in the same relationship to the activity of the pastoral magisterium and to its declarations as any other believer with a sense of the church. The moral theologian's task is the scientific investigation of moral-theological questions, and he or she is a teacher in such questions for those who are willing to learn. Since the task is not pastoral, the moral theologian does not speak to the church as to the people of God. Still less does he or she attempt to determine what is to count as sound and defensible teaching within the church.

This latter determination is the pastoral task of the magisterium. On the other hand, the magisterium is not active in an authoritative manner in the sphere of moral theology. Rigali criticizes the growing custom of speaking as though "theological dissent" vis-à-vis the teaching of the magisterium arises only in the Christian and moral theologian, and not in the form of a "theological" dissent within moral theology. For moral theology, the teaching of the magisterium, though certainly important, is one source among many other sources of moral-theological reflection.

Rigali's remarks about moral theology must be understood formally; otherwise, they can be confusing. We are accustomed, today, to understand the moral theologian as a moral-theological scholar who has received a commission from the pastoral magisterium, for example, from the bishop, for research and teaching at a particular institution. Such a moral theologian is not only a moral theologian in Rigali's sense, but also one who participates in, or exercises, the pastoral magisterium of the church. As such, and not simply as a moral theologian, he or she teaches in and for the church and is accountable in research and teaching to the church's pastoral magisterium. This distinction, however, between the moral theologian simply and the moral theologian in the name of the church is less common in other countries than in Rigali's United States.

The magisterium as pastoral ministry.

The magisterium, unlike moral theology, is an ecclesiastical ministry. It also teaches in questions of moral theology. Church councils say that it is competent in questions of faith and morals. This competence does not mean, according to Rigali, that the magisterium is competent in the same way in questions of faith and questions of morals since, according to the explicit teaching of Vatican I and Vatican II (*Lumen Gentium* 25), its competency extends exclusively to the *depositum fidei* (the formal revelation) and to that which is logically bound to this source.

According to Vatican Councils I and II, the starting-point of the doctrine of faith is the Christian tradition, which is to be set forth and defended among Christian believers. The starting-point of individual morality, however, is the conscience and created human realities; particular morality is addressed to humanity. Even when the church believes that it ought to give a hand in moral questions to believers and all humanity in the light of the gospel and under the assistance of the Spirit, it (the church) must do this without having a direct relationship to, responsibility for, or competence in, all questions of morality corresponding to that which it has in questions of faith. The bishops should respect the example of Vatican II (*Gaudium et Spes* 33, 43) and actually say this to the faithful.

Moral theologians can and should support and help the bishops carry out their magisterial task; they can and should accept the commission to share in the bishop's magisterial task (e.g., in seminaries and university faculties). But even then, they must honestly draw attention to the limits of the statements made by the bishops or by themselves in the bishops' name.

It follows that the conduct of the magisterium vis-à-vis moral theologians in general will be distinct from its conduct vis-à-vis the moral theologian who has accepted the commission of the magisterium. The relationship of the magisterium to moral theologians in the first case is like its relationship to any other member of the church, while its relationship to the moral theologian who is active in the name of the church remains within the sphere of the authentic and authoritative magisterium.

THE STYLE OF THE MAGISTERIUM
IN ITS RELATIONSHIP TO MORAL THEOLOGY

The magisterium understands itself as commissioned by God with leadership and the defense of the truth, a commission that includes the realm of Christian ethical teaching. It knows that it has received the Holy Spirit in a particular way for this task. Its ethical teaching must, therefore, count as the authentic and authoritative interpretation of the ethical will of God. Thus, the magisterium presents itself authoritatively to moral theology and is convinced that the faithful also expect it to give a clear and authoritative exposition of God's will. This view of the magisterium is the teaching that they have received.

There are moral theologians and many believing Christians who have been formed in and profess this attitude. This attitude, however, brackets the question of how the magisterium receives direct access to the ethical will of God without a particular revelation. The brackets are necessary because direct access to God's will does not exist. The magisterium and moral theology alike are confronted with the task of interpreting the self and the world in a way that promotes and accepts ethical conduct as the presumptive will of God. The Spirit of God assists the magisterium and moral theology to make this interpretation in the way that is most appropriate to each.

If the magisterium comes forward in concrete moral questions as proclaimer of the will of God—and it does very frequently—then it must permit the question from whence it has this knowledge of God's will. It can appeal to the revelation of general ethical truths, and it can point to the anthropological implications contained in faith that are significant for particular ethical questions. But ultimately, the persons who may and must be considered as belonging to the magisterium must seek and find the answers to questions about the foundations of this knowledge in their own personal endeavors. The answer "God's will" is in no way more certain than the outcome of human endeavors in faith and the Spirit to search for valid ethical answers. The expectation that moral theologians or believers will attach a higher qualification to a magisterial answer that appeals to the "will of God" is an expectation that does not correspond to the theological character of the magisterium.

We are therefore left with the question of how certain the ethical teaching authority of the magisterium is in reality. To what extent does a sufficient theological foundation exist for the extremely harsh words that are often heard at some moral theology congresses or in papal discourses? To what extent does a theological justification exist for ecclesial interventions in moral questions and solutions, and for interventions in the case of nominations to professorships in moral theology?

Richard McCormick, a professor at the University of Notre Dame in Indiana, has been a tough and persistent opponent of Roman interventions in moral questions for many years. He has pointed out, in an article that appeared in *America* in October (1988), that the magisterium (above all the Roman magisterium) often seeks to evade genuine moral-theological problems, and seeks in this way to hang on to its authority vis-à-vis moral theology.[6]

McCormick points to seven "syndromes" of such an evasion. First, the magisterium speaks of the "confusion" that has arisen among the faithful in moral questions, a confusion that the magisterium would remove rather than admit that there are cases of genuine dissent. Second, it is a tendency of the magisterium to emphasize basic ethical values in ecclesiastical documents (*Humanae Vitae, Donum Vitae*), which emphases divert attention from the extremely concrete and decisive statements that may possibly lead to dissent. Third, an evasive magisterium appeals repeatedly to the traditional and permanent teaching of the church, though it is in no sense binding. In some cases, church teaching does not exhibit continuous development, and in some cases, it has even undergone genuine change (for example, in cases of religious freedom or freedom of conscience).

Fourth, McCormick notes the magisterium's tendency to emphasize that the church is not a democracy and to overlook the steps the magisterium is bound to take—steps that could also be called "democratic" in some sense—to come to a valid decision in theoretical or practical questions ("due process"). Fifth, the magisterium often says that theologians are only "speculating" and that their activity is meaningless. Therefore, it is free from the necessity of taking the significant insights of moral theology into account in its own magisterial conduct.

Sixth, the magisterium can appeal to its own exclusive magisterial knowledge and experience, which (it says) the faithful and, above all, theologians lack, and therefore it can disregard the insights that others have. Seventh, it accuses theologians of lacking respect (or of insufficient servility) in the tone they adopt vis-à-vis the magisterium, and thinks that it is justified in paying little heed to the substantial observations of moral theologians.

Using these seven syndromes, McCormick draws attention to the fact that the style of the magisterium in its relationship to moral theology and the honest and serious communication of the two institutions with one another are still capable of development, and must be developed.

THE CONDUCT OF MORAL THEOLOGIANS VIS-À-VIS THE MAGISTERIUM

Rigali identified the starting-point of the magisterium's moral teaching in faith and revelation and the starting-point for the moral theologian in the conscience that has been given to all human persons. I am not altogether happy with this formulation. Ultimately, the conscience is also the starting-point for the magisterium, since it also consists of persons with conscience; and faith and revelation are the starting-point for the moral theologian too, who as a Christian reflects on the consequences of faith.

The task of the moral theologian is the scientific investigation of the ethical endeavor of Jesus, Paul, and the tradition, including also the magisterium of the past and present. Besides the faculty of reason, the moral theologian also has Jesus, Paul, and the magisterium and other sources from tradition and life. He or she is a moral theologian only when consciously at work in the ecclesial community, which also implies that one takes the magisterium into consideration, though one should note here that the church and the magisterium are not simply interchangeable terms.

In keeping with its nature and experience as a religious institution, the magisterium is inclined to read these various sources with less criticism and interpretive acumen than the moral theologian who does not belong to the magisterium and does not share its responsibility. So much the more, then, does the moral theologian have the duty to take the critical and hermeneutic endeavor seriously and to set out the results for the magisterium in every possible way, through writings and personal contact.

The magisterium and its teaching are binding also on the moral theologian. This authority can become problematic, above all when the magisterium determines its own competence and limits. The problem is particularly acute when the discussion concerns the ethical natural law. In this area, the moral theologian must determine with scientific precision what the Councils have really said in their teaching on the church's authority "in questions of faith and morals." The studies of A. Riedl, W. J. Levada, and J. Schuster are important here. Moral theologians must also take seriously the explicitly determined limitations of the magisterium in its pastoral endeavors in particular questions of morality (*Gaudium et Spes* 33, 43). Such careful attention is significant both for the moral theologian's own work and for the help that he or she can and ought to offer the magisterium.

To be a moral theologian with the commission of the magisterium, that is, to be entrusted in some manner with the church's faith in one's teaching and research, is fundamentally a great and inspiring vocation. This vocation is a service of and to the Church, and it can, in certain circumstances, be a service to the magisterium. It is based on the theological and philosophical foundation of moral theology, on argumentation used in moral theology, and on moral theology's normative and casuistic sphere.

But the moral theologian with the church's commission also has particular difficulties, because it is not one's own moral theology that one is concerned with, but the moral theology of the church; therefore, one must render an account of oneself to the church and its magisterium. Some years ago, I came across an institute of moral and pastoral theology in the United States that proclaimed as its program: only the magisterium and the whole magisterium. I do not believe that such a program can responsibly be the church's commission to moral theologians in a faculty or a seminary. The moral theologian is charged to present the teaching of the church and to introduce the fullness of moral theology.

Certainly, one will present as the church's teaching whatever is exclusively and truly the teaching of the church. But if the moral theologian is acquainted, from personal experience or through others, with difficulties in the questions or argument taken by the church's teaching, then that theologian will only give genuine service to the church by informing it about such problems and by telling it what moral theology can and cannot grasp. This genuine service, however, will never be undertaken in the intention of convincing Christians to accept a position against the teaching of the church.

I have occasionally said or written that I do not say things that I myself do not believe, but also that I do not always say everything that I believe. The desire to provoke is, in general, a mistake. In the face of potential difficulties to be expected from the magisterium, one must become sensitive to what may, and even sometimes must, be said, and what things are better not expressed.

$$* \quad * \quad *$$

Some questions concerning the relationship between the magisterium and moral theology should be decided—or at least discussed—by other than moral theologians. If an institution like the magisterium follows a philosophy of its own or has established for itself a firm *modus procendi* for many problems, then it is not easy for bishops or university faculties to introduce a change. These difficulties can affect the whole church as well as priests who are active in the apostolate and academic teachers with their students and institutions. But the application of these remarks to those fields must await another time.

NOTES

1. "Il ministero del Papa dopo i due Concili Vaticani," *La Civiltà Cattolica*, 2 November 1985, 209-221.

2. G. Mucci, S.J., "La competenza del magistero infallibile," *La Civiltà Cattolica*, 2 August 1988, 17-25.

3. F. A. Sullivan, *Magisterium. Teaching Authority in the Catholic Church*, Dublin 1983, 150-152; F. Böckle, "Le magistère de l'Eglise en matière morale," *Rev. Th. de Louvain* 19 (1988): 15.

4. "La Competenza," 25.

5. N. J. Rigali, "Moral Theology and the Magisterium," *Horizons* 15 (1988): 116-124.

6. R. A. McCormick, "The shape of moral evasion in Catholicism," *America*, 1 October 1988, 183-188.

PART 3

Conscience and
Moral Objectivity

10

Conscience and Conscientious Fidelity

A considerable discussion between the Catholic Church and moral theology has taken place in recent years concerning the concept of the conscience. Some fear that a current trend overvalues the conscience, as "kind of apotheosis of subjectivity," or as "subjectivity elevated to the ultimate criterion" against which there is no "appeal to authority."[1] Others denounce an undervaluation of the conscience on the part of certain authorities. In reality the conscience is not sheer subjectivity, but a reflection on objectively available facts and discoverable evaluations that strives responsibly to reach the conclusion of ethical discourse in order to make a responsible decision. Its decision is the ultimate authority, justified subjectively and objectively, for all who act responsibly.[2]

The present discussion on the ethical significance of the conscience is, however, concerned with less fundamental and general issues. Rather, its one-sided interest concentrates to a high degree on the significance of the conscience in the face of authentic (i.e., official, but not infallible) decisions or declarations of the church's magisterium—in the form of declarations or occasional statements of the pope, the Congregation for the Doctrine of the Faith (or other Vatican bodies), the bishops or episcopal conferences, and even of some prominent theologians. At the moment, this discussion concerns above all questions of moral theology (and thus of theological ethics).

The problem of overvaluing the conscience is raised above all by official representatives of the magisterium and by theologians who see themselves as bound in a particularly close fashion to this magisterium. The problem of undervaluing the conscience is seen especially by many representatives of Catholic theology and by priests and laypeople who sense that the traditional teaching on the significance of the conscience (concretely and in general) has been called into question.

My interest is not to provoke a confrontation—this article is not entitled magisterium or conscience. The task is rather to clear up the concept of conscience and thus to lay the foundations of a solution that pays heed to objective reality and satisfies both sides of the discussion.

Contributions to the discussion (including the magisterium's) that appear unfair to the traditional concept of the conscience ought to be documented precisely, and as far as possible, quoted literally. But these contributions include not only texts of the magisterium but also texts by theologians who follow a certain line and texts by authorities in the Catholic Church. It seems, therefore, less appropriate and even impossible to quote them precisely and individually in each case.[3]

VARIOUS CONCEPTS OF CONSCIENCE

In recent discussions, not only is the concept of conscience frequently insufficiently clarified, but various concepts of conscience are employed simultaneously.

We frequently run across the traditional concept of the conscience as the "voice of God"—a concept that belongs to the religious sphere and is even somewhat mystical. It is interesting that no problems are felt to lie in the realm of the possibility of an erroneous conscience, nor in the fact that even atheists and agnostics, despite their lack of faith in God, are admitted to have an experience of conscience. Especially since the Second Vatican Council (*Gaudium et Spes* 16), it has become common to describe the conscience as a *sacrarium* in which we find ourselves responsibly before God—*solus cum solo* (alone with the alone). This description is understood above all (though certainly not exclusively) in a Christian and religious sense. However, the question not posed is whether it holds true for agnostics and atheists who, by the very fact of being human, are likewise held to have a conscience.

The two statements, that the conscience is the voice of God and thus has an absolute validity requiring obedience, and that the conscience can err (as we know from experience), are often placed together without any explanation. The dignity of ultimate authority is attributed to the conscience in the fullness of its situation, to which only it can have access as the voice of God. Nevertheless, the will of God, ethical norms, and statements of the church's magisterium as objective realities, often have an authority superior to that of the conscience, an authority, in fact, that functions as a check on the objective competence and significance of the insights given the conscience. In general, there is scarcely any attempt to find a satisfactory solution to this problem.

Other understandings of the conscience exist that are not specifically Christian or religious: first, it is described as an experience and insight into the objective and absolute ethical requirement that always exists a priori in the human person, an insight that cannot be rejected; and second, it is described as an organ, not an oracle. For some persons, conscience is responsible for finding the correct norms and concrete solutions for life's many decisions, and it is the organ that makes these decisions (R. Spaemann). For others, conscience is only a responsible readiness to "listen" to the given word without any "creativity" of one's own in a purely perceptive sense, that is, to accept this word in a basically passive and humble way (A. Laun), to obey it—and thus, ultimately, to obey God (C. Caffarra).

Recent discussions are unanimous in rejecting an understanding of the conscience as a pure superego or as a purely biological instinct (behavior research), and they are equally opposed to a concept of conscience as the exclusive result of sociological facts and developments or as the product of education alone. In general, a one-sided response to such proposals—although without noticeable attention to the enormous significance they have on the formation of the conscience—is an appeal to the idea that the ethical order that comes from God's wisdom is written in the heart and nature of the human personal being (whatever one understands by this). Almost without exception, the significance of faith in God and acceptance of the Jewish and Christian revelation is held to have the greatest importance for a deeper understanding of the phenomenon of conscience.

It is often unclear which of the various functions of conscience is intended in these individual affirmations: it could be its deepest source (the "fundamental" conscience); or its care for the ethical goodness of the person and the moral rightness of what the person does and how he or she behaves; or the instruction given by the conscience in the moment of decision ("situational" conscience); or the ethical knowledge that precedes the situational conscience by indicating first and general ethical principles and more concrete ethical norms. Presumably this question is seldom considered precisely; therefore, it is an open question whether particular statements are to be understood of the entire realm of conscience, or only of determined functions—and what these functions are.

CONSCIENCE AS THE VOICE OF GOD

What we call, or can call, the conscience expresses itself in various ways, in accordance with the distinctions presented in the preceding paragraphs. We shall now consider this in greater detail.

Fundamental conscience.

At the basis of everything is the fundamental experience that alone makes it possible to talk about morality and ethics: the experience that we—who have only a "share" in absolute personal freedom—are moral beings; that is, we have a freedom that is absolutely oriented not to arbitrariness but to what is objectively good and right. One can call this "the voice of God," as is often done, but not in the sense of an experience "infused" by the Creator rather than accomplished in a personal manner. That is, we are speaking of a personal self-understanding that has been made possible in the created human person as truly the person's own—even if it is often present only in a stage of knowledge and acceptance that is as yet unreflected.

This experience can be taken up into explicit intellectual reflection, even if its correctness cannot be forcibly demonstrated in such reflection. Thus, absoluteness and objectivity (nonarbitrariness) always stand a priori in conscious acceptance as the criterion before, or in, everything that has to do with morality and the conscience. Various philosophies, world views, ideologies, and religions have attempted to give a theoretical explanation of this phenomenon of conscience. The catholic theological explanation points fundamentally to the character of the human person as created by God in God's own image, in intellect and freedom. But it also knows that the Holy Spirit of God and the word of revelation can be, and are already, at work in this fundamental experience.

The experience of the "fundamental conscience" immediately allows us to understand two things. First, the personal human being who is aware of one's own being in the fundamental conscience must seek in the free development of life to act in accordance with what the fundamental conscience experiences. In earlier times, this action was called "being good"; today it is customary to refer more precisely to the *ethical goodness* of the person as such. To this goodness there belongs also the inner readiness to behave rightly in the personal structuring of one's life and world, to take account in one's actions of the reality that exists.[4] For this reason the distinction is made today between the ethical goodness of the person—morality in the truest sense of the word—and the *ethical rightness* of action or behavior.

Knowledge of one's goodness and of the rightness of one's action or behavior ought to coincide, but on occasions they fall apart, because of the possibility of error in what is ethically right. The rightness of behavior is still often characterized de facto as the "good." The significance of the distinction between the "good" as a person's ethical *goodness* and the ethical *rightness* of one's actions in the judgment of conscience is already seen in the fact that the evaluation of personal ethical goodness is *infallible*, while the evaluation of the ethically right action or behavior remains exposed to the possibility of error. Therefore, only the former judgment, not the latter, can be called the "voice of God," that is, can be derived directly from God through one's creation as a person in God's image.

The formulation that the conscience, however one understands it, is the place in which the human person is illuminated by a light that comes, not from one's own reason (since reason is created and always fallible), but from the wisdom of God in whom everything is created must, accordingly, be too simple. It cannot stand up to an objective analysis nor prove helpful in the vocabulary of Christian believers.

Situational conscience.

In neo-Thomist theology and in the moral theology of the church's magisterium, conscience is often spoken of as the ultimate interior ethical "judgment" of the person who makes a decision for action or conduct. This judgment is *simultaneous* with an ethical decision as its "light"; therefore, its priority over the personal decision is understood chronologically, not logically. Conscience understood in this way is often called the "situational conscience" or even simply "the conscience." In this concrete experience of a "judgment" of conscience, the fundamental conscience of the person who makes the decision is, of course, always present as the ultimate origin of the judgment.

It is the fundamental conscience that requires the responsible formation of the situational judgment and makes it take into account all available helps and personal circumstances and to seek an objectively correct decision. If the situational conscience is often called the "voice of God," then the term is only partly correct: the word of the fundamental conscience contained therein—the command to seek responsibly for what is objectively correct and to decide in favor of it—is infallible and is, in this sense, "the voice of God." The contents of the ethical judgment of the situational conscience (which directs the concrete act or behavior) may also allow or require something that is incorrect, and therefore cannot be called the "voice ofGod" in the same sense.

Principles and norms.

Naturally, it is not possible to deduce the contents of the behavioral directive of the situational conscience from the experience or insight of the fundamental conscience, for between these two lies the immeasurable width of human, worldly, and historical reality on which the human person (including the one who believes) reflects when called upon to help shape it. Persons always do reflect on the entire context of the human and ecclesiastical society in which they live in order to discover how they can give their actions and the world the correct form. They do not begin to reflect only in the moment in which the situational conscience demands that they make a concrete decision; rather, they are always already engaged in the search for ethical self-understanding and in the attempt to orient themselves to the near and the far future, and always under the experience, insight, and requirement of the fundamental conscience.

Thus, it is often and correctly said that seeking and finding takes place "in conscience" (*Dignitatis Humanae* 3; *Gaudium et Spes* 16) although it is otherwise customary to attribute the recognition of ethical principles and norms to the practical reason. Thus, the human person arrives at very concrete ethical norms that can provide one with an enormous and decisive help for the formation of the situational conscience. The concrete interpretation, evaluation, and ethical judgment of the wide human world is thus possible for the personal being in a manner that is proper to the person without any guarantee of infallibility, that is, not "simply" as the voice of God.

Thomas Aquinas understood the fundamental conscience (*synderesis*) in a different manner, namely, as a certain and infallible insight into a small kernel of ethical first principles.[5] De facto principles, such as "doing what is good," "not behaving arbitrarily toward one's neighbor," and so forth, are initial formulations of the fundamental conscience and just as much infallible (and hence the voice of God). It follows that the principles that one must not behave "arbitrarily" in the construction of one's life and in interpersonal and societal relationships (that is, in situations involving justice, fairness, and sexuality) are tautological, infallibly true, and, in this sense, the "voice of God." But it is not possible to state with equal clarity, cogency, and infallibility what such principles or ethical norms intend to say about concrete behavior in the larger human world. And a yet broader question is what such concrete norms can mean in the situation of the person who, externally and internally, is true to, and truly, oneself: in the last analysis, their solution can be sought and found only "solus *cum solo*." But the contents of this solution are not unambiguously the "voice of God."

SUBJECTIVITY AND OBJECTIVITY

As fundamental conscience, the conscience is subjectivity that is oriented absolutely and infallibly to ethical objectivity. It follows that a discussion about too much subjectivity or objectivity cannot be referring to the fundamental conscience, but to what is generally characterized simply as "conscience,"chiefly the "situational conscience," and the insight-experience vis-à-vis concrete ethical norms.

Subjectivity.

Romans 2:14-16 states that gentiles, too, at least in part, live according to the contents of the torah, the law of the covenant that God revealed to the Israelites as a gift. Thus, the gentiles show that although they do not have the law, they are an ethical law "unto themselves," that is, their law was formed on the basis of an inner act of understanding and this ethical law was "written on their hearts." In this context, Paul uses the Greek word "conscience" and the Hebrew word "heart." He does not mean that the gentiles, in the multiplicity of ethical ideas, have received a "partial," passive "infusion" of ethical knowledge. He means that the gentiles (i.e., all human persons) have been created with the capacity to arrive at the concrete and objectively correct knowledge of morality, prior to and in the exercise of the situational conscience. It is quite clear that Paul intends an "interiority" of the conscience-heart.

In its declaration on religious freedom, the Second Vatican Council indicated that persons discover the objective ethical order by their own active search, and that they should do so, to arrive in this way at a true judgment of conscience (*Dignitatis Humanae* 3). In its pastoral constitution, the same council dedicated a whole paragraph to the conscience (*Gaudium et Spes* 126), strongly emphasizing the interiority and the created subjectivity of the conscience, which nevertheless shows itself to be the locus of an absolute and objective requirement, that is, one that is not "given" by the conscience itself. Thus, a person knows from within oneself about the essential obligation that the ethical conscience lays on one.

The ethical requirement in question here is not only the word of the fundamental conscience: Vatican II, taking up the statement in Romans 2:15, formulates it thus: "the human person has a law that has been inscribed by God on one's heart. . . . In the conscience, one recognizes in a marvelous way the law that is fulfilled in love for God and for one's neighbor." The fact that this law is written on the heart means, according to the council, that the human person can "recognize" the ethical order with objective correctness in the conscience. This interpretation becomes even clearer when the text speaks of searching (in the conscience) "for truth" and for a "solution, in keeping with truth, to all the many moral problems that arise both in the life of the individual and in living together in society."

Here it is a question of seeking and finding "objective norms of morality"; but this seeking and finding, we are told, does not exclude inculpable error, since the translation of the fundamental conscience into objectively correct norms of behavior, and the translation of the correct contents of the situational conscience, do not take place automatically or through a purely logical deduction. A risk always attaches to norm-giving ethical objectivity, even in the conscience (and even in the conscience of the believer [*Gaudium et Spes* 43 and 33]), the search for the objective norm does not mean that this objective norm already exists "somewhere" waiting to be found by us, and correspondingly (since it already exists) needs only to be sought and found.

The Constitution also states that "the conscience is the hidden center and sanctuary in the human person, where one is alone with God whose voice can be heard in this, one's most interior place." Do these words mean that there is a *solus cum solo* in the conscience, especially in the situational conscience, in which one discovers the divine commandment in God's holy presence and hears God's commanding "voice," giving the sought-for answer to the human person who seeks and is required to act, so that all one has to do is obey? But we know that it is possible for an erroneous conscience to exist. We have, therefore, an obligation to lay down the path to the correct solution "creatively" in a responsible research that takes into consideration all the available realities, knowledge, and known evaluations (including those of the church and the church's magisterium), and finally to be equally responsible in breaking off this process of seeking once it has been "sufficient," thus arriving at genuine conviction.[6]

Such a conviction would not contain the direct voice of God, a voice that one need only "hear" perceptively and then obey; rather, it would be the last word of the situational conscience reflecting on its own reality, containing not the infallible voice of God but the human person's attempt to give a concrete "body" to the absolute requirement of the fundamental conscience. This creative attempt would not be a subjectivist *sola cum seipsa* (alone with itself) on the part of the conscience (as has sometimes been said), but an active and living *solus cum solo*, that is, alone with the Creator-God who is present in and through the fundamental conscience and who urges one to make one's own search for what is correct.

The outcome would not be the *ipsissimum verbum* of God. Nevertheless, it would be what God requires as the only possible "objectivity" in the "sanctuary" of the conscience of God's human image; that is, it would be a created share (and hence a share by participation) in God's eternal wisdom and "eternal law," and precisely for this reason, something that demands unconditional obedience. As we have already noted with R. Spaemann: the conscience is not an oracle but an organ that actively sketches out projects and seeks what is right.

Objectivity.

Because of the constant awareness of the fundamental conscience, the personal human being seeks to discover in the conscience, as an active organ, how to deal with given human reality in order to be ethically "good." In order to reach an objectively justified judgment, one must have sufficient knowledge of the nature of the person and the nature of the reality that is to be lived in a personal manner. Today's humanity knows more about the latter than its ancestors did, and one must naturally pay proper attention to this knowledge in the search for the ultimate word of the situational conscience.

The realities of the self and world are not meaningless, purely "material" realities that one seeks to develop in a "material" manner. On the contrary, this world, as the creation maintained by God, is the expression and bearer of spirit and meaning in its present form thanks to a long development and to the interventions of the human person in giving it form. To live in and make use of this reality is an activity oriented to the future, but always on the basis of what the reality is at present as the point of departure. Thus, in the very act of decision, the person in the world of reality, spirit, and meaning is in the presence of the creator God who always maintains the world in being. This objectivity not only involves the question of what reality means "in itself" and materially considered, for what can reality say about itself without any relationship to the human person? It also involves the question of the spirit and meaning contained in the world of human persons and society, for particular human relationships and for individuals in their particularity.

To undertake this act of understanding through interpretation, using the ethical principles, evaluations, and norms that have already been discovered or that lie to hand to arrive at a justifiable ethical judgment and decision about behavior and activity that must be taken now though oriented to the near or far future—this is the work of the personal subject in the conscience, which seeks to find a creative and objectively justified word in the situational conscience. This activity is anything but a pure "subjectivity" that would be improper for an organ; but it is also anything but a pure listening to an "objective" oracle.

FIDELITY TO THE CONSCIENCE

If one seeks, in keeping with the available possibilities, to discover in the conscience the objectively correct directive for ethical behavior, one will be evaluated by one's fundamental conscience as "good" in the sense of personal morality. Such a person does not entrust oneself to any arbitrary subjectivism. This care is also the case with the inculpable erroneous conscience: the one who errs inculpably holds an objective error to be what is objectively correct; therefore, one is not ethically bad despite the incorrect judgment and fidelity to it in conduct (*Gaudium et Spes* 16). If one avoids this suggested distinction between "good" and "correct," but still wishes to avoid saying that one who does what is incorrect out of error is simultaneously good and not good, then one would have to follow Thomas Aquinas in saying that one's error "excuses" one with regard to "not good" behavior; however, because of the linguistic equation of "good" and "correct," one cannot simply call this person "good."

THE CONTEMPORARY DISCUSSION

Matters are somewhat different in contemporary discussion; here the complaint is made that in today's society (including the society of the church and moral theology) an appeal is often made on one's own behalf and on behalf of others to the conscience against "the commandment of God," against the "objective" moral norms, and against the ethical natural law. This complaint is, however, justified only if the appeal to the conscience is made against an ethical order that is called objective in an arbitrary or irresponsible frivolity (*Gaudium et Spes* 16).

This complaint raises a certain difficulty because it presupposes that God's commandment, the ethical norms, and the solutions of the ethical natural law are somehow and somewhere objectively "present." But since God has not given them to us directly (we shall speak later about moral norms in the church), such ethical normative statements in human society exist only thanks to human ethical knowledge "in the conscience." They are neither "invented" nor "created" but experienced and recognized "creatively," in the (merely) created human participation in God's own wisdom. To hold *absolutely* that one must adopt these norms simply because they express what it is customary in our society, is to fall victim to the logical error of deducing an ethical "ought" from an "is." Nevertheless, ethical prudence demands that one should not reject an ethical ordinance that is widely accepted or prescribed by a high authority; rather, one should be open and attempt to understand or accept such a norm, since it can contain great experience and lofty wisdom, even though it is not infallible.

On the other hand, the adoption of ethical norms that are widely accepted in society or prescribed by an authority always takes place within personal responsibility.[7] In the same way, the rejection of an ethical norm or ordinance comes under personal responsibility. It follows that the adoption or rejection of ethical claims or prohibitions always takes place via the responsible, decision-making function of the personal conscience. To close one's mind against ethical reasoning proposed by authorities and others, can be as much a sign of frivolous or idiosyncratic arbitrariness as of an honest and great sense of responsibility on the part of the conscience.[8] Thus, it is not necessarily a sign of disobedience to God who is represented as the authority behind the rejected moral ordinance; it can also be the sign of a conscience quite aware of its responsibility.

The formulation that ultimately only the individual can, in conscience, know and decide what he or she is to do, is not simply false. Although many things and many persons may advise one and seek to persuade one to abandon a conviction, this advice must pass through the responsible judgment made by the conscience of the individual before it can be adopted or rejected in prudent responsibility. The individual can err, but so can those who advise the individual. Has one no criterion by which to distinguish unambiguously between truth and error in the conscience? If there is no criterion, it would not be possible for an erroneous conscience or erroneous advice to exist—not unless infallible authorities exist. R. Spaemann goes beyond the problem of such a criterion to ask whether there is any indication of the genuineness of the decision of conscience, and answers affirmatively: "the willingness of the one concerned to pay the price of an unpleasant alternative."[9] Is such an indication anything more than the great exception?

Conscience and fidelity to the church's magisterium.

For the believing Catholic, a moral utterance of the church's magisterium is a significant element that must be considered in the responsible formation of the conscience. But in contemporary discussion, the statement that the church's magisterium was founded for the illumination of the conscience is, while not simply false, a deliberately chosen ad hoc and one-sided statement. The magisterium functions above all to preserve and defend the word of God, the foundation of the faith that has been deposited in the church. The magisterium can also render this service in an infallible manner to the faithful. The believing Catholic will give the church's moral utterances a decisive role in the formation of conscience.

But this protected area within which infallibility operates does not include the many concrete ethical questions of natural law that concern our activity in the world, questions that also have significance in the formation of conscience. Because of this significance, the magisterium can certainly seek to teach Catholics (and others) in an official manner about such concrete ethical truths (even if they have not been revealed), lest people too easily fall into the danger of giving an erroneous expression to the Christian faith in the shaping of earthly realities.

Nevertheless, the magisterium does not deduce these truths from the faith: it knows them from the exercise of the practical reason that is enlightened by faith. Such truths therefore lie outside the realm of infallibility. But since such ethical teaching directives have come into being in the community of the Holy Spirit, and since they have been proposed by the office-bearers who are called to lead this community and are therefore assisted by the Spirit, they have a great significance in the church, and the spirit of fidelity that is required in the church obliges one to be receptive to them in the internal discourse that is the formation of conscience, and to give them a certain preference over other considerations—even one's own. This receptivity is required by the responsible conscience itself. An aspect of the full fidelity of those who belong to the church is that they bear witness to such concrete ethical statements.

This, at least, is how matters stand usually; this restriction is necessary because the conscience also bears the responsibility, embedded in the fundamental conscience, not to accept anything into itself, if the necessary discourse, carried out with sufficient competence (and thus not disobediently) within the context of the church's community shows that there are very serious arguments against it that cannot be overcome even with the greatest measure of personal openness. The dilemma "conscience or magisterium," about which one frequently hears, does not exist. There exists only living fidelity in the church as the hierarchically ordered community, but this in turn cannot exist without the responsible conscience of those who bear the fidelity, for it is only via the responsibly formed conscience that the magisterium can achieve significance in the life of the person.

This reciprocity and faith is Catholic tradition; in normal circumstances, it ought not to create any problem. If problems arise, then it is necessary to repeat and adhere to what was previously said about fidelity to the conscience. However, Thomas Aquinas (in opposition to Peter Lombard) provides the extreme example, which should not be passed over in silence. When an ecclesiastical decision that is evaluated in conscience as certainly unacceptable is proclaimed under the threat of excommunication, one may not under any circumstances follow it, even if noncompliance means that one must die excommunicated.[10]

Noncompliance would, in such a case, indicate a genuine decision of conscience.

And even such decisions of conscience lie within the sphere of responsible fidelity to the church's magisterium. One is always glad to take the hand that is offered, and one seeks, even in a seriously doubtful case, to discover responsibly how far this offer can be a genuine help for the correct shaping of the concrete world by a Christian in a particular case. The individual under certain circumstances is justified, and even obliged in conscience, to contribute the results of a particular moral judgment to the church that wishes to help those in difficulty and which is, in any case, the community one wishes to follow.

The question whether such an attempt at helping the church may or should be made in public, raises problems that go beyond the limits of the questions posed in this essay. But here, too, the indication given by R. Spaemann is appropriate. If we wish to know whether such attempts are derived from a genuine concern in conscience, we may ask whether the person in question is willing "to pay the price of an unpleasant alternative" But a further question is also necessary: What freedom do moral theologians have in scholarly discussion? Here it is perhaps necessary to distinguish between moral theologians who work outside the commission of the church, and those who teach and do research in the name of the church's magisterium.[11] Research, however, entails evidence of reflection and discussion that, in turn, demands fidelity.

Fidelity always signifies the encounter and cooperation of two partners: the individual and the church and its official representatives. Normally speaking, fidelity in the church, which is filled with the Spirit, ought to be a spiritual necessity that is carried out in thankfulness. The magisterium must make such a view of things possible by offering a service that is officially helpful rather than authoritarian— although even the latter does not mean that its utterances would be the product of complete arbitrariness. The magisterium should offer a service of loving mutual cooperation in the church, working through invitation (an invitation that is constantly repeated) rather than through official ecclesiastical imposition of demands for obedience. Certainly the magisterium should not assume the form of a commandment proceeding directly from God so that even in cases of grave difficulty a responsible discourse in the conscience would necessarily ipso facto be disobedience.

Further, since the concrete norms of conduct are derived from the practical reason illumined by faith, rather than from the Christian faith itself (and hence are universal in principle), the magisterium in its invitation to fidelity should attempt cautiously and persuasively, to make clear to those who are willing to follow, that such norms are reasonable. They are not based on a theologically unjustifiable use of scripture, a particular distorting ideology, a naturalistic fallacy, or an excessively juridical understanding of the magisterium (for example, that one must always follow the teaching of one's own bishop, and not the teaching of another bishop, which may in particular circumstances be different).[12] Rather, such norms are based on reasons that are generally plausible and capable of being communicated to others.

Both partners—the individual and the church—must meet, if fidelity in conscience and to the magisterium is to become possible. Some years ago, Val J. Peter, a North American moral theologian, pointed in this context to Thomas's teaching about *pietas*.[13] *Pietas* is the virtue that undergirds justice; it is owed to the church as to one's own "mother," and thereby to the church's magisterium. But "mother" church and her magisterium likewise owe *pietas* to those who follow them. According to Yves Congar, *pietas* implies a *ius communionis*—and thereby not only a common seeking but occasionally also a serious struggle. But these struggles are always within the realm of *pietas* and *communio*.

SEARCHING FOR A SOLUTION: RICHARD A. McCORMICK

For many years, Richard A. McCormick has lived the problematic of conscience and magisterium, and discussed it privately and in public, both within the society of moral theologians and in his relationships with the official church. Those who have followed his writings, above all his "Notes on Moral Theology," have noted how this dialog has developed through a slow crescendo to become a central issue.

The dialog began with McCormick's first reflections on the justification of concrete ethical norms of conduct. P. Knauer's 1965 study on the principle of the action with double effect as the basis of practical morality had initially provoked McCormick to contradict him, but a process of further discussions on this issue and further essays in moral theology pointed McCormick more or less in the direction indicated by

Knauer. McCormick slowly became one of the strongest defenders of proportionalism. In this spirit, he analyzed ethical norms of conduct and tested the soundness of the reasons adduced for them. For McCormick, as for many other moral theologians, the encyclical *Humanae Vitae* (1968) had a galvanizing effect.

McCormick believes that the true purpose of negative norms of conduct is to avoid as much as possible doing something evil in the human construction of the world and the life of humanity. Therefore, the evil to be avoided should be recognized as a nonmoral evil; it would be a moral evil to carry out such an evil without adequate reason. It would also contradict personal ethical goodness and salvation in Jesus Christ. This theme, in turn, raises another: how far do the formulations of negative ethical norms have validity? Is their validity in every case as absolute and without exception as their habitual formulation seems to indicate? McCormick's analysis denies this claim.

However, when the magisterium condemns particular concrete norms of conduct, it usually states its formulations precisely in this absolute way—which poses for McCormick the question of his attitude to such formulations. In the case of individual problems that seemed to him to permit no other intellectually defensible solution than a norm different from the norm upheld by the church's authority, he took the side of academic freedom. He believed that he was not only permitted but also obliged to dissent—in theory and in practice. And, he was willing to pay the price of vexations for his stance—an indication, as we have seen, of a genuine conscience.

Behind McCormick's defense of academic freedom, therefore, stands the problem of the ethical conscience. He is concerned with what is ethically permissible and obligatory. He will not have overlooked the fact that other moral theologians have made the problem of conscience the explicit and clearly stated rationale for their "divergent" solutions—even in Italian and Roman Catholic books, periodicals, and newspapers (even in the *Osservatore Romano*), without (as far as one knows) provoking unpleasant reactions. The opinion has been stated that only in conscience can one fully see the totality of the reality to be realized in action or behavior; therefore, only in conscience can one evaluate the defensible (inner) spectrum of the validity of ethical norms of conduct.

As was remarked at the beginning, the theme of the conscience and its relationship to the ethical statements of the magisterium, especially in the sphere of norms that must be justified in terms of natural law, has become more acute in recent years. In fact, this problem has been explicitly moved to center stage by certain theologians and also by the magisterium itself. According to Catholic tradition, just as there exists an obligation of fidelity to the conscience, so is there an obligation of fidelity to the magisterium—even in cases of noninfallible moral utterances. McCormick's further work in moral theology will be devoted to the search for a balanced solution—in *pietate* and in *iure communionis*.

NOTES

1. J. Ratzinger, "Der Auftrag des Bischofs und des Theologen angesichts der Probleme der Moral in unserer Zeit," *Int. Kath. Zeitschrift "Communio"* 13 (1984): 524-538.
2. See Robert Spaemann, *Moralische Grundbegriffe*, Munich 1984, 75ff.
3. Cf. "Der Auftrag des Bischofs." In his analysis of conscience, Cardinal Ratzinger refers above all to R. Spaemann, *Moralische Grundbegriff*, but also to A. Laun, *Das Gewissen: Oberste Norm sittlichen Handelns*, Innsbruck 1984. Compare also the keynote lecture "Humanae Vitae: 20 Years Later: Quis sicut Dominus Deus noster?" by C. Caffarra, director of the John Paul II Institute for Marriage and Family, at the exclusive congress of moral theologians organized by this institute and by the "Centro Academico" of Opus Dei in November 1988. Pope John Paul II's address at this conference on 12 November 1988 is also significant (*L'Osservatore Romano*, 13 November 1988).
   Further, see the informative interview Caffarra gave to the newspaper *Stampa Sera* on 28 November 1988. Significant too is the essay (unsigned, and therefore very official) "Sull'autorità dottrinale della Istruzione 'Donum Vitae,'" in *L'Osservatore Romano*, 24 December 1988, 1-2. The long pastoral document of the Italian episcopate dated 1 January 1989, *Comunione, comunità e disciplina ecclesiale*, deals in detail with the problem of the conscience vis-à-vis the magisterium (*L'Osservatore Romano*, supplement A, nr. 8, 11 January 1989).
4. R. Spaemann, *Moralische Grundbegriffe*, 91.
5. S.T.I.79.12f.; *De veritate*, 16f.
6. See *Moralische Grundbegriffe*, 77: "Thus the individual must decide when he departs from the endlessness of weighing things up, ends the discourse and passes over with conviction to action. We call this conviction, which permits us to end the discourse, conscience."
7. Ibid., 76: it is the individual who "in the last analysis must bear the responsibility of such "obedience."
8. Ibid., 82f.
9. Ibid., p. 84.
10. In 4 Sent.38.2.4.q.3; In 4 Sent.27.3.3.expos.textus; In 4 Sent. 27.1.2. q.4.ad3.

11. On this distinction, see N. J. Rigali, "Moral Theology and the Magisterium," *Horizons* 15 (1988): 116-124.

12. This question has become acute also in the contemporary discussion about the teaching competence of the bishops' conferences (and the question whether this binds the individual bishop); see the discussion by G. Ghirlanda and J. F. Urrutia in *Periodica de re m.c.l.* 76 (1987), especially 602f., 637, 649.

13. V. J. Peter, "The Pastoral Approach to Magisterial Teaching," in *Moral Theology Today: Certitudes and Doubts*, Saint Louis 1984, 82-94.

11

"The One Who Hears You Hears Me": Episcopal Moral Directives

Jesus' logion related by Luke, "the one who hears you hears me" (Luke 10:16) has moved many Christians over a long period to trust the bishops' teaching on moral questions and to feel themselves bound by this teaching. The logion has presumably also confirmed many bishops' belief in their episcopal commission and obligation to proclaim the moral teaching of the church of Jesus Christ (or their understanding of this teaching). No doubt Christians and bishops in past years have read and understood these word of Jesus in a very simple manner—perhaps all too simply, without much exegesis, hermeneutics, or reflection on ecclesial reality. May not the same be true today?

On 14 January 1992, the bishops of Pennsylvania in the United States published a pastoral letter, with a foreword by the Archbishop of Philadelphia, Cardinal Bevilacqua—emphasizing the moral obligation to provide artificial nutrition with food and liquid (water) for comatose persons, that is, for those who live in a purely vegetative condition.[1] The bishops issued this letter, they said, to carry out their episcopal obligation to proclaim to the faithful the teaching of the church and Christian moral theology. Prior to this pastoral letter (and simultaneously) several other bishops in the United States were publishing pastoral letters on the same theme, likewise carrying out their episcopal obligation vis-à-vis the faithful, but the majority of these bishops had arrived at the opposite conclusion.[2] This dichotomy confronts the faithful (above all hospital personnel, doctors, and families) with questions about the value and binding character of episcopal directives in ethical questions.

THE ETHICAL DIRECTIVES OF THE BISHOPS

The Christian community possesses its own morality. The community lives this morality and is familiar with it to some extent. Early Christians who came from Judaism knew something about morality on the basis of the law of the covenant; they were instructed by teachers of the law (although their teachers belonged to various schools). Jesus, too, followed the law, as it was understood at the time, but he opposed certain individual misunderstandings of it that had their origin in the hardness of human hearts. Early Christians who came from the gentiles also knew in principle how to distinguish between good and evil and were greatly helped by moral philosophers and itinerant preachers.[3] Paul, too, was familiar with the moral views of gentile Christians and their teachers.[4]

Jesus and Paul insist that Christians live according to the ethical law: it is a condition for belonging to the kingdom of God. Jesus, Paul, and the other disciples who teach are de facto the custodians and guarantors of the community's morality. They provide relevant counsels or directives when hitherto unknown ethical problems arise; for example, what are the consequences of Christian freedom? how are the marital relations between Christians of different backgrounds or between Christians and non-Christians to be organized? and how does one preserve one's Christian identity in the larger world of Christians, Jews, and Gentiles? (In New Testament terms, these questions are mainly about foods, slavery, and celibacy.) Above all, these teachers give instruction about the Christian horizon and the deeper Christian meaning of particular ethical modes of conduct (e.g., 1 Cor 6:12-20).

After the apostolic period, bishops marked by philosophical and theological learning were the leading ethical figures in the first Christian centuries, although some laypersons with similar background were also among them. These leaders represented the community in discussions with non-Christian ethical teachers; on the one hand, they were ready to adopt valuable ethical insights from those teachers, but on the other hand they also had to defend the community's ethical truths. In general, individual Christians followed these leading figures in their ethical views.

In the course of the centuries, the bishop's teachings became more *pastorally* than philosophically oriented (a magisterium of pastoral care and administrative governance), although they continued to include concern for the moral doctrine of the Christian community. Doctrinal guidance (the teaching and researching magisterium) was generally carried out by nonbishops (priests and laypersons) with a philosophical and theological schooling. Naturally, the latter were also subject to the pastoral magisterium of the bishops, only a few of whom were theologians. Clearly the two magisteria, with their different orientations, depend on one another for the sake of fruitful cooperation; but their different orientation can also lead to tensions, above all when the issue involves competence in the matter of ethical truth.

Even today, the Christian community and individual Christians see the bishop as their shepherd and "pastor." Thus, the bishop embraces many moral questions concerning the way Christians structure their lives and carry out their professional tasks. Christians often expect a concrete word of leadership from their bishop and sometimes even bring unjustified pressure to bear on him to speak, thanks to an incorrect understanding of the episcopal task and the bishop's responsibilities. This pressure is all the more unjustified, when Christians' own orientation is lost or changing.

Among the many innovations in the world, in society, and in the church, the mentalities and outlooks on life held by many Christians have become extremely pluralistic in moral questions. All the more do they look for an "authentic" directive word from their bishops. But the opposite tendency also exists among Christians: "What can an episcopal directive mean for us, when the bishop cannot have sufficient knowledge of the facts underlying today's ethical problems but bases his judgment on inherited traditions and perhaps even imposes this judgment as an authentic position of the church?" It is clear that this question is not wholly unjustified.

What are believing Christians to do when the directive of their bishop is different from the directive of other bishops? What is the primary point: obedience to the bishop who has been set over this diocese as pastor, or the correct and true solution of the ethical problem that confronts us? Clearly, the latter is the more important, for the bishop's pastoral task stands at the service of the moral solution. What are Christians to do when neighboring bishops decide differently from their own bishop? When a bishop in the United States stated a few years ago that his magisterium had exclusive competence in his diocese for ethical teaching, his (remarkable) statement must be heard as prescinding from the primary question, which concerns truth; but then obedience to one's own bishop as such cannot be absolutely binding.

Either one's own insight (in the Holy Spirit and in union with other trustworthy Christians) will lead one to understand which of two mutually divergent episcopal directives states the truth, or else one will grasp that while both directives intend to indicate the truth, only one of them (at most) is right. The consequence is that one's link to truth is not unconditionally guaranteed by one's own bishop (and perhaps not through another bishop either); and therefore Christians must attempt to discover, in the light of the means available to them, in which of the episcopal directives (or indeed in what other place) the true solution to an ethical question is to be sought.

Christians must make their own decisions. In principle, Christians must willingly obey the ethical directive of their own bishop, but this obedience is not a demand admitting of no exceptions. The only thing absolutely obligatory is the honest search for the true solution to an ethical problem, and in this search the episcopal directive has a significant, indeed a presumptive value, but not an absolute value. A highly placed Catholic politician recently stated in public that, despite his personal conviction, he had voted in an ethically and politically significant referendum in accordance with the directive issued to Christians by the pope. His attitude of Catholic loyalty does him honor, but he was presumably not wholly clear about the problem attaching to the status of an episcopal directive.

One could widen this question: an auxiliary bishop owes obedience to his diocesan bishop and his ethical directives. But his absolute will to seek the truth is more binding on him than this obedience—even if he were to perceive that the truth lies rather in the directive of another bishop than the bishop of his own diocese, or even simply in his own judgment. Through episcopal ordination, he has been appointed in the Holy Spirit to care for Christian doctrine. A similar judgment must be made even about the obedience of the bishops to the ethical directives of the Bishop of Rome—with the exception (which is not to be presumed) of an infallible decision.

It has often been said that the problem of obedience or nonobedience vis-à-vis episcopal directives is really concerned not so much with the ethical principles as with the practical applications of these principles to innumerable individual ethical problems. The Second Vatican Council pointed out that the church's pastors do not always have an unambiguous answer to manifold ethical problems, or to new problems as they arise, and also that Christians with a firm Christian faith and responsible conscientiousness can legitimately arrive at different solutions to such problems.[5] This last statement holds true not only of Christian laypersons but also of priests and bishops. Was it not the case in the past, that many ethical problems were continuously discussed and yet remained open? Not everything has always been known in a clear and unambiguous fashion; rather, lengthy periods, even years, have been necessary in the church and in the episcopal hierarchy, to arrive at unambiguous and more or less universally accepted solutions for the manifold applications of ethical principles to concrete ethical problems. And the same is true today.

It is possible for this problematic to exist under certain circumstances with regard to ethical principles themselves as well as with their concrete application. The fundamental distinction between principles and their application is that the principles are less concrete, and therefore less capable of making statements than the applications are. Precisely for this reason, the principles can be grasped more easily and with a greater measure of agreement. It follows that the distinction between principles and applications does not completely solve the problem of which insights and statements are unanimous and which ones are not. Thus, in the church's history, problems have occurred not only with the applications of the principles of sexual ethics but with the principles themselves, for example, with the problematic of the "meaning and purpose of marriage." Indeed, many ethical principles are more or less universally accepted in the church that only in their concrete application in the world of human persons finally undergo so many transformations as to become problematical and to call into question unanimously held solutions.

Let me be more concrete. A few years ago, when questions about the ethical permissibility of the production, possession, and use of nuclear weapons were still very acute, no unambiguous or unanimous position was taken by Catholics and their theologians, or by bishops and episcopal conferences about nuclear weapons; that is, nothing was said about the ethical principles that are almost universally accepted in the church on this issue. And the statements made by various bishops and episcopal conferences diverged partially from one another. Indeed, in order to clear up this embarrassing situation, a meeting was organized between representatives of the United States' episcopal conference and some European episcopal conferences in the Vatican. Finally, in 1983, the United States' episcopal conference published its celebrated pastoral letter, "The Challenge of Peace." However, the bishops stated at the same time that some individual bishops could not assent to this document on a number of concrete questions. American Christians were confronted with the question whom they were to follow among their episcopal hierarchy.

The bishops in the conference had foreseen this question. They indicated that the principles in the document that are universally accepted in the church are naturally binding, whereas the concrete applications of these principles are not binding in the same way. Believers ought to be willing to take these applications into consideration, but they do not demand an unconditional assent. This observation by the bishops, and the public dissent on the part of some bishops, ought to teach Christians that their obedience to the ethical directives of their own bishop (or bishops) has limits in certain circumstances, and is not demanded in a manner that knows no exception. However, the North American bishops did not state specifically in their pastoral letter which of their ethical statements were absolutely binding principles and which were only concrete applications to the immensely difficult and almost impenetrable problems of nuclear ethics.

On the evening of the decision by the United States episcopal conference, the president of a European episcopal conference remarked in a discussion that his conference, unlike the United States, published only unanimously accepted documents. Naturally, this does not exclude the possibility (confirmed by another bishop belonging to another European episcopal conference) that there may also be dissenting bishops (like himself) behind such "unanimous" pastoral statements, who do not wish to limit the "unanimity" of an episcopal document, or perhaps do not wish to state their dissent openly in the presence of the other bishops.

Accordingly, it would be better if episcopal directives in ethical questions were issued as the expression of the bishops' pastoral concern to help the faithful reach decisions, rather than as authoritative directives, at least in those cases in which the bishops cannot be sure of moral unanimity in the church. The faithful ought not to feel that they are being exhorted to a greater degree of obedience than is theologically justified. In their pastoral letter on *Humanae Vitae*, the German episcopal conference sought cautiously to keep things within this limit.

THE BISHOPS AND BIOETHICS

The problematic of episcopal moral directives is present in the acute discussion in the North American Church concerning the question of the obligatory or nonobligatory giving of food and water to human persons who live permanently in a purely vegetative condition—a hotly debated ethical question in the United States, unlike many other countries. In the United States, this question is disputed among doctors, in the various official authorities dealing with matters of civil law, and also within Catholic theology and within the hierarchy of the Roman Catholic Church. As we have noted above, a number of bishops have made statements about this question, arriving at substantially different results that are, at least in part, mutually exclusive. The most recent lengthy pastoral letter was the one previously mentioned issued on 14 January 1992 by Cardinal Bevilacqua, Archbishop of Philadelphia, and the other bishops in the state of Pennsylvania. We shall draw on this letter chiefly to grasp the problematic of the present essay.

The chief aim of this pastoral letter, according to its explicit statement, is to communicate the teaching of the church to those who have been charged as its pastors and to their faithful, and thus of leading them to a deeper understanding of "the reality of God's plan for our salvation." The bishops admit that the magisterium at Rome has not yet explicitly adopted a position on the question at issue, not even in its significant 1980 document on euthanasia. While important principles for the correct solution to the problem were set forth in this document, it contains no explicit application of these principles to the present question.

It is not without reason that the Pennsylvania bishops refer to that decrees of the Congregation for the Doctrine of the Faith, since they consider the refusal of artificial nutrition with food and liquid to comatose persons to be euthanasia, that is, the conscious (though not intended) causing of death through omission (at least in the case, first, that such persons are not already dying and, second, that their organism can still digest the artificially transmitted nourishment, for otherwise it would obviously be meaningless to give them this nutrition). They understand the artificial nutrition of human beings who lead a vegetative life as developing in a binding manner the traditional medical ethics, in a mode that has become possible only in our own time. They believe that, as teachers and spokesmen of the church, they must ensure, in the way that is available to them, that this is done.

This tradition of medical ethics is, however, perhaps not so certain as the bishops seem to believe. In a recent article, Professor John J. Paris, S.J., has pointed out that this ethical tradition does not really exist.[6] He refers to the great ethical writers of the sixteenth century (D. Soto, D. Banez, F. de Vittoria), but also to the much more cautious statements by significant moral theologians of the more recent past, such as

the American Jesuit Gerald Kelly, for example. Professor Paris holds—
as do other bishops and moral theologians—that even the Vatican's
1980 declaration on euthanasia is to be read otherwise than some bishops read it. The former group quote above all the sentence from the
Roman declaration in which it is affirmed that it is permitted to discon-
tinue artificial methods of treating sick persons when these methods
will not lead to the hoped-for result (to the extent that this can be reasonably foreseen). Here it is no doubt primarily treatments like artificial respiration that the document has in mind as not being the
equivalent of killing ("suicide").

Bishops like Bevilacqua, however, do not consider artificial medical nutrition with food and water to be this kind of medical "treatment," but to be quite simply the continuation of the normal nutrition
of a human person. The Roman document, however, continues; "'such
a treatment' is to be understood as an acceptance of the human situation and as the intention to avoid an application of a medical treatment
that is disproportionate to the result expected, or as the intention not to
impose any excessive burden on the family or on society." But in Professor Paris's view, it is not only artificial respiration that must be seen
as an excessive burden without any hope of success: the same view
must be taken of artificial nutrition (e.g, feeding the patient through a
tube or in another way), since this can be continued for many weeks
and even for years. This result, however, would be "disproportionate,"
to use the word of the Roman document. This word clearly replaces
and clarifies the traditional formulation of the lack of obligation to use
"extraordinary" means of treatment, since it takes into account not
only the manner of treatment as such, but unambiguously includes the
total reality and situation of the sick person who is to be treated and
this person's milieu. For there is not doubt that nutrition as such is not
disproportionate but normal and natural, though medical treatment
with an artificial and invasive feeding method is certainly disproportionate.

The result of refraining from artificial nutrition is, indeed, that
the patient soon dies; ultimately, however, this death is the outcome of
the pathological situation of the permanently comatose person who is
incapable of taking food and drink without a disproportionate artificial nutrition that lasts over a long period and is therefore scarcely
obligatory.

The Pennsylvania bishops and the theologians and philosophers
who are close to them clearly work with a concept (typical for one par-

ticular school within today's philosophical and theological community) according to which human life, even purely vegetative life, is a
"basic good" given to the human person by the Creator. As such, life
may never be attacked, but must always be respected and protected. In
the light of this theory, the artificial nutrition of permanently vegetative human persons continues to serve a human and basic good,
namely, life, which the sick person thus retains. Thus the artificial
maintenance of (purely vegetative) life is seen as a good deed done to
the sick person.

But this view does not take into account that while human life is
indeed a gift of God, it is at the same time accompanied by a particular
task and goal that is to be fulfilled on this earth. Accordingly, a good
deed for this person can only be one that somehow helps the person to
fulfill that for which he (or she) is determined here on earth. This, however, is not possible by means of the continuing artificial nutrition of a
purely vegetative human life. These bishops, theologians and philosophers admit this to a limited extent; they do not hold the doubtless
meaningless feeding of a person who is already dying or who is no
longer able to lead a vegetative life as something obligatory. The real
problem, however, is not posed by these two exceptional cases: the real
problem lies in the question whether the permanently comatose
patient lives in a pathological situation that of itself necessarily leads to
death unless artificially prolonged—because then an artificial prolongation of the pathological condition also occurs by means of medicinal
artificial nutrition—and whether this prolongation can be considered a
proportionate means to achieve the desired goal.

The fact that this problem has been discussed in the church and
the larger society, and that it remains an object of discussion, makes it
appear extraordinarily questionable that official church authorities
would appeal to their authority in the church as permitting them to
state the unambiguous teaching of the church, and hence unquestionably the will of God, in the present ethical question. Beyond any doubt,
they may form their opinion on this question and make it known—as
their opinion. And they may also make known that they personally
hold a particular opinion to be the teaching the church, and hence
God's will for them. But may they, in the present doctrinal situation
and variety of opinions, impose this opinion of theirs, whatever it may
be, in a binding manner on the faithful? May they give the faithful the
impression that they are obliged to follow this episcopal directive in
making the decision? Or may not the well-instructed faithful follow

the result of their own reflection on the basis of serious information and responsible discussion, even when it does not correspond to an episcopal directive?

If these arguments are correct, then it can scarcely be denied that not all bishops—and even fewer of the faithful—agree with them completely. Does it follow, although the opposite is often maintained today, that a hypertrophy of magisterial thinking has developed, and that we are "caught fast" in this? Richard McCormick, S.J., recently coined the formulation "magisteriolatry," which may perhaps be too sharp.[7] But at any rate, a little less magisteriolatry could help promote a conscientious autonomy and a calm and balanced judgment, so that mutually opposing episcopal statements and claims may be less inclined to confuse the faithful.

NOTES

1. "Nutrition and Hydration: Moral Considerations," *Origins*, 30 January 1992, 541-553.
2. Bishop W. Bullock of Des Moines (Iowa), in *Origins*, 30 January 1992, 553-555.
3. Cf. Rom 2:14-16.
4. Cf. the lists of virtues and sins in his letters.
5. *Gaudium et Spes* 33, 43.
6. J. J. Paris, S.J., "The Catholic Tradition on the Use of Nutrition and Fluids," in *Birth, Suffering and Death, Catholic Perspectives at the Edges of Life*, ed. K. Wildes, S.J., F. Abel, S.J., and J. C. Harvey, Dordrecht/Boston/London 1992, 189-208.
7. "'Moral Considerations' Ill Considered," *America*, 14.3.1992, 211.

12

Ethical Self-Direction?

Parents and educators often have the very painful experience of seeing young persons connected to them behaving otherwise than they themselves did when they were young. In important areas of life, young people deviate from the life their parents and educators presented and declared to be the only correct way to shape one's life. In many families, such behavior can lead to a distressing lack of understanding on both sides and even to deep conflicts. Yet it also happens that many educators consciously and intentionally deviate in particular areas of life from the familiar standards and attitudes they learned from an earlier generation. They may also deviate from the way of life expected from them by an institution hitherto regarded as competent in a tradition or authority once considered to be binding.

These same young persons may regard their present behavior as incorrect because of traditional standards and perhaps consider themselves to be guilty. No doubt such was the case in the society of the recent past and even more so in the more or less closed societies of earlier periods. The mentality expressed in such an attitude has changed to a great extent in the intervening time.

1. The word "self-direction" (*selbstesteuerung*), which is often meant as a maxim for life, indicates that inherited authorities, traditions, and institutions are no longer looked on as a valid source of orientation for the construction of one's life. A transformed mentality holds that each person should provide one's own direction, not only in the sense that one must freely decide whether or not to observe inherited regulations without bothering too much about the authority and the justification of such regulations (this attitude has existed at all periods); but also in the sense that one looks on such inherited directives as sheer authoritarianism, to which no objective justification, and hence

no justified authority for the direction of each individual life, can be attributed.

Each one, alone, is the authority for oneself. This viewpoint presupposes the conviction that it would be a false anthropomorphic understanding of God, and thus authoritarianism, to postulate that God had, at some time and place, formally and positively imposed commandments on us as obligatory directives for living. Consequently, the tradition usually presented and preached as an authoritative regulation for living can only be the human self-understanding of those who present it and preach it.

One asks oneself why this tradition should in principle have more authority than one's own ideas that are held, perhaps in fellowship with others, as leading to the correct behavior appropriate to the reality of human existence, activity, and individual life. Should it not be possible for the individual or a group to recognize its own ethical truth and understand it more deeply than an authority or institution that gives direction from outside? Why may not a group of like-minded persons or a "movement" that does not treat ethical questions in a superficial manner but tackles them conscientiously and seriously (without ignoring the potential significance of authorities and institutions), be capable on their own of correctly finding and grasping ethical truth, even in cases of complex matters that cannot be guaranteed by societal custom, institutions, and other authorities?

On a visit to Germany a few years ago, I had a discussion with a university chaplain friend about his students' position on certain questions that were the object of much discussion at the time—problems similar to those raised in *Humanae Vitae* in 1968 and by *Persona Humana* in 1975. During the conversation, my friend made it very clear that for many students, these concrete questions needed to be newly answered from some source or by some person, despite the fact that Rome's authoritative statements were well known.

Many students had the attitude: "Who can presume authoritatively to offer or impose on us a valid solution to our ethical problems?" To them, Rome's ethical pronouncements were sheer authoritarianism. Thus, the students' own solution and need was for conscientious self-direction. To a large extent, they believed that the concern of authoritative decisions was not primarily to establish ethical truth but to establish conformity or nonconformity to what the authorities, institutions, and traditions already say anyway; that is, the fundamental aim of authority was to defend past authority and therefore also its validity for today—despite the obvious temporal disjunction in technical knowledge and in consciousness. This authority, however, lacks substantial justification in the field of ethical truth and is merely an unacceptable authoritarianism.

The problem indicated here does not affect all ethical questions, but it does affect many that are significant, including questions involving political decisions requiring a high degree of responsibility and questions of corruption on a large and small scale; questions like divorce and extramarital relationships, abortion and euthanasia; and various questions concerning the sexual conduct of young people.

Naturally, the "solutions" to such questions can also be, and often are, determined wholly or in part by egotistic tendencies. But this egotism is not necessary and not always the case. It is also perfectly possible to be convinced that particular alleged regulations are determined by insufficient technical knowledge, by decisive mentalities in society, and by influences from other groups. Therefore, those who uphold the principle of ethical self-direction react strongly against every form of fundamentalism.

Must one not also concede that attempts at self-direction are largely based on a genuine intention and a genuine readiness to be totally open to contemporary perspectives and evaluations (including those that are untraditional), especially in a period of obvious societal and ethical pluralism? And when a comparison is made on the basis of what we know today, and between inherited convictions and insights stemming from new reflection and experience, isn't a reasonable evaluation justified in giving the preference to the latter—indeed, isn't it compelled to do so? This evaluation is all the more likely, because the untraditional tendency, despite strong opposition, is widespread in our society. It is not easy, therefore, to justify disqualifying the honesty, upright intention, convinced insight, and argumentative acuteness of the many who believe they must depart from tradition.

Certainly many proponents of ethical self-direction are genuinely convinced of the correctness of their views. Nor does this certitude necessarily require that the convinced and convincing insight be supported by arguments—very few persons are capable of strictly logical argument. Genuine insight does not always presuppose explicit argumentation, just as it is possible to arrive at argumentative conclusions without true insight. One holds firm to a convincing insight, and one must do so; one defends it and lives it.

The attempt at ethical self-direction, the sincere endeavor to arrive at one's own insights and solutions to problems, is not an answer based on conclusive evidence any more than were the ethical insights in differently formulated statements made in the past, and recently, by institutions and authorities. Both have the same validity as statements that we are accustomed to attribute to the natural (ethical) law. They are called a participation in God's insight, will, and commandment, but they are God's knowledge and insight only in human knowledge and insight. And since traditions, institutions and authorities can only participate in human insight, the genuine validity that such sources of authority have as binding statements in individual epochs and cultures as well as in today's concrete individual situation is only a relative validity.

To the same degree and for the same reason, one cannot deny in principle a similar positive weight to the well-intentioned insights and convictions of the proponents of ethical self-direction, however much they deviate from directives laid down by tradition or authority. The dissimilar ethical statements made today by obviously noncontemporaneous mentalities ought in principle to have the same justification; the same holds true of the individual persons and groups who believe that they may or should hold to the particular conviction. The attempt to make our own mentality, insight, and conviction "plausible," or a matter of "insight" to one another, instead of casting suspicion on or condemning one another, will open a path in this situation. The attempt to communicate "insight" implies a corresponding endeavor in education and private dialog as well as public attempts to open up access-paths to correct insights and convictions.

2. What has been said here corresponds to the traditional and correct doctrine concerning the conscience. Strong tendencies have existed in the past to tie the formation of the individual's conscience in an absolutely obligatory fashion to the norms laid down in advance by institutions and authority, and such tendencies still exist. But what the conscience ought to seek—while naturally also paying due heed to inherited norms—is not conformity to established norms but an absolutely ethical truth. Established norms are insightful results in exactly the same way as directives acquired on the basis of conscientious ethical self-direction: both are God's original, foundational, and hence infallible ethical insight though mediated as the possibility of (merely) human insight. Such insights in an honest conscience are not, however, absolutely oriented to the fixed point of an absolute norm that is the only norm possible, since human insight, as a merely created possibility, is not aware of the totality of human reality and its own possible interpretations at every moment and in every situation.

Precisely for this reason, the possibility exists that proponents of ethical self-direction—individuals, groups, or entire cultures—will believe that they are obliged to uncover an insufficiency or something erroneous in the mediation of norms carried out by institutions or authorities For this reason, they can believe that they discern, in their very nonconformity to norms mediated in the past or in the present, something good not only for their own lives but also for society. One should bear this possibility in mind, particularly if one is aware of having a one-sided tendency to see evil and "the evil one" at work in unusual and "new" elements in the proponents of ethical self-direction. A high degree of good will and responsible discretion is required in the proponents of ethical self-direction and the upholders of the authority of traditional norms.

This sensitive discretion is also required when the inherited or established ethical utterance clearly displays a decisive substantial truth that must, in order not to remain merely "approximate," be further nuanced. This discretion, too, is ethical self-direction. In other periods it has been given the name *epikeia* and especially in the sphere of law, but recently *epikeia* has begun to be at home in moral theology, too.

The Roman Catholic Church as institution and fellowship, and not least as theology and authentic magisterium, is the decisive institution and authority to which in certain circumstances the proponents of ethical self-direction take on a negative relationship. It must be noted, however, that the church also practices ethical self-direction, apart from a few cases of revealed truths. Especially in the field of concrete ethical questions, few, if any, concrete ethical statements are laid down in advance. And when because of its biblical foundation and institutions that have come into being in the course of history and the Spirit, and because of its doctrinal traditions, authentic magisterium, and, ultimately, the attempt of Christian people to preserve Christian reality as faithfully as possible, the church believes that it ought to make authentic statements, then in the last analysis these statements are no decisive ethical direction of Christians *ab extra*, but a help for their own necessary ethical self-direction, which the church recognizes as the only concrete ethical direction that is ultimately valid.

Therefore, ethical self-direction is not only a task of the church as a whole but also of various groups and individuals. Moral theologians can attempt to give valid information to believers and to the magisterium only along the path of self-direction; that is, they must do the painstaking work of seeking and finding within life all that can be helpful. Theologians can offer their results to believers, to the ecclesial fellowship, and also to the magisterium, only as a result (and, one can only hope, a trustworthy result) of their own ethical self-direction. However, since these results are a question of ethical self-direction, mutually exclusive results cannot be absolutely excluded. We are more than familiar in today's church with the crises provoked by this possibility.

An obvious recourse in times of crises caused by the ethical pluralism among theologians, is for groups of believers and the individual to trust to the decision pronounced by the authentic magisterium—and no doubt this reaction is the correct one. But not even this solution is free of problems. For concrete ethical truths have not been handed over to the magisterium by some higher (or indeed, divine) ethical authority; the only possibility for the magisterium to guarantee the truths of the faith and also exercise an authentic concern for truth in the sphere of ethics (despite much assistance and aid from the Spirit of God) lies exclusively along the path of its own activity of insightful argumentation in the light of faith, that is, along the path of ethical self-direction. Precisely because no absolute guarantees exist, the possibility remains that some Christians (including some moral theologians who think seriously) will not be convinced by the results presented by the magisterium but may indeed be convinced by the opposite position.

Moral theologians who are required or who wish to make an ethical judgment on concrete problems and those who bear responsibility in the magisterium and believe that they can evaluate or judge an ethical position, will be confronted by doctrinal positions of theologians that are not in conformity with the tradition. To assess these positions or even to express an authoritative judgment on them is an important task to carry out in the church but also one that can only be carried out through ethical self-direction. The result will not have absolute certainty, nor may one overlook the fact that ecclesiastical (even authentic) statements made in the past have not always been repeated. Some have fallen into oblivion or been subjected silently and even openly to an interpretation in the opposite sense.

The Viennese exegete Jakob Kremer has written an important article in which he clearly demonstrates the extent to which statements of the Hebrew Bible and New Testament (including ethical statements) have necessarily corresponded to the mode of thought, the ideas, and the style of earlier times.[1] Some statements, that is, have more in keeping with the world views and mythical categories of earlier times, with their supposition of the existence of many spirits (rather than natural forces) and the remarkable occurrence of miracles. Kramer points out how many biblical narratives have been falsely read and interpreted in the church through a lack of historical awareness, and how, even today, they can alienate people from the faith, if one erroneously considers their content as teachings valid for today.

Thus, we have not only a question of "the sacred *preservation*" of the human word in which the divine word dwells, but also of its "faithful *exposition*," as the Second Vatican Council explicitly demands in the decree *Dei Verbum* (9, cf. 24); the word of God must be "kept open for the truth of the past, as well as for new and unforeseen knowledge." However, "in view of the complexity of the societal and cultural contexts," the process of exposition can lead "to divergent perceptions and judgments."[2] In "the theological elaboration of the truth of revelation, the appropriate freedom should be permitted."[3] It is always a question of ecclesial self-direction in the exposition of the human word that gives expression to God's word.

In his book *Nel cuore della Chiesa e del mondo* ("In the Heart of the Church and the World"), the Archbishop of Milan, Cardinal Martini, likewise insists that one should cultivate not only *obedience* to the doctrine (*obbedienza dottrinale*), but also an interpretative understanding (*intelligenza interpretativa*).[4] He fears that the average Christian demands, above all, an exact teaching about what is allowed and what is not allowed in human behavior, and that this demand is made even by those who from the very outset are unwilling to live in accordance with this distinction when it is recognized. The Cardinal calls such a morality a "rabbinical" morality, which he sets in antithesis to a "pauline" morality. The rabbinical morality is also called moralistic and legalistic; the pauline morality is also called evangelical.

In the pauline morality, the accent does not lie primarily on establishing what is allowed and what is not allowed, but on the evangelical ideal that drives the Christian to transcend oneself, that is, to live dynamically with Christian enthusiasm. When he is asked about sexual ethics in the course of the debate, the Cardinal refers to a deutero-pauline text from the letter to the Ephesians: "But fornication and all impurity or covetousness must not even by named among you, as is fitting among saints. Let there be no filthiness, nor silly talk, nor levity, which are not fitting; but instead let there be thanksgiving" (Eph 5:3-4). Cardinal Martini sees in this text the primary Christian interest. He explicitly emphasizes the necessity for the church to have a firm hand on ethical questions. But he also discerns one of the most serious crises of the church in the duality of a particular moral teaching and the genuine situation of the people, and consequently he demands above all that stronger attention be paid to cultivating a pauline and evangelical moral proclamation as the church's ethical self-direction.

NOTES

1. J. Kremer, "Kein Wort Gottes ohne Menschenwort," *Stimmen der Zeit* 117 (1992), 75-90.
2. Position paper by the working team of German-speaking dogmatic and fundamental theologians on the instruction on the ecclesial vocation of the theologian by the Congregation for the Doctrine of the Faith (24 May 1990), prepared by D. Wiederkehr in the name of the team, in *Wie gesbhieht Tradition?* (Quaestiones Disputatae 133), ed. D. Wiederkehr, Freiburg i. Br. 1991, 175.
3. Ibid., 176, quoting Vatican II, *Unitatis Redintegratio*, 4.
4. C. M. Cardinal Martini, *Nel cuore della Chiesa e del mondo. Dialogo con Antonio Balletto e Bruno Musso*, Genoa 1991, 77.

13

The Faithful Must Not Be Unsettled

The title "The Faithful Must Not Be Unsettled" reproduces a familiar warning. And we know well who, in these terms, are the warners and who are the warned. Many people, however, regret this customary interpretation, certain that it is sometimes justified to ask whether the one who warns ought not to be warned and perhaps often.

The generally accepted understanding of the formulation of our title is found in many statements made by the church's hierarchy—by individual bishops and the Vatican—and in theological utterances of a decidedly traditional orientation (although traditions of other periods and other intellectual and Christian milieus are not in every case an absolutely valid criterion for today). The view is also found among Christians (clergy and laity) who are more concerned with the guarantee of personal certainty than with an honest search for truth as the basis of their lives.

The warning concerns all issues in the broad realm of believing, theological, and moral thinking. In the most recent period, however, its primary focus has been on questions of ethical conduct in individual, interpersonal, and social life.

"Weak" Christians (see Romans 14) may think that they are strengthened by being told, for example, that many ethical norms are "God's commandment" that cannot be altered. They believe—falsely— that this proclamation is to be understood in the sense that God has revealed these norms directly to us. In the same way, they are strengthened in their "weakness," by the belief that the acceptance and observation of all these norms is a touchstone of their "Christian faith." They *believe* they are strengthened, even though this notion is surely a false touchstone.

When the "weak" are confronted with opposing formulations, they easily become unsettled. The question is who has unsettled them. Is it those who make opposing assertions, or those who hold such assertions to be false, or at least open to misunderstanding? Or simply those who say such things publicly?

THE FAITHFUL

1. If one speaks of the faithful's right not to be unsettled, then one must be clear in some way about who the faithful are.

Shortly before the revolution in Rumania broke out, a North American daily newspaper observed that should this revolution break out, the only European dictatorship left would be the one whose leader demands more strongly than others a nondictatorial respect for human rights: the Vatican. Naturally, the observation was intended maliciously, but even Catholics noted it with a benevolent smile. Catholics do indeed know the reply, which is quite correct despite being stereotypical, that the church is not simply a state institution and was not founded by the Lord as a democracy. But this reply does not solve the problem.

The foundational kernel of the church and its structural and permanent development on the basis of Jesus' lordship is indeed something other than a democracy; but despite this principle the form of its leadership in every age including today ought to be more "democratic," without contradicting its fundamental essence and indeed perhaps corresponding more deeply thereby to this essence. Would Catholics who think this way still belong to the faithful, the group of true Catholics whose preservation from being unsettled concerns us here? Or ought one to understand them as already unsettled, or even as people who are only selectively Catholic?

In the United States, we find one group of Catholics among others, whose collective name is Catholics United for the Faith (CUF). Catholics who belong to, or sympathize with, this group see it as their task to safeguard the orthodoxy of statements made about theological and ethical questions, in part by reporting on these matters to the central authority. Some theologians who belong to this organization (e.g., Baker, Grisez, Roach) have publicly demanded—for example, at the celebrated congress of moral theologians at Rome in 1988—that moral theologians who think differently be disqualified as theologians or even excommunicated. Are Catholics and theologians who are painted in such terms believers in the true sense; that is, are they among those who should not be unsettled?

The customary and usual criterion for being a genuine believer is one's agreement with the official teaching of the magisterium on questions of faith and morals. Leaving open, for the time being, the question about the meaning of the term "moral questions" in this context, we may ask whether all statements of the magisterium genuinely share in the unity derived from its collegial unity? It is, after all, quite a well-known fact that not all members of the magisterium always have the courage to state their true opinions. For example: a few years before the Second Vatican Council, Pope Pius XII upheld in a modified form the traditional (negative) position of the church on religious freedom. Many bishops, including those from North America, let it be known at the Council, despite this Pope's opinion, that they had never identified themselves with this position. Ultimately, it was their opinion that determined the contents of the Council's decree on religious freedom. We must still find an answer to the question about the meaning of the word "believer" and, accordingly, about the meaning of the warning, that one "must not unsettle" them.

2. Believers are those who, out of a free personal decision (called forth by the Holy Spirit), are willing to accept God's loving self-communication in Jesus Christ and to construct their lives in keeping with it. Again, let us for the moment put aside the question of what, more precisely, is the content of this free personal decision. The important point here is that we are concerned with a decision that is taken in freedom. Although this decision may be subject to conditions, it is not subject to any external coercion and is not ultimately reducible to any coercion of social or personal origin. Since the possibility of a free decision affects the meaningfulness of the whole of one's earthly and eternal life, it is not surprising that this decision is often taken only amid great inner difficulties and remains in the long-term subject to these difficulties.

Free faith presupposes "hearing" the faith in a Christian or ecclesiastical community. Only in this way does faith go back to Christ; but having gone forth from Christ, faith enters upon a long development as tradition in a community that has its origins in, and continues to be in history—and here and there geographically—clearly not a process of development like that of a straight line.

From what has been said, it will be seen that a believing self-identification with the historical self-communication of God and the continuation of this identity in the Christian community's life poses new problems. The abundantly rich continuation, which is not linear at all points, of the Christian community's understanding of faith and above all of its adherence to morality, which has many individual details, certainly requires many believers. Some believers who are perhaps only more or less aware of what they are doing, and some who are very much aware, may behave in a selective manner without thereby being unfaithful to their fundamental Christian faith which they hold with honest devotion. The urgent question here is to what extent the quality of genuine Christian faith depends on the full acceptance of the moral doctrine that is taught in the church. To what extent, how, and by whom is it possible for a detailed moral doctrine, the content of which is not simply based on faith, to be presented as obligatory for the sake of faith to the believers whose faith is exclusively rooted in a free decision supported by grace?

3. Beyond doubt not every conceivable lifestyle is in keeping with the faith of believers. Indeed the opposite is true: every arbitrary ethical style or norm contradicts faith in the creating and redeeming God of Christian revelation. This assertion seems to be what the Second Vatican Council meant when it characterized the object of the magisterium as the revealed faith and the conduct of life in keeping with it (*Lumen Gentium* 25). Or did the Council wish to go beyond this assertion and indicate that in a Christian community of faith, an ethos proper to it will necessarily develop an ethics that is in some measure its own? If the latter, then those who watch over the doctrine of the faith must pass judgment on the compatibility of this proper ethos and ethics with the revealed faith.

Or—a third possibility—did the Council see the entire realm of ethics in the Christian community (or communities) in its incalculable mass of details as entrusted to the decision of the church's authority? If so, then every moral detail must be seen as within the competence of human reason as it is illuminated by faith in revelation. Many rather emphatic statements made by the magisterium seem to affirm or to presuppose that this third position was the Council's clear intent. Neither the First nor the Second Vatican Council, however, attempted to clarify this question, although both Councils contain pronouncements that would appear to exclude such a wide-reaching competence of the church's magisterium.[1]

Thus, the question of truth in the church does not concern only the magisterium, but also and above all the entire believing community; the magisterium is, after all, only the people's official and ministerial representative. But the Second Vatican Council acknowledges that justified differences of opinion on ethical questions, despite a seamless faith, can exist among the faithful who are the primary bearers of the truth of faith.[2] Therefore, it follows that these differences of opinion can also exist among moral theologians and even among bishops. Believers, then, are those who ought to be familiar at least to some extent with their own ecclesial reality with regard to the truths that are to be accepted; at any rate, this reality ought not to be withheld from them.

4. It is not only the irresponsible proclamation of various doctrinal opinions, especially when these appear to contradict the church's official teaching, that contribute to the unsettling of the faithful. More is done in this direction by an insufficient or even theologically incorrect instruction of the faithful about the true authority of the various entities in the magisterium and their limitations. For it is easy to feel oneself "unsettled" when one is confronted with the plausible arguments of conscientious teachers who have the appropriate competence but are not exclusively conformist if one believes that authority not only gives helpful guidance in moral questions, but also that one is absolutely bound by this authority. If one has been taught to be so bound, no matter by what persons, and if one therefore does not know or misunderstands one's own freedom with regard to the formation of the individual conscience, then one is also "bound" to be unsettled. But the faithful have a right to be given appropriate instruction about their true reality within the church through public teaching and thus to be "made certain" in their behavior which is justified and responsible, even if it is occasionally nonconformist. This freedom should apply both in individual cases and in individual corporate statements. Believers have a right to live as Christians without anxiety and uncertainty within determined limits.

The warning of those who warn others ought therefore and in a significant manner, be addressed to the warners themselves.

THE CHURCH'S MAGISTERIUM

1. How does the magisterium come into play in this question? If it is the magisterium's primary task to safeguard faith in God's self-communication, what then, is its task in regard to judgments about moral-

ity and moral teaching in the church? If the magisterium is the body that watches over the Christian doctrine of faith, then it is doubtless also in some sense the body that watches over the Christian conduct of life, to ensure that it is in keeping with the faith that it proclaims in God. Here, however, it is basically the people who must make judgments, while for its part the church's magisterium watches over those judgments, reflects on them, and ultimately makes a statement. The magisterium must see that people live in keeping with the fundamental ethos and ethics of God's word, to the extent that this ethics is more than time-conditioned.

But the magisterium must also see how the community (including itself) has authentically interpreted and understood the ethics of God's word in the course of time: whether (falsely) as an ahistorical doctrine that remains static, or (correctly) as the historical ethical evaluation and judgment of given historical realities in the light of faith. It must also note how from time to time, individual points in the biblical ethics are adopted as in keeping with the Christian faith and with the circumstances of a particular period and how they must sometimes be reinterpreted or replaced by something else. Finally, it must also establish whether and for what reason individual ethical statements that had once been adopted or reinterpreted, have to be reinterpreted yet again: is it because of better understandings of scripture or because of new historical circumstances and possibilities of understanding?

2. In the light of these remarks, is it possible for the church and its magisterium to arrive at a knowledge of nonrevealed moral questions and a proclamation that correspond in the same way to scripture, to historical tradition, and to present-day historical reality? The magisterium must always remain aware that the support of the Spirit of God, which is promised to the magisterium, does not include the promise that its final word today will in every case be the final and absolutely definitive word.

How does the Christian community, and above all how does the church's magisterium arrive at a sufficiently certain knowledge of matters on which Christians must make a decision, in both the smallest and most important questions of life? The Spirit of God is given to them and is present, not, however, as the revealer of ethical truths, but as light and support in one's search for these answers. The Spirit aids our attempt to use all available aids and authorities to interpret human realities as the realities and possible understandings that exist here and now, thus and not otherwise, and to evaluate these realities and to judge them in an ethical perspective.

From this point of view, the bishops and pope are no exception to what has already been said; Christian doctrine does not justify, in the case of their proclamation of ethical norms, an appeal to the Spirit who guarantees the truth. For example, neither the authentic interpretation of the humanly possible and meaningful realizations of human sexuality (about which new knowledge has continually developed in the course of history, even within the church), nor the authentic interpretation of the humanly meaningful application of force (opinions about warfare have changed in the course of history and also in the church) is in the realm of ecclesiastical and magisterial authoritative competence. Indeed, authority relevant to these matters has not been clearly bestowed on any group.

These reflections do not mean that a believing Christian, faced with ethical questions, cannot begin by turning, on the grounds of an already-existing presupposition, to the utterances of the church and its magisterium—because the support of the Holy Spirit is promised to them in a special manner. This turning to the church's utterance can be a genuine act, yet still lie only on the level of presupposition, since the church's search for the truth of ethical norms takes place along the path of human knowledge. Some Protestant denominations assert that they cannot accept this appeal, because of the fallibility of the human person who bears the mark of sin and is therefore inclined to egotism; instead, they say, they must first appeal in all ethical questions to scripture as God's word.

It appears, however, that they are not giving sufficient consideration to the fact that one's appeal to the bible also requires one's own interpretation, since the bible does not interpret itself for us, and since it does not deal concretely with the multiplicity of today's ethical questions. We require, therefore, only an analogous use of scripture. And always the believing person who carries out the interpretation and the analogous act of understanding even then always remains a sinner inclined to egotism. One could almost say that, in the Catholic understanding, we solve concrete ethical problems by means of reason illuminated by faith (*ratio fide illuminata*), and in the Protestant understanding by means of faith illuminated by reason (*fides ratione illuminata*). Is there, after all, much distance between these two positions?

3. These reflections on the magisterium have consequences for the behavior of those who represent this magisterium vis-à-vis believers (who include the members of the magisterium). The magisterium must leave believers in unimpaired possession of their rights in the church or else establish them in these rights. That is, it must under-

stand believers to be adults in the full sense of the word. The preceding reflections, together with the rights of believers and the duties of the magisterium deduced from these considerations show that not every dissent in the realm of moral and theological statements involves a lack of the loyalty to the magisterium. A one-sided fundamentalism is no part of genuine orthodoxy, and not all the ethical statements that are proclaimed are in themselves truths of salvation.[3] A historical mentality does not denote any contradiction of fidelity owed to the Christian tradition and to scripture, and unity in the church, which the magisterium oversees, does not in the least require full (and, ultimately, life-destroying) uniformity.

The well-known warning in our title ought therefore to be turned around and directed against some members of the magisterium. It ought, for example, to warn them that the Second Vatican Council would have been incapable of writing the 1950 encyclical *Humani Generis* and that not even *Lumen Gentium* 25, is a sufficient, let alone definitive, solution to all the problems it implies. Otherwise, the failure to reflect on the relationship between the magisterium and the faithful in questions of morality could lead to the "abuse" of authority, a danger that was pointed out a few years ago by Bishop B. C. Butler, a member of the magisterium.[4]

An abusive use of authority—whether caused by a failure to take seriously and openly the faithful and their rights in the church, or by a fear of full information and communication, or by a concern to preserve one's own authority and, at the same time, the fullest unity possible (in the sense of uniformity)—is certainly capable of unsettling the faithful in their conscious and happy position within the church.

THE CHURCH'S MORAL THEOLOGY

1. Christian ethics, which is generally called moral theology by Catholics, does not have the ecclesiastical authority of the official magisterium. This lack of ecclesiastical authority, however, does not affect its professional competence; in many cases it can and does take precedence over ecclesiastical authority. Moral theology can and should place its competence at the service of the church's teaching authority, to the extent that the authority asks for this service or at least shows itself willing to make use of it, which is not seldom the case. Via the church's authority, moral theology can, in some cases, acquire a signifi-

cant influence on the community of the faithful. But this influence can be hindered by a lack of harmony between the representatives of authority and the representatives of moral theology as when both hold themselves to be competent at the same time, although in mutually opposite directions. In this case, it is usually the church's authority that has to decide—at least for the moment, if not always. As this situation and lack of harmony is likely to unsettle believers who hear of it, responsible behavior on both sides is imperative.

Naturally, the personal activity of moral theologians in this age of mass media, is not confined to the writing-desk and to books that are little read: it is carried out also in public lectures given by professors, and in contributions to newspapers. In this way, moral theology has a more or less direct influence on moral questions, although this influence is frequently determined by the media.

When this publicity accords with one's fundamental position, the moral theologian can be confronted with the same problems as representatives of the church's magisterium. Then it is the theologian's task to beware of unsettling the faithful either through excessive reservation or through insufficiently grounded assertions and ethical demands. In this matter, the moral theologian—like all Catholics—owes the magisterium the presupposition of obedience that was mentioned earlier, and he or she will also not proceed independently, that is, without sufficiently taking heed of the positions and arguments of other moral theologians.

One is not obliged, however, to avoid public discussion and obvious differences of opinion. If the Second Vatican Council has explicitly acknowledged the possibility of such differences of opinion, and if the faithful are given more instruction in keeping with this possibility, then the public difference of opinion will not unsettle anyone, let alone lead to scandal.[5] The ideal for which we must aim, although we may never attain it completely because of the various presuppositions of individuals, is, of course, the greatest harmony possible among moral theologians themselves and with the church's magisterium. Each one must always take the other seriously, although never too seriously. This harmony would without doubt be the best means of excluding an unsettling of the faithful.

2. One of the most important tasks of moral theology in the service of the faithful (not only, but above all in service to Catholics who are intellectually awake) is to liberate them from supposed (but unfounded) "absolute obligations" to moral theological positions that

are broadly represented in the church. These positions may be the product of a particular tradition or particular theological tendencies or, above all, of decisions by the church's magisterium. The doctrine of the ecclesiastical privilege of occasional infallibility in teachings of faith gives no theological justification whatsoever for the "infallibilism" of all moral teachings asserted within the church (above all by the magisterium), though such an infallibilism is still maintained by many of the faithful.

A few years ago, the Vatican Italian periodical of the Jesuits, *La Civiltà Cattolica*, published an essay against such a "Byzantine infallibilism," which has nothing to do with the official teaching of the church about the occasionally infallible doctrine of faith or else presents a false interpretation of it.[6] Opposite tendencies, such as those of Catholics United for the Faith, the North American group that was mentioned earlier, are capable of unsettling the faithful in their faith or in their sense of belonging to the church without any justification. Someone has called Catholics United for the Faith, "the tired nostalgia of the marginalized right." On the other hand, it is regrettable that the author of the essay in *La Civiltà Cattolica*, who is secretly known to be an ecclesiologist, has found himself "led" to defend a more extensive significance attaching to the church's moral doctrines.[7]

Above all, moral theologians must check the reasoning that supports ethical statements and, to the extent that it is possible, "give certainty" to critical believers in their difficulties. This task applies to moral questions and forms of argument that concern scripture, the church's tradition, and especially statements that are based on the so-called natural law when it is surreptitiously applied to ethical statements on the basis of arbitrary interpretations or evaluations of nature that are based on a common fallacy.[8]

Such an activity by moral theologians can lead to the justification of dissent whether by theologians or believers who are influenced by theologians, from an officially taught or widely held position in the church. The legitimacy of such an occasional dissent has never been absolutely excluded in the church and has also been mentioned positively in an official document of the Second Vatican Council.[9] Since the church's moral doctrines in their multiplicity (which comes from natural law) do not belong to the privileged realm of infallibility, dissent can be not only a sign of genuine vitality in the struggle for Christian truth and life, but also a sign of something that has a positive and beneficent meaning in the church.

It has often been said, above all in the past, that such dissent should remain secret and only be communicated in confidence to the magisterium. But such secrecy cannot be carried out in an age of mass media, and would, in any case, render the dissent meaningless, since it would not be communicated to the very believers who are caught up in the suffering of such a dissent and are therefore unsettled in their feeling of being Christians. It may be presumed that it is easier for theologians to express dissent than for many bishops who may perhaps have equal grounds for dissenting—this at least is how things are at present.

When moral theologians proceed in the serious manner appropriate to the search for truth, a certain dissent exists and thus an absolute avoidance of a moral-theological *pluralism* is a possibility that is not to be expected, although many Catholics expect it to be avoided. In the search for truth, moral theologians are not determined exclusively by the ethical problem (the object) that led them to undertake the search; they also necessarily bring themselves with their unavoidable personal characteristics into this search. Such a pluralism impels an untiring and unending reflection on the ethical arguments adduced. For example: are the data of nature as such ethical justifications, or are they only relevant to the intellectual and ethical justifications that must be found by the subject? Are the concrete applications of ethical principles nothing other than numerical applications, or are they also a broadened knowledge of the contents of the full meaning of the principles themselves?

Such a pluralism, understood correctly, is not the unsettling of the faithful, but the act of "giving them certainty." Vatican II explicitly confirmed the justified freedom of research.[10] John Paul II did the same in a significant address at his first visit to the Pontifical Gregorian University. Thus, the principle holds good that the faithful have a right not to be unsettled, either by irresponsible ethical assertions that diverge from the church's moral doctrine, or by an unjustifiable indoctrination of the faithful.

NOTES

1. Compare the corresponding relevant limitation of the magisterial competence at Vatican I (according to the official statement of the Relator of the Deputatio de fide, Bishop Gasser (Mansi, Vol. 52, 1124, a), and the limitation of magisterial infallibility at Vatican II in *Lumen Gentium* 25: "the deposit of faith."

2. See *Gaudium et Spes* 43 and 34.

3. Cf. J. Fuchs, "Moral Truths—Truths of Salvation?" in *Christian Ethics in a Secular Arena*, Washington/Dublin 1984, 48-67 (German original in *Stimmen der Zeit* 200, 1982: 662-676).

4. B. C. Butler, "Authority and The Christian Conscience," *The Clergy Review*, 1975, 3-17.

5. Cf., for example, *Gaudium et Spes* 43.

6. "Il ministero del Papa dopo i due Consili Vaticani," *La Civiltà Cattolica* 136 (2 November 1985), 209-221.

7. G. Mucci, "La Competenza del Magistero infallibile," *La Civiltà Cattolica* 139 (2 July 1988), 17-25.

8. Cf. J. Fuchs, "Naturrecht und naturalistischer Fehlschluss," *Stimmen der Zeit* 206 (1988): 407-423.

9. *Acta Synodalia Sacrosancti Concilii Vaticani II*, vol. 3.8.88: Modus 159 and the reply of the Theological Commission.

10. *Gaudium et Spes* 62.

14

Spiritual Foundations of the Structural Change in Western Society

The manifold structural shifts in our society have a variety of causes—economic, technical, social, political and, not least, spiritual. This essay investigates the intellectual bases of this structural shift from the viewpoint of moral theology, or theological ethics. The concept of "human dignity" serves as our starting-point.

THE SHIFT TO THE FUNDAMENTAL VALUE OF THE "DIGNITY OF THE HUMAN PERSON"

The emphasis on "human dignity" has slowly become more than a fashionable phrase of the first period after World War II. The dignity of the human person is now mentioned not only in officially formulated catalogs of fundamental rights; it is also given an important role in all areas of life and it orders the most varied concerns of society. Its presence in public life signifies a decisive structural shift, when compared to the preceding epochs of dictatorships and to the periods that went before these, and a contribution to a gradual structural shift within our society that is ongoing. Its chief concern is to provide for the interests of individual persons and groups in the realms of the state, economics, technology, and other social and cultural realities, including the spheres of family and marriage.

Although talk of the necessity of providing for the dignity of the human person is universal, it is not at all clear what various partners in the dialog mean when they speak of this dignity. Even the basis of this dignity, attributed in Christian theology to God, is understood in a broadly different sense by catholic and evangelical theology. Doubtless to most of our contemporaries (although not all), "human dignity" refers to the predominant position that human persons have within earthly reality, and in most cases (to a greater or lesser extent following Kant) the quality of the human person as a subject and an end in itself, as one who can never be merely the object of another's intentions.

It follows that this dignity is inherent in the human person. Thus, it is not quite correct, not fundamentally, to attempt to prohibit an attack on the dignity of another person, for this dignity can in reality be damaged only by oneself when one is not true to oneself or one's own personal reality. One's reality is attacked when one fails to live in accordance with this inherent worth and indeed contradicts it through undignified behavior. Even if others inflict damage on the value and rights that correspond to one's dignity, one does not thereby lose this dignity.

It is precisely because of one's dignity that one has particular values and rights as one's own possessions. It is, however, possible for persons and societies to draw too close to this personal realm and to damage "what is one's own." When damage is done to "one's own," and to that which should have been securely protected, that is, one's rights and justified expectations, one trespasses on something that is derived directly from one's human dignity, and in this sense (and properly only in this sense) one trespasses on that dignity itself. It follows that the right to the dignity of the human person is not only a right alongside other human rights, but the foundation of them all.

One frequently hears, however, that particular forms of conduct are unacceptable in society, in the family, between marriage partners, and so forth, because (we are told) they contradict the dignity of the human person. One ought rather to show more carefully why a form of conduct in fact contradicts the rights or the justified expectations of a human person or group; if it is possible to demonstrate this reason or to see it, then one can also say that a form of conduct somehow contradicts the dignity of the human person or group.

What contradicts the dignity of the human person understood in this way, and what corresponds to it? Widely divergent answers are given to this question, not only in successive epochs, but even in our own age. In many questions, a measure of fundamental consensus nevertheless leaves open the possibility of various concrete realizations. To justify these various possibilities, corresponding attempts at evaluation are offered for comparison; and while these never produce universal conviction, they lead to a broad fundamental consensus, which is often entirely justified, or at least makes possible a legislative arrangement built on compromise.

As a practical matter therefore, all the forces of society and of the various realms within society should aim at the public recognition of the best forms of public and private conduct in which to respect the dignity of the human person. The emphasis on the dignity of the human person must be more than a well-intentioned proclamation. Certainly, this proclamation has shown its efficacy in many areas, for example, in a concern (which is more than a little self-interested) in the underprivileged; nevertheless, it always finds its resolute opponent in unjustified private interests.

THE DIGNITY OF THE HUMAN PERSON IN SOCIETY AND STATE

The personal human being, whose dignity is written large today, must of course be understood in a manner other than individualistic. In one's essence, one bears an interpersonal and social structure; these adjectives are therefore not supplementary to the description of a person's essence. One's relationship to others, the group, and society are an extension of oneself. Fundamentally, the individualistic concentration on the individual self or on the group of one's own interest are a self-alienation of the personal human being, and thus contradict the preservation of human dignity. This concentration is a basic misunderstanding of one's dignity as a person, but it exists today and will always exist.

Respect for one's own dignity as a person is expressed when the human person tends, now more strongly than in other periods, to claim that it is various forces in society (which are basically older than the state) that should give structure to society, rather than a force above society (such as the state itself). In the struggle of intellectual and moral forces within a society and of corresponding groups (which also have power), clarity is sought about what the good for this particular society that wishes to determine its own concepts of value and to create its own cultural and material possibilities for the development of the human persons in it and within all human society. The being of the human person, as interpersonal and societal, demands that this struggle should take place in the attitude of solidarity and subsidiarity, not in an individualistic or group mentality.

The distinction between society and state that has just been discussed has always existed; in earlier decades, it was emphasized more strongly in the United States than in Europe. Many European social scientists were surprised when the Second Vatican Council's decree on religious freedom—not independently of North American influence—attributed the care for the common good, not to the state but to society, while attributing to the state only the preservation of public order as a part of the common good and, above all, the preservation of the rights that exist within the society. The state is therefore understood fundamentally as a power that provides good order. Human persons in a society must themselves discover and decide what they wish and what they are responsibly able to make of themselves and their society.

On the other hand, the reality of our contemporary industrial and pluralistic society demonstrates that the state, as the power providing good order, must take over many activities, perhaps in subsidiarity with society, without which it cannot be sufficiently effective in providing order. It is not a priori evident where the boundaries of such activity lie; for example, must the state become a welfare state and judge over morality? Society creates the state for the common good. On the other hand, the various forces of society, bearing in mind their dignity and their own interests, are skeptical about many interventions of the state. They frequently believe that they can see in them an attack on the principle of subsidiarity, which they must oppose.

Naturally, specific concepts of value generate the decisions taken by superior authorities. The authorities of the state (parliament, congress, or government), which today are composed of pluralities and controlled in a pluralistic manner, are not called or even empowered to be active in creating values. The individuals who bear the state's power are not servants of a particular concept of value but of the common good of this concrete society. While they do have their own concepts of value in ethical responsibility, they are not expected to promote the acceptance of these concepts, but only the public order and the common good. This expectation is true in economics, technology, and culture, and also in penal law and public morality. Today's society observes the conduct of officers of the state very exactly and critically, although society itself is not capable of a full consensus. The tension between society and state will always remain alive.

ABSOLUTE VALUES AND THE
DIGNITY OF THE HUMAN PERSON

Both society and the state are continually confronted with the question whether any absolute values exist that they would logically have to recognize, acknowledge, and enforce. But if everything were to depend on them, then it is obvious—as is often said—that there would be no "objective order of values." Of course, such an order does exist, but only in the realm of the spirit. As a valid order, it can exist only in recognition and acknowledgement by the human persons who make up the society and the state. Such an absolute order of values does exist as recognized and acknowledged—at least, in its most general sense, in the fundamental values of justice, honesty, faithfulness, solidarity and subsidiarity, and the need for sexuality and marriage to be the object of culture. But there is no absolutely identical answer, either for all periods and situations or for our contemporaries, to questions about the manner and extent to which these fundamental spiritual values are to be made concrete and realized in practice.

This lack of consensus does not imply any relativity of value such as one might suppose; rather, it implies that the interpretations and evaluations that influence the conduct of citizens are honestly and correctly sought in relation to various objective and subjective circumstances. We must not overlook the fact that human persons, in accordance with their innermost essence, are historical beings. The just wage of the worker, for example, must be measured against different criteria in agricultural and industrial situations; and the same is true of the whole realm of economics and technology. The correct culture of sexuality will be determined in different ways in various periods in keeping with the changing knowledge of the essence of human sexuality and with the conduct that can be justified sociologically in each particular situation.

The majority of citizens in our society know more or less clearly what has been said here about the relative character, not relativism, of values, and many behave accordingly. Their behavior is, therefore, not determined by the denial of an objective order of values; the personal dignity of the human person is unquestioned as the basis for a human order of values, nor is there any denial of the relevance of the concrete human circumstances in each case for the discovery of the correct conduct in relation to these circumstances. But it is not accepted that everything that belongs concretely to an order of values worthy of the human person has been laid down once for all, nor is this simply accepted from state or society, or from moral theology or the church.

There is no cause to be surprised by this discussion or the mutual contradiction within our society. There is, however, a great need for the virtue of tolerance—the tolerance that grasps that not all values are simultaneously "relevant" (or *aktuell*, in Karl Rahner's word) for all periods and situations, or for all the members of this society with their various characteristics. There must be no ethical compromise here; the only compromise concerns what is to be enforced for the political common good and, in certain circumstances, with the sanctions of the state and society's penal codes. In the Vatican document about the problematic of abortion, issued in 1974 in a correspondingly precarious political situation in Italy, the condemnation of abortion—including its political condemnation—is absolutely demanded, but not likewise an absolute penal law admitting no exception. The document does not even begin to discuss the question of the extent of the indemnity that was foreseen.

FREEDOM AND DIGNITY OF THE HUMAN PERSON

The widely observed emphasis on personal freedom in our age is in keeping with the emphasis on the dignity of the human person. In a positive sense, this emphasis means that one is left free, indeed, that one is called to personal decision and development. In a corresponding negative sense, it means opposition to bonds or manipulations that hinder freedom understood in the positive sense. The will for freedom is seen in a mentality that is lived publicly, in various "movements," and in opposition to established circumstances in society. Such a will can certainly signify an awareness of the personal dignity of the human person without implying an equation between personal being and individualism; one must not overlook the fact that the personal human being exists in relationship to other persons and society. Basically, such a will for freedom must be welcomed in all its manifestations.

But freedom, because of its ambiguity, can also be misunderstood as a will for arbitrariness. One can be aware of this will for arbitrariness in its negativity, but an *apparent* arbitrariness also exists, which can be generated by a correct but insufficiently enlightened perception of bonds that must be rejected and insufficiently clear goals and ideals. Many tendencies and movements of our age give an impression of irrationality, although they are not simply or exclusively irrational in their depths.

The student unrest of 1968 and the following years is over, but a great deal of liberation from those years remains. The universities have not been completely restructured, but they are not simply the professors' universities that previously existed. This change has also meant the loss of values that were present once, but other values have been introduced that no one is willing to lose. Emancipation has also begun in relationship to traditional understandings of the state: one may, for example, compare the penal code then and now, and even the undeniably unjust oppression of women in society is justifiably giving place.

The pressure for liberation from illiberal and insufficiently justified church laws, which reduce the realization of personal freedom, has not remained fruitless. In marriage legislation today, a stronger guarantee than was earlier the case exists that one will have free choice of a partner. Many marriages that were formerly forbidden in the church on religious grounds are no longer excluded; ecumenical weddings are now allowed as are purely civil and even nonpublic weddings. Thereby greater allowance has been made for religious freedom.

If one has open ears, one can hear everywhere in society that in the realm of morality—and perhaps especially in the realm of the Catholic Church—a change of mentality seeks a path of freedom. Here it seems often to be overlooked that the formation of structures, for example, in the state, technology, economics, or industrial law are also extremely important elements of a human and Christian ethics. But when people speak of structural change in the field of ethics, they do not speak so much about these areas.

Rather, they point above all to sexual morality. It is true that in earlier times, many things were done by human persons, including believers, which both were and are officially forbidden. The difference today is that either these things no longer cause concern or they are considered completely justified. Today we see a widespread refusal to accept prescriptions from an outside authority about what in each case is justified or unjustified conduct. "One" knows that much of what was traditionally considered to be gravely sinful is no longer held to be such; therefore, it no longer requires sacramental confession. This perception is also influenced by frequent reception of the eucharist—also without the necessity of preceding sacramental confession. Naturally, these facts are not unknown to the professional representatives of the church's moral theology.

If one takes the church's moral theology to be absolutely binding, with no exceptions, one can only regret this situation. If, however, one knows something about the insufficiency of reflections and justifications within the field of sexual ethics, and something about today's biological and anthropological knowledge concerning human sexuality, then one will certainly not say that only a cheap arbitrariness is at work in the attitudes and positions in contemporary sexual ethics that diverge from the church's teachings. At certain points a process of genuine liberation has developed that corresponds better to the dignity of the human person in his or her private and interpersonal reality than the traditional, "imposed" order.

FREEDOM OF THE PERSON AND CREATURELY NATURE

The tendency exists to favor an anthropocentric liberation (corresponding to the personal dignity of the human person) from a strongly cosmocentric understanding of the human person that was held in other ages based on a false concept of creation.

The human being is a person, a created reality in a human and created nature that is also the world as a created reality. One must not overlook this fact that the human personal being is created reality. Although only the unitive human being exists, there reigns an order between these two coprinciples of person and nature. The person is not subjected to nature, nor does the person rule over nature, or simply have it at one's disposal. Although we often hear today that animal, plant, and material nature, also have "rights" in relation to ourselves, this assertion is not correct unless one understands "right" in an analogous sense; namely, plants, animals, and materials are introduced by the personal human being into the totality of the human world and are to be respected in their individual relevance.

The human being is not only person but also nature. As a person, one may intervene in one's own nature and integrate it meaningfully into the totality. The person (and human society) must interpret and evaluate nature to discover what can and should be done. One may not dispose arbitrarily over nature, nor let oneself be dominated by natural circumstances as though they were moral norms. Greater emphasis is laid today than at any other time on this last statement.

The state, too, according to Cicero and later to Thomas Aquinas, is not a product of nature but an institution of the personal human being. Likewise, for Thomas, private property is not an institution of nature but an institution devised by human beings. The same is true of marriage (prescinding from the texts in Genesis 1 and 2). The natural data of human sexuality show us only what man and woman are and how they spontaneously function; they do not solve the ethical question of how we are to realize our sexuality. The data are relevant to the ethical solution, but they cannot demonstrate it.

The last-named supposition is, however, frequently made even in declarations of the church's magisterium, although it is nothing other than a naturalistic fallacy that is above all powerless to justify any absolute norms.

In addition, we never merely possess our human nature. It has come into being in the course of human history informed by the human person, including the human sinner. Many realities of this world are marked by the sins of human persons—those committed in history and in our time—and many realities must also be constructed by human persons whose weaknesses are determined by sin or by a society marked by structures of sin. But this construction must take place in such a way that human persons and human society—despite all the structures of sin and injustice—are able to exist humanly, although they must at the same time strive to eliminate the consequences of sin as far as possible (see, for example, John Paul II's encyclical *Sollicitudo Rei socialis*).

Further, we have this nature only and always as a nature that has already been interpreted and evaluated in a particular way by persons and society. This fact may not be overlooked when one reads the 1987 Roman document on questions of bioethics, which bears on the question of the total rejection of *in vitro* fertilization and on the treatment of embryos (though here it must also be noted that this document—like the 1974 document on abortion—does not make any definitive statement about the beginning of personal human life).

The considerations that have just been presented also make it clear that norms of concrete ethical conduct in the responsible structuring of state, economics, technology, culture, and sexuality are not commandments deriving directly from God that would have been explicitly imposed on the human person somehow or other even without revelation, although it does speculate when and where. The few normative statements in scripture do not even begin to cover the entire ethical realm within which the contemporary human person lives. Concrete ethical norms and individual decisions are not derived directly from a God who makes laws and issues directives, but from God as the creator. This God, however, creates the human person (society) to be the very image and likeness of God—albeit created—and therefore also limited and fallible. This image must interpret its own and the rest of creation and carry it further by realizing it. It follows that an essential dimension of the personal dignity of the human being is the free and responsible search and discovery of ethically defensible systems of order and the norms for concrete individual decisions. The human person today is right to insist in this question too on his or her God-given dignity and responsibility.

Further, the human person never exercises this vocation only as an individual: thanks to one's interpersonal and social being, the human person always acts also in relation to religious experiences and traditions that develop in the course of history in society and church and in the dialog between human persons and society.

DESTRUCTION OR CHANGE?

One may wonder whether the spiritual foundations of contemporary society are being changed or destroyed. I hear this question frequently and with mixed feelings. In the reality of the world of the human person no sphere is free of history; the world changes—sometimes slowly and imperceptibly, but today very quickly and to an enormous extent. Indeed, the human person is a historical being, always coming forth from yesterday in order to shape it creatively and make it tomorrow; this contingency determines to a greater or lesser extent the changes both in individuals and in society. Change necessarily implies a destruction, even though it were only the destruction of yesterday's reality through its integration into the new tomorrow, which is certainly more than a mere repetition of yesterday.

A first question: has our society lost its ability to acknowledge an absolute (in the singular)? If one understands the absolute as a personal God, especially in the Christian understanding of God, then the process of a nonexplicit acknowledgment of God, which began a long time ago, has accelerated (even if not necessarily in the form of a denial of God). This change (like humanity's various images of God) has consequences for the acknowledgment of values, but does not in the least determine a complete denial of values and an empty space for morality. One may, for example, think of Kant's ethical theses and of the ethics of many humanists who are not believers. I also suspect that even the explicit atheist, even without a reflection of what he or she knows conceptually, nevertheless is deeply aware of a personal God. An awareness of an absolute that is not thought of in personal terms, an awareness that is expressed in the experience of ethical obligation, seems to be widespread, even if it is interpreted in various ways in conscious reflection.

The second question: what about the absolutes, or values in the plural? Have the changes in our time created empty spaces, that is, a destruction of virtues, of ethical values, of right forms of conduct in the entire realm of human life and work? If history and the historical character of the human person necessarily imply change, then this change is necessarily expressed in the destruction of values that are no longer contemporary (or not *aktuell*). Does this necessarily create empty spaces? Perhaps, but it is also possible that newly filled spaces come into being. What de facto happens will not always be evaluated in the same way by human persons who, though they live as contemporaries, do not always think and evaluate in a contemporary fashion.

We go along our path through time; but we do not go alone, nor do we start each day afresh from zero. All that one does is also determined by one's tradition and the traditions of the larger society; only so is history possible. Change, however, will place limits on the significance of tradition, and we must also accept that when the change occurs, it can be followed by an extreme swing of the pendulum back to the opposite. Some may even be comforted to interpret the changes in our time in this way. On the other hand, we cannot free our society from the necessity of reinterpreting the truth as our knowledge grows (instead of possessing the truth once and for all). Only thus can we arrive at new insights and evaluations. The criterion of the communicability of truths and evaluations between persons, which is highly praised in contemporary philosophy, can help here. But who, despite much good will, is able to step completely out of prejudice and the world of self-interest into pure "openness"?

15

Law and Grace: A Theme of Moral Theology

"Law and grace" is a fundamental theme in dogmatic theology. It is also a decisively important theme in moral theology. While it is true that as Christians we "belong to the Lord" (1 Cor 3:23), we are also "free men and women in the Lord" (1 Cor 7:22). "Everything belongs to you" (1 Cor 3:21), and "everything is permitted to me" (1 Cor 6:12; 1 Cor 10:23). On the other hand, this freedom demands an ultimate responsibility. Belonging to the Lord must bear its own proper fruit: "nothing is to have power over me" (1 Cor 6:12), because "not everything is of profit to me" (1 Cor 6:12). "For you were bought at a high price, and you do not belong to yourselves" (1 Cor 6:19f.). "Do you not know that you are the temple of God, and that the Spirit of God dwells in you?" (1 Cor 3:16, cf. 1 Cor 6:19). This dynamic is why the "commandments" (1 Cor 7:19) and everything that is recognized as a commandment (e.g., the natural law; cf. 1 Cor 6:8-11) are valid even for those "who belong to Christ" and are therefore "slaves of Christ."

NEW TESTAMENT TEXTS

Some New Testament (especially pauline) texts will show more precisely in what sense the theme of law and grace is significant for moral theology.

Paul writes in the Letter to the Romans: "Sin is not to have dominion over you; for you do not stand under the law, but under grace" (Rom 6:14). Clearly, Christians can sin, and therefore the law is also valid for them, but the law does not determine their lives. What determines one's life as a Christian is grace. The law is only a letter; it does not give one the power to live to the letter of the law. Grace, however, is spirit, the Spirit of God; it gives one the life that is expected in keeping with the law. The law as mere letter—that is, as lacking the Spirit that gives life—kills ("death" here means distance from God); it leads to sin. At 2 Cor 3:6, Paul says briefly and clearly that "the letter kills, but the Spirit gives life" ("life" here means union with God), and more concretely at Rom 8:2: "the law of the Spirit and of life in Christ Jesus has set you free from the law of sin and death."

One who understands the law in this way, will also grasp the observation at 1 Tim 1:9: "the law is not laid down for the righteous person, but for lawless and disobedient persons, for the godless and sinners, for those without faith and reverence." "For the law was given through Moses, but grace and truth came through Jesus Christ" (John 1:17).

In the formulation "law and grace," it is plain that "law" does not have the meaning that it has in contemporary speech; rather, it must be read within the binomium "human person of sin and of death" and "human person in the Spirit of Christ, in grace." This is clearly expressed in the brief résumé of Jesus' preaching (Mark 1:14f.): "Jesus proclaimed . . . the gospel of God and said, 'the time is fulfilled, the Kingdom of God is near at hand. Repent and believe in the gospel!'" Thus, the person without grace and faith is also without the kingdom, that is, in sin and death. He or she needs repentance, not only in *lifestyle* but in *life* so that one actually becomes another. Instead of the "old person" (without grace and Spirit), one must become a "new person, a new creation" (2 Cor 5:17): "Thus, when one is in Christ Jesus, one is a new creation. The old has passed away, the new has come. But all this comes from God" (2 Cor 5:17).

The apostle says something similar about Christians on the basis of their baptism: "We know that our old person was crucified with him, so that the body" ["body" here refers to the personal human being] "which was dominated by sin might be destroyed, and that we might not remain slaves of sin. For the one who has died has been set free from sin. If, then, we have died with Christ, then we believe that we shall also live with him" (Rom 6:6ff.).

Paul continues this theme in the eight chapter of the Letter to the Romans. Here he sets "flesh" and "Spirit" in antithesis to each other. "Flesh" (and the "fleshly human person") mean the human person in his or her egotistic tendencies, closed in upon oneself. "Spirit" and ("spiritual human person") mean the opposite": the person who is open to grace and to God's kingdom. "All who are determined by the flesh fix their thoughts on what is in keeping with the flesh, and all who are determined by the Spirit fix their thoughts on what is in keeping with the Spirit" (8:5), "for the striving of the flesh is enmity with God, it does not submit itself to the law of God, and indeed cannot do so" (8:7). "But you are not determined by the flesh, but by the Spirit, if indeed the Spirit of God dwells in you" (8:9). "The law of the Spirit . . . has set you free from the law of sin and of death" (8:2).

THE PROBLEM: LAW AND GRACE

In the binomium "law and grace," *law* means above all the law of the Hebrew Bible, the torah, which is the very type of every law that makes demands but does not also give the Spirit that fulfills the law, namely, grace. Paul, accordingly, takes this law as his theme, but what he says applies equally to every law, whether positively given or not (the natural law).

The effect of the law depends largely on the human person for whom it is to have validity, that is, on whether one is fundamentally a person in Christ, in grace and the Spirit, or a person without grace and the Spirit, a sinner who neither will nor can submit to the law. In the latter case, the law is a (merely) external law, since it does not give the inner powers to correspond to the will that presses one forward to grace and the Spirit, that is, to the law of the person in Christ. The law of the person in Christ, on the other hand, is an inner law, something that presses forward from within and gives one the power to do the good contained in the law.

Grace is the Spirit of Christ, who works in those "who belong to the Lord." The type of "grace" is the new covenant, the good news of Jesus Christ. Grace does not alter the contents of the law, but the inner life of the person who "belongs to theLord." If one "belongs to the Lord," and the law concerns that person, it will be accepted because grace always orients one to the good that belongs to the law. In the one who belongs to the Lord, the law presses forward to the things of the Spirit, to the fruits of "being in the Lord," to that which the law requires (Rom 8:4) and its works. This law of grace is totally an "inner" law, and it also internalizes the law that by itself is only a letter.

The necessity of both, law and grace.

Among Christians, the necessity of grace is evident. Without it, the human person would be a sinner, and the law would be the law of sin and of death.

It has sometimes been held that, for Paul, the law is superfluous for the Christian: Is not everything allowed? and is not the law for those who are godless? The law, to the extent that it is a mere letter, the law of sin and of death, may be superfluous for Christians, but not insofar as it contains directives: Paul points even those who are in Christ to the commandments and to the requirements of the natural law, to everything that is useful and uplifting. Against all this, however, there exists no law (Gal 5:23). We do not live under a law according to the type of the old law (the letter), but according to the type of the new law (grace). The law kills if it remains letter and external law; it gives life if it receives life from the Spirit of grace and thus becomes an internal law.

Paul says at Rom 2:14-16 that even the pagans know a moral law within themselves; but this interiority refers only to their knowledge. If, however, this "moral" law remains without grace, it is only an *external* law, a law of sin and death. The same is true of the commandment of love: taken purely as a commandment, it is an eternal law, but as the gift of grace, it is an internal law and gives life.

Thomas Aquinas.

Following John, Paul, and Augustine (*De spiritu et littera* [PL 44, 199-246]), Aquinas treats the problematic of law and grace under the title: "The new law of Christ," mostly in his commentaries on texts of the New Testament and systematically in the *Summa theologiae* (I-II.106-108). He does this within the traditional distinction of *lex vetus, lex nova, lex naturalis*. In each case, *lex* denotes a situation of the history or dispensation of salvation.

According to Thomas, the new law of Christ contains various elements. The most important element (*elementum principale*) is the grace of the Holy Spirit, which moves the human person from within, helping one to love and to do for love what the law requires. The secondary (but still essential) element is everything that is not the grace of the

Holy Spirit and hence does not move the human person from within. To this secondary element belong not only commandments and laws, but also the sacred books, the sacraments, the church, the commandment of love, the natural law—all these are only the external law.

Grace is the specific element in the type of the "new law," as the specific element in the type of the "old law" is the *law* itself. But Aquinas is aware that even in the history of salvation in the Hebrew Bible, in the *lex vetus*, the grace of the Holy Spirit—the type of the "new law"—was present and at work, for example, in holy persons. In the same way, even in the dispensation of salvation in the New Testament, the *lex nova*, the law of sin and of death—the type of the "old law"—is present and at work in sinners. He knows also that the grace of the Holy Spirit, the principal element of the new law, is present and at work even beyond the dispensation of salvation in the Hebrew Bible and the New Testament (I-II.107).

ETHICAL CONSEQUENCES

"The one who is born of God does not sin" (1 John 5:18). The theme of "law and grace" is very schematic and formal. It has already been observed that the new law of the Spirit is the "type" of grace, while the old law (the torah) is the "type" of law. But if one speaks, not per typum, but in terms of the concrete reality, then the one can be found in the other. More concretely: "How can we, who died (through baptism) to sin, still live in sin?" (Rom 6:2). And "we know that the one who is born of God does not sin" (1 John 5:18). The one who is under grace does not sin. And yet the apostles never cease to warn Christians against sin: "So let the ones who think that they stand take heed, lest they fall" (1 Cor 10:12). We have the Spirit, but only as the firstfruits of the Spirit (Rom 8:23), and this is why we always lives in the hope of fulfillment (1 Cor 8:4). Thus, the life of those who are in Christ is an enduring struggle. Our victory (or the kingdom) is indeed present, but it is also "not yet." The struggle signifies permanent growth and permanent conversion. But it remains true that whoever stands under grace, does not stand under the (external) law, and does not sin.

The use of the law.

The theme of law and grace was present in Christian theology up to the time of the Reformation: in Paul and John in the first century; in

Thomas and Bonaventure in the Middle Ages; in Seripando at the time of the Council of Trent. The theme has become common to all Christians in the decades of ecumenism. But the terminology has changed: instead of speaking of "law and grace," we agree in speaking of "law and gospel," that is, the proclamation of the law in the Old Testament and the proclamation of grace in the New.

Luther sought to interpret particular formulas of Paul. According to him, the primary use of the law is its theological use: the law serves sinners, it draws their attention to the situation in which they stand and leads them to despair (because they cannot free themselves from sin), but thereby also to hope in the grace of Jesus Christ and in justification. In addition to the theological use of the law, Luther also acknowledges a second use, which, however, is purely political or civil; knowledge of the law preserves egotistical humanity from chaos, but according to Luther, the law has no theological significance in this function. The Lutheran Melanchthon, however, concedes a further significance to the law for those who belong to Christ, the so-called third use of the law that permits the Christian to understand what works (or deeds) ought to be the fruit of being in Christ. Calvin makes this third use the first, assigns the second place to the theological use (for the sinner), and the third place to the political or civil use.

We stand closer to Calvin than to Luther. The law is good and holy (Rom 7:12). It helps Christians to recognize more easily what are the works of the Spirit's urging and the fruits of being in Christ. But the law can—in an analogous manner—have a theological use even for the Christian. For we have the Spirit only as firstfruits, and the power of the flesh is still at work in us. There is no doubt about the civil significance of the law, but this law is not only civil; it also serves the correct construction of God's kingdom in the categorical world.

LAW AND LAWS

The law is a secondary element of the new law of Christ. We are inclined to understand the law as a sum total of many laws or commandments. But it is more than this: it is everything that is not the grace of the Holy Spirit, including also the possibility of a multitude of laws and commandments. The grace of the Holy Spirit must create an expression for itself in its secondary element, the law. Since the multiplicity of laws and commandments also belongs to the law, grace must create an expression for itself in this multiplicity, that is, in a normative morality.

The multiplicity of laws and commandments does not come directly as a fruit from the grace of the Holy Spirit as the primary element in the new law of Christ; nor does it come from scripture as the spring from which the divine revelation flows. Rather the laws and commandments of a normative morality are the ethical self-interpretation of the human person. That is, they are the self-interpretation of the "human person in Christ," even when this interpretation does not take place as the search for what is actually the work of salvation.

No matter how true it may be that normative morality—the morality of laws and commandments—has its place in Christian morality, Christian morality is not primarily law and commandment. But it is necessarily interested in the correct laws and commandments of a normative morality as the expression of its own self. These laws and commandments are not the primary element of the new law of Christ. For example, Romans 6 insists that the essential point for the Christian is to be one who does not sin; but we are not given a list of sinful works and corresponding ethical norms. Explicit guidance is not a theme of Christian proclamation.

Some know the content of the moral law on the basis of the Hebrew Bible; others, from Christianity's self-understanding; and still others (the gentiles) know it from the human person's self-understanding—the heart (Rom 2:14-16). John 14:15-24 demonstrates the relationship that exists between love for God and Jesus on the one hand and the ethical commandments on the other; John does not reflect on what these commandments are as the object of a list of things to be expounded in treatises, although he does indeed understand them as the content of the commandment of love.

According to 2 Cor 5, the only thing that counts for the Christian is to become a new creation in Christ. This renewal, however, comes entirely from God who has reconciled us to Godself. Therefore, we no longer live for ourselves, but for the one who died for us. What this means in concrete terms, the Apostle does not say. That meaning is not to be discovered in the theme of "law and grace."